THE AGE *of*
DOUBT

TWAYNE'S
AMERICAN THOUGHT
AND CULTURE SERIES

Lewis Perry, General Editor

THE AGE *of* DOUBT

American Thought and Culture in the 1940s

WILLIAM GRAEBNER

Twayne Publishers • Boston
A Division of G. K. Hall & Co.

Copyright 1991 by William Sievers Graebner.
All rights reserved.
Published by Twayne Publishers
A division of G. K. Hall & Co.
70 Lincoln Street
Boston, Massachusetts 02111

Copyediting supervised by Barbara Sutton.
Book production by Gabrielle B. McDonald.
Book design by Janet Z. Reynolds.
Typeset in Janson
by Compset, Inc., Beverly, Massachusetts.

The paper used in this publication meets the minimum requirements
of American National Standard for Information Sciences—Permanence
of Paper for Printed Library Materials, ANSI Z39.48-1984. ∞™

Printed and bound in the United States of America.

Library of Congress Cataloging-in-Publication Data

Graebner, William.
The age of doubt : American thought and culture in the 1940s /
William Graebner.
    p.   cm. — (Twayne's American thought and culture series)
Includes bibliographical references.
ISBN 0-8057-9061-6 (alk. paper). — ISBN 0-8057-9070-5 (pbk. :
alk. paper)
1. United states—Civilization—1918–1945.   2. United States—
Civilization—1945–   3. United States—Intellectual life—20th
century.   I. Title.   II. Series.
E169.1.G698   1990
        973.917—dc20   90-42941
                                    CIP

0-8057-9061-6 (alk. paper) 10 9 8 7 6 5 4 3 2 1
0-8057-9070-5 (pbk. alk. paper) 10 9 8 7 6 5 4 3 2 1
First published 1990.

For Jerry Clore, Judy DeLoache, and Mary Lee Sargent

Contents

Foreword

The American Thought and Culture Series surveys intellectual and cultural life in America from the sixteenth century to the present. The time is auspicious for such an extensive survey because scholars have carried out so much pathbreaking work in this field in recent years. The volumes reflect that scholarship, as well as valuable earlier studies. The authors also present the results of their own research and offer original interpretations. The goal is to bring together books that are readable and well informed and that stand on their own as introductions to significant periods in American thought and culture. There is no attempt to establish a single interpretation of all of America's past; the diversity, conflict, and change that are features of the American experience would frustrate any such attempt. What the authors can do, however, is to explore issues of critical importance in each period and those of recurrent or lasting importance.

Today the culture and intellectual life of the United States are subjects of heated debate. While prominent figures summon citizens back to an endangered common culture, some critics dismiss the very idea of culture—let alone *American* culture—as elitist and arbitrary. The questions asked in these volumes have direct relevance to that debate, which concerns history but too often proceeds in ignorance of it. How did leading intellectuals view their relation to America, and how did their compatriots regard them? Did Americans believe that theirs was a distinctive culture? Did they participate in international movements? What were the links and tensions between high culture and popular culture? While discussing influential works, creative individuals, and major institutions, the books in this series place intellectual and cultural history in the larger context of American society.

This book on the 1940s is the first to appear, though not the first chronologically, of a number of volumes on separate decades of the twentieth century. In some quarters the division of cultural history by decades is controversial. The same may be said for division by century, presidential administration, business cycle—or virtually any other way—since cultural history is not determined by calendar, politics, war, or prices. Or is it? In the twentieth century it is certainly common practice for Americans to conceive of their cultural life as changing with the decades. While we may be skeptical about that sense of sudden and inevitable shifts in moods and values, it is also undeniable that trying to discern the central issues and tensions of a decade can be a good approach to understanding modern America.

William Graebner in these pages is not locked in by the dates of the decade. He points out trends from earlier decades that helped to define the 1940s and, even more usefully, trends of the 1940s that came to fruition (bitter or sweet) in the 1950s, 1960s, and beyond. He also uncovers some unifying themes in a decade we often think of as sundered at 1945. Some of these themes have to do with gender roles, consumerism, and material welfare; others, with artistic style in fields as diverse as film noir and abstract expressionist painting. He examines Americans' fundamental attitudes toward the role of chance in human life, the anxieties of the self, the lessons of history, the sources of unity, the meanings of freedom and dependency. He turns to such varied topics as religious revivalism, games theory, cybernetics, anticommunist liberalism, and the Kinsey report to depict an age of doubt. Not only does he show how disparate events and pronouncements were joined in their historical moment; he also uses the 1940s as a prism for seeing both fissures and connections in modern American culture.

LEWIS PERRY
Series Editor

Preface

From the relatively comfortable and secure perspective of the present, it can be difficult to appreciate the level of uncertainty that permeated life in the 1940s. The trauma of war and cold war, the shattering revelation of the murder of millions of European Jews, the discovery of nuclear fission and the use of an atomic bomb on civilians at Hiroshima and Nagasaki, the Great Depression that threatened to return any day—these were the events that held Americans in a decade-long state of anxiety. Never before had progress seemed so fragile, history so harmful or so irrelevant, science so lethal, aggregations of power so ominous, life so full of contingencies, human relationships so tenuous, the self so frail, man so flawed.

To be sure, the forties were witness to considerable prosperity and to the nation's rise to the pinnacle of world power. But neither achievement generated the culture of optimism, confidence, and security that has generally been seen as characteristic of the decade. Instead, uncertainty reigned. Americans agonized over the nature of man, over an appropriate role for science and the expert, over the dangers of "mass culture," over the function of chance in human affairs, over the relative importance of reason and emotion, over whether the solutions to the dilemmas of the modern world were in the field of organization (in what I have labeled "the culture of the whole") or in the realm of the self ("turning inward"), even, and no less important, over the relationship between a new television set and happiness.

From the 1946 film *The Best Years of Our Lives* to theologian Reinhold Niebuhr's *The Irony of American History* (1952), many of the characteristic products of this culture of uncertainty were either ironic or concerned with the pervasive irony of the American experience, a sign of the society's general failure to work out the most crucial issues before it. Yet there were also efforts, embodied in phenomena as disparate as beat subculture, the evangelism of Billy Graham, the abstract expressionism of Jackson Pollock, and the existential determination of Frank Bigelow in the film noir classic, *D.O.A.*, to transcend doubt and stasis and to affirm that humanity might still act with resolve and moral purpose.

Though our own moment in history lies nearly a half century removed from the intellectual and cultural crisis of the forties, the events of that decade, and the anxieties they precipitated, constitute a most significant part of our cultural heritage. While the cold war has modulated, we remain hostage to the paranoia it engendered and chattel to the bureaucracies it spawned. In television productions like *The Day After* (1983), we imagine our own Hiroshima. The piles of corpses that Senator Alben Barkley saw at Buchenwald have been cleared away, but their meaning is etched in our memories. As the comic strip protagonist Pogo (1949–) would later announce in another context, "we have met the enemy, and he is us."

What we have not imported from the forties is the courage—or should we say common sense?—to act despite, perhaps even because of, our doubts. We lack the sneering defiance of Tennessee Williams's Stanley Kowalski, the brazen confidence of fictional detective Mike Hammer, the audacity of composer John Cage, the bravado of Snoopy, the gall of psychologist B. F. Skinner, the persistence of Camus's Sisyphus, the pointless guts of Mister Roberts, the thirst for power of Norman Mailer's Sergeant Croft, the self-reliant perseverance of James Cain's Mildred Pierce. We lack the ability to dream that drove Eric Hodgins's Mr. Blandings, Frank Capra's hero George Bailey, and whoever it was that decided that it wouldn't be long before all cars would fly.

These days many students of culture, among them literary scholars and a small but growing number of historians, approach the study of culture from the perspective of experience. That is, they assume that nothing exists except experience, and therefore that one cannot know culture, or really accurately describe or analyze any text, without knowing how contemporaries experienced, and interpreted, that text. According to this view, a cultural *production* (a play by Arthur Miller or a performance by Charlie Parker) contains little or no inherent meaning that one can derive from reading the play or listening to the live or recorded performance. Because every reader and every listener brings to the production different values and needs, the essential reality is the reality of *consumption*: how the play or performance is received by the individuals and groups that make up its audience. Since one way of assembling that sort of evidence is to ask people what their experiences were, this view of culture is in part responsible for the current enthusiasm for oral history.

There is much to be said for this consumption-based approach to culture. As a set of logical propositions, especially, it has the ring of truth, and, used sparingly in conjunction with other methods, it can help shed light on culture, past and present. Nonetheless, I believe the approach to be flawed. It is flawed in the practical sense that it is virtually impossible to do. It is one thing to gather the fresh interpretations of youth who have just seen a Madonna video, but quite another to generate a trustworthy oral-history account of what it was like—and what it meant—to listen to Charlie Parker in 1944. Moreover, if the historian cannot be trusted to read the original performance accurately, what is to ensure that that person's reading of interpretations of that performance will be any better?

A second, more important flaw lies in consumption theory's central concept of experience. While one might agree with the idea that all truth is the truth of experience, it does not follow that the document and experiences of it are entirely distinct, or that, in the absence of a public opinion poll, one is helpless to interpret the text. By understanding the document and the historical context in which it was created, one can approximate the experience of contemporaries; one can see, for example, why most of those who saw Alfred Hitchcock's *Rope* in 1950 went away shocked at a crime committed in the name of reason. More than that, a contextual approach, in which a document is interpreted in the light of many other contemporaneous texts, allows the scholar to understand the document in ways that might be only dimly understood, if at all, by a surveyed moviegoer, a critic assigned to review a film, or even the director of the production. The categories that constitute the chapters of this book, including contingency, the whole, and freedom, are the final product of this contextual method.

This contextual approach, however, places considerable demands on the scholar. One's ability to generate accurate readings depends on one's knowledge of the culture—on knowledge of the range of ideas and values it normally generates—and that, in turn, can come only from familiarity with a wide range of historical research and with numerous documents and performances, not all related in any obvious way to the text under consideration. For example, one's reading of *Rope* can be checked, ratified, broadened, and refined by a knowledge of Dwight Macdonald's "The Responsibility of Peoples" (1945), on the Nazi concentration camps; of Theodor Adorno's *The Authoritarian Personality* (1950); of the science fiction of Robert Heinlein; and of film scholar Dana Polan's discussion of science and cybernetics in *Power and Paranoia*.

At bottom, culture as perception would seem to be based on lack of confidence, on a failure of nerve. Too many scholars, perhaps convinced of their own inability to understand the past in larger ways, have essentially given up the ghost, taking refuge in techniques of inquiry that at best can produce only modest truths. As the reader must know by now, I have chosen a different path. Though perhaps no less strewn with booby traps, the contextual approach to the history of thought and culture at least assumes the possibility of understanding and rendering the American 1940s as a coherent cultural moment.

Acknowledgments

As my references should demonstrate, I am indebted to many fine scholars whose work on the forties has preceded my own. I wish to thank the State University of New York at Fredonia for a leave of absence that made it possible for me to examine certain primary materials, and for the sabbatical that freed me to write the book with the kind of concentration the task required. A Graduate Research Initiative Visiting Professor Grant from the State University of New York at Buffalo funded research into the iconography of the forties and gave me access to the considerable research skills and analytic abilities of Ted Pelton and John Ulrich. I am especially indebted to Lew Perry and Robert Westbrook for their thoughtful and perceptive readings of an earlier draft of this book.

one

War and Peace

It seems simple and obvious enough. Unlike the 1930s—the decade of the Great Depression—and unlike the 1950s—the decade of the Eisenhower "equilibrium"—the 1940s seems not a decade at all. It might easily, and reasonably, be understood as two half-decades, neatly separated in 1945 by the death of Franklin D. Roosevelt (12 April) and the laying to rest of the New Deal, the use of the atomic bomb on Hiroshima and Nagasaki (6 and 9 August), and the end of World War II (7 May in Europe, 15 August in the Pacific). Seen in these terms, the first half of the forties was a culture of war: public, nationalistic, pragmatic, and realistic; championing the group and its political equivalent, democracy; committed to production and to the new roles for women it required; and, torn by the inevitable separations, sentimental. The second half was a culture of peace: private, familial, characterized by a dawn-of-the-new-day idealism; favoring the individual and its political equivalent, freedom; committed to consumption and the consequent reversion to traditional gender roles; and, the far-flung populace brought back together, blissfully domestic.

Provided that one does not take these categories as sacrosanct or chronologically precise, they can be useful in isolating several of the dominant axes of the age. The transition from the public, institutional climate of a nation at war to the private tone of a people living in peace (even in the shadow of cold war) was real enough. So was the wartime focus on democracy and the group, the culture of sentimentalism, and the movement from production to consumption. Women spent the decade meeting the needs of men and capital; filling the factories as producers, then, after the war, soothing the fragile male ego, doing housework, and heading the family's department of con-

1

sumer affairs. And, as we shall see in later chapters, the postwar turn inward toward aspects of the self—characterized by renewed interest in psychology and psychiatry, by the anxiety of the lonely, fragmented individual, by a philosophic posture that favored freedom over egalitarianism and social democracy, and individualism over state, community, and the group—would be in full swing by midcentury.

During the war years, American culture was decidedly democratic—at least on the surface. Just as they had in the First World War, Americans fought the Second in the name of democracy. From the Library of Congress, where Archibald MacLeish furnished the "Democracy Alcove" with the works of John Stuart Mill and John Locke, to the public schools, where students were urged to participate in newly created student governments and in school clubs that taught democratic behavior, Americans understood the war as a struggle between the American way of life, labeled "democracy," and absolute tyranny, known as "totalitarianism."[1]

Beginning in the mid-1930s, when Nazism and fascism first appeared as serious threats, Americans indulged in a frenzy of democratic institution making. At every level of the culture, they looked to democratic systems of governance and decision-making to draw the line between the United States and Hitler's Germany and, during the war, to demonstrate that American values remained intact despite the military draft (1940), government price-fixing (1942), the evacuation and relocation of West Coast Japanese into interior "concentration" camps (1942), government censorship of Hollywood films, and other examples of wartime coercion. Radio-listening discussion groups, first used in England in the 1920s, numbered an estimated fifteen thousand in the United States in 1941. Using such groups, wrote Emory Bogardus in *Democracy by Discussion*, "the whole nation could participate in national affairs in a truly intelligent manner. Democracy could come into its own in a new and vitalized way." Beginning in 1942, the Office of Civilian Defense orchestrated a series of supposedly spontaneous Saturday "Town Meetings for War," whose purpose was to give the mobilization for "total participation for Victory" a democratic gloss.[2]

Though much of the economy was regulated by law during the war, the Department of Agriculture experimented with democratic methods of increasing production and modifying patterns of consumption. The University of Iowa social psychologist Kurt Lewin helped the government by designing an experiment that used group-discussion leaders and other "democratic" methods to convince housewives to contribute to the war effort by serving their families kidneys, brains, and other odd cuts of meat. Even those in the service, whose lives were necessarily highly regimented, came into contact with democratic methods. Hundreds of United Service Organizations (USO) facilities presented democracy in the form of group singing led by a social worker with a baton in one hand, a booklet called "Music: USO" in the other.

"Singing," the booklet said, is "primarily a weapon, a medium through which men march straighter, give better commands, fight harder, work longer and move coordinately." Unfortunately, none of this happened naturally; the "right leader" was required to "develop the habit of group singing" and to "encourage general participation." Even the relocated Japanese were subject to democratic community activities programs, designed to ensure a proper "adjustment" to "life on the outside."[3]

One purpose of the wartime emphasis on democratic systems was to demonstrate the absolute necessity of sublimating the self to the larger whole, of melding the individual into the life of the group. Signals of this sort were everywhere. In selecting George Marshall as Man of the Year for 1943, *Time* magazine applauded the chief of staff for a recently released report that did not contain a single "I"—*The Team* is General Marshall's concern." Readers of the popular comic strip "Terry and the Pirates" opened the 17 October 1943 Sunday paper to find their usually active hero, who has just earned his wings as a flight officer in the army air force, passively listening to his superior officer dispense the folk wisdom of the day: "It wasn't you who earned those wings. . . . A ghostly echelon of good guys flew their hearts out in old kites to give you the know-how"; and Terry's skills as a pilot are useless without the transport pilots who delivered every bullet and gallon of gas. Children learned about the value of the group in books such as *Susie Cucumber* (1944), which features a dog, squirrels, and neighborhood boys and girls engaged in a letter-writing campaign that involves division of labor, mass production, and the cooperation of all in the achievement of a common goal. In the back of the book was an envelope, and the reader was invited to exercise a democratic right (or was it an obligation?) by writing his or her own letter.[4]

Hollywood elevated the group and downplayed individualism in several wartime genres. The combat film narrated a shift from the individual and pluralistic heterogeneity to the heroic unified group, headed in *Bataan* (1943), for instance, by a "natural leader" (Robert Taylor). The message of *Bataan*, as film scholar Jeanine Basinger explained, is that

we are a mongrel nation—ragtail, unprepared, disorganized, quarrelsome among ourselves, and with separate special interests, raised, as we are, to believe in the individual, not the group. At the same time, we bring different skills and abilities together for the common good, and from these separate needs and backgrounds we bring a feisty determination. No one leads us who is not strong, and our individualism is not set aside for any small cause. Once it is set aside, however, our group power is extreme.[5]

"Commitment" films described the process through which individuals sloughed off the old skin of the self for a new, more responsible, social outlook. *Casablanca* (1943) features Humphrey Bogart as Rick, an isolated and

3

cynical saloon-keeper who more than once spurns requests for his help in the effort against the Germans with the line, "I stick my neck out for nobody." However, as the film ends, Rick finds the strength of commitment, sacrificing a lifetime love for the cause. Gary Cooper plays the reluctant hero in *Sergeant York*, a story loosely based on an actual Appalachian pacifist who saw the light in time to kill some twenty German soldiers in World War I. Eleanor Roosevelt and other luminaries at the film's 1941 premiere witnessed York dispensing with a deep-seated, highly personal, Biblical pacifism to participate in a national cause: a "whole people's struggle to be free."[6]

Music proved an especially fertile ground for the cultivation and dissemination of the group values that were so central to American culture in the first half of the 1940s. Wartime film musicals often developed the theme of group unity around a vaudevillelike, family-based group such as the Four Cohans in *Yankee Doodle Dandy* (1942). The breakup of such a troupe, usually precipitated by the selfish ambition of one member, signaled a general moral collapse and stood for the consequences of anything less than complete commitment to the whole. Marching bands experienced a substantial revival in high schools and colleges, attracting eminent classical composers such as Samuel Barber ("Commando March" [1943]). In 1942, the Music Educators' National Conference issued a new version of "The Star-Spangled Banner" pitched in A-flat so that "the melody is now within the reach of all." A 1943 report of the education faculty at Stanford University noted the prominence in Germany of a concept of harmony that "subordinates the individual to the mass" and approvingly cited the American dance band for its revival of "harmonic group improvisation." The Stanford scholars also mentioned a means to unity called "alternation of group activity," through which each element of a symphony orchestra would, in turn, give up "some of its 'sovereignty' in order to achieve a balance or ensemble."[7]

In *Made in America: The Arts in Modern Civilization* (1948), John Kouwenhoven applied ideas of the group and the individual to the dominant popular music of the war years: the dance music of the big bands of Benny Goodman, Woody Herman, Tommy Dorsey, Les Brown, Jack Teagarden, and hundreds of lesser lights. According to Kouwenhoven, big band jazz was something of a folk art; it arose out of a culture both technological and democratic. He argued that big band music reconciled the demands of individual expression (the solos) with group performance (the arrangement). Kouwenhoven probably overemphasized the elements of freedom and individualism and overlooked the elements of pattern and coercion, not just in jazz but in other cultural forms, including modern architecture. The solos offered within the big band framework were anemic displays, circumscribed by a highly choreographed musical presentation not far removed from the regimentation of the marching band. In fact, big band jazz hardly deserved to be called "jazz." But perhaps it expressed all the individualism a nation at war could afford.[8]

As much as the war had to be understood and marketed as a group endeavor, millions of Americans experienced it as intensely isolating and individualizing. Indeed, soldiering not only meant denying the willful self to ensure the survival of the company, the platoon, and ultimately the nation, but it meant separation from home, family, friends, and community—a wrenching uprooting similar to what turn-of-the-century immigrants experienced. For those who were left behind—wives and lovers, sons and daughters, mothers and fathers—separation imposed a different but equally compelling set of emotional demands. The churning chaos of wartime affected even those whose relationship with the conflict was less direct. "There were no apartments to be had anywhere," recalled Alfred Kazin, who in 1942 had become an editor of the *New Republic*.

It was all homeless now—a series of "transient" hotels: West Side, East Side, Brooklyn Heights, the Village—surrounded by that unending wartime crowd I had seen being pushed out of Washington's Union Station, or waiting around the clock to get on a train. War-crowded New York threw back my splintered image from every store window. I could not stop walking the streets, round and round, looking for myself. It was not just my old reasons for everything, my sense of home that I missed; it was a world in which the old invisible connections still existed.[9]

Of the numerous strategies for dealing with the problems of separation—what Kazin described as a lack of "the old invisible connections"—two stand out. The first, typified by war correspondent Ernie Pyle, was to put one's emotions on the back burner. In a syndicated column and several best-selling books, Pyle presented the war in a gray prose that avoided the precise descriptions and narratives that might have made the war a vivid emotional experience for those on the home front. Pyle wrote about the ever-present reality of death, but real soldiers did not die on his pages; he wrote about suffering men without presenting their agony; he wrote about "insecurity, discomfort, [and] homesickness," but without getting much beyond the words themselves. Pyle's soldiers approached the war with the author's cold and mechanical fatalism. In *Here Is Your War* (1945), Pyle described the reaction of pilots to the virtual disintegration of a plane on a bombing run over a Tunisian port—the victim, apparently, of a direct hit on the craft's load of bombs: "Fellow fliers of the ill-fated American crew were naturally pretty blue over the incident. But, as they said, when anything as freakish as that got you your number was just up regardless. And they went on with the war as usual." Pretty blue. Number was just up. As usual.[10]

The other way of dealing with separation was sentimentality. The sentimental, no more realistic than Pyle's prose, was just as surely a way of avoiding contact with aspects of the wartime experience that were too difficult for most people to confront. Where Pyle sidestepped tragedy or potential tragedy by ratcheting down the emotions, the culture of sentimentality did the same by inflating emotion—making emotion into spectacle, if you will—thereby bypassing or displacing genuine experience. Like the Currier and Ives prints that hung in the parlors of nineteenth-century homes, the wartime sentimental culture presented hearth and home as a fortress and sanctuary, a compelling emotional space capable of overcoming separation and, metaphorically, of transcending death itself. Director David O. Selznick's *Since You Went Away* (1943) opens on the empty leather chair of advertising executive Tim Hilton, gone to war; it closes with a Christmas Eve phone call announcing Tim's safe return, another shot of the chair, and, to the music of "Adeste Fidelis," an exterior shot of the snow-covered house and the final caption: "Be of good courage, and He shall strengthen your heart, all ye that hope in the Lord." When, as in *Tender Comrade* (1943), a boyfriend or husband fails to return, grief is momentary (Get on with your life! Set the table!) and soon displaced by a different and more positive set of emotions, with death as a field of triumph for a new generation and the values of freedom and democracy.[11]

Children had their own sentimental tales. Robert McCloskey's *Make Way for Ducklings*, winner of the Caldecott Medal for best children's book of 1941, features Mr. and Mrs. Mallard and their eight ducklings, searching for suitable housing and otherwise trying to make a go of life in the Boston area. Like Tim Hilton in *Since You Went Away*, Dad departs ("One day Mr. Mallard decided he'd like to take a trip to see what the rest of the river was like, further on"), vaguely promising to return and wishing Mom success in the task of raising the ducklings as a temporary single parent. "Don't you worry," Mrs. Mallard replies, "I know all about bringing up children." When she has finished teaching her brood how to avoid bikes and scooters and to stride in step behind her (many wartime children's books had a marching scene that emphasized coordinated group activity), they make their way to the Public Garden, where the waiting father is reunited with the family.[12]

Wartime music was often sentimental, a fact that irritated the federal Office of War Information's music committee, which would have preferred to have Americans humming energetic, nationalistic songs on the order of the World War I hit, "Over There." Americans were not in the mood. What they wanted—and got—was what historian John Costello has called "sentimental bullets": mawkish, nostalgic ballads that played on the themes of separation, anxiety, and loneliness. The isolated self experiencing these feelings was apparent in the many wartime song titles that began with "I" or—projecting the self into an uncertain future—"I'll": "I Love You," "I'll Be Seeing You," "I'll Get By," "I'll Walk Alone" (all 1944), and "I'm Making Believe" (1945). Another set of titles posed the problem of separation in the vocabularies of time and space: "Sunday, Monday, or Always" (1943), "Long Ago and Far Away" and "Together" (both 1944), "It's Been a Long, Long Time," "Till the End of Time," and "It Might as Well Be Spring" (all 1945), and "Sentimental

Journey," a funereal and perhaps ironic ballad from the summer of 1945 that obliquely raises the chilling possibility that a dead man is taking the journey described ("I'll be waitin' up for Heaven").[13]

The war brought another change, no less dramatic than separation. For the first time in decades, Americans understood themselves as producers, as part of a supply-based economy whose function was to produce useful goods rather than to generate wages for the purpose of consumption. Since the turn of the century, the economy had spawned huge advertising and public relations industries, the former designed to create demand (i.e., to foster consumption), the latter to facilitate public acceptance of the corporation by shaping it into easily consumable images. In the midst of the prosperous 1920s, theorists of the "new leisure" bemoaned an economy whose technological prowess had overreached consumers' pocketbooks. By the mid-1930s, with the country mired in the Great Depression, most approaches to recovery—from Keynesian economics to the old-age revolving pension plan of the Townsend movement—involved getting more money into the hands of those who would spend it, whether government bureaucrats or consumers.

Cutting against this long-term trend, the early 1940s reprised the nineteenth-century economy of production. After an uneven start, a mobilized wartime economy produced three hundred thousand airplanes and one hundred thousand tanks and armored cars. Most industries operated seven days a week, around the clock, and factories flew banners proclaiming, "This is one part of the arsenal of democracy." At San Quentin, prisoners demanded and won the right to bid on war contracts; they were soon producing submarine nets and nightsticks for the National Guard. With labor in short supply, women replaced men in shipyards, ordnance plants, and aircraft factories, contributing to the boom and generating the image of Rosie the Riveter. *Time* called the results "the miracle of war production," and Soviet leader Joseph Stalin agreed, in 1943 toasting American accomplishments with the words, "To American production, without which this war would have been lost."[14]

One can overdo the "production" theme, of course. Wartime prosperity provided many Americans with the money to buy not only necessities but some luxuries. And the experience of women—who might have been called upon to produce during the conflict but were expected to return to the sphere of consumption when the war came to an end—suggests that the production mania was not intended to bring any basic alteration in the shape of the society and in its culture. Nonetheless, the production mania made its mark on U.S. culture, if only temporarily. Michael Curtiz's *Mildred Pierce* (1945) plays the modest producer desires of the protagonist Mildred against the insatiable consumer passion of her daughter Veda; film theorist Mary Ann Doane has described Veda as a "consumer vampire" whose excesses—both economic and sexual—threaten the production economy of scarcity. In the theater, Arthur Miller's play *All My Sons* (1947), first produced at the Coronet

Theater in New York City, was close enough to the war and its issues to establish the protagonist as a producer—the owner of a factory making airplane parts—and to ground the dramatic action in a moral dilemma involving the quality of the parts. (From Coca-Cola to ball bearings, just about every product was sold during the war with the claim that it was a well-produced, "quality" item.)

In contrast, the postwar years of the late forties featured a renewed interest in consumption. Miller's 1949 play, *Death of a Salesman*, features Willy Loman as a salesman occupying a space between production and consumption—making a living by selling himself (by turning himself into a commodity to be consumed). Cheesecake changed, too. The wartime ideal, representing the collective desires of American fighting men, was the leggy Betty Grable, whose pinup was a portrait of activity: upright, full of potential energy, ready to move on those long legs, ultimately a producer. But Grable was replaced by an altogether different ideal: the bosomy, supine, postwar female, foreshadowed during the war in Jane Russell's performance in *The Outlaw* (1943), seems incapable of producing anything but milk and babies (that is, more consumers).[15]

Separated by time and space and uncomfortably engaged in new roles as producers, wartime Americans indulged in another form of the sentimental: they dreamed—Bing Crosby's dream of a "White Christmas" (1942); George Bailey's (Jimmy Stewart) dream of college, a life of adventure, and escape from Bedford Falls in Frank Capra's classic film, *It's a Wonderful Life* (1946); the American male's "impossible dream" of the Varga girl; the dream that Superman (1938), Wonderwoman (1941), or even God might see fit to intervene and bring a measure of order to a chaotic universe. In 1942 and 1943, magazine advertisements featured the simplest of all dreams: the dream of a future that would someday arrive, despite what seemed an interminable present. "This is an American child," read an advertisement for Ipana toothpaste. "This is an American home. Lucky young American. No child in the World has so bright a future."[16]

Most often, Americans dreamed the capitalist dream of the postwar world as a consumer paradise. As early as 1943, David Cushman Coyle was "Planning a World of Plenty" for the readers of *Parent's Magazine*, anticipating a "brave new world . . . made possible by the speeded-up production of [the] war years." Revere Copper and Brass struck a similar note, suggesting in 1942 that the "new machines and new metals" required for the war effort would lead to "the unbounded promise of the years that begin with X-DAY." In 1944, Libby-Owens-Ford offered housewives the glistening modernism of the "Kitchen of Tomorrow." And from 1941 through 1946, *Ladies' Home Journal* published designs by nationally known architects for their "dream houses."[17]

When the postwar world finally arrived, it brought with it a reversion—half-hearted in some ways, and incomplete, to be sure, but a reversion nonetheless—from wartime emphases on the group and democracy to an emphasis on the individual and freedom. The change was perhaps most noticeable among postwar intellectuals, who found one reason or another to pull away from a variety of leftist political sympathies—Marxism, communism, socialism, the industrial unionism of the Congress of Industrial Organizations (CIO)—that had been highly attractive during the Great Depression. Some had been repulsed by Stalin's vicious purges in the Soviet Union in the 1930s. Others became disenchanted with Marxism and communism when the Soviets signed a nonaggression treaty with Hitler's Nazi Germany in 1939, or when aggressive postwar Soviet behavior in Eastern Europe seemed to have unilaterally brought on a cold war. The relative prosperity of the postwar years seemed to many Americans to reduce the need for the militant policies of the more radical labor unions; some also felt that the aggressive social and economic policies of Franklin Roosevelt's New Deal were no longer appropriate. Many intellectuals, disturbed by the growth of bureaucracy, by cultural homogenization, and by the dangers they perceived in a burgeoning mass culture, were much more interested in challenges to individual autonomy than in making critiques, as they had in the 1930s, of the unequal distribution of wealth and the condition of the working class under capitalism. While old-age security, unemployment insurance, the minimum wage, and other New Deal innovations were not eliminated by future Democratic or Republican administrations, the ameliorative fervor of the depression decade for the most part disappeared during the war and afterwards.

For a time during the presidential campaign of 1948 it seemed that Henry Wallace and his Progressive party had the potential to reunite radicals and old-line New Deal liberals in a revitalized alliance of the political left. The self-proclaimed candidate of the "common man," Wallace called for a more vigorous and far-reaching welfare state. He also continued to hold out the possibility of working with the Soviets on an international level (in the foreign trade sphere, for example) and with American Communists domestically. In the end, the cold war proved fatal to his candidacy; a "vote for Wallace," wrote James Burnham in a typical smear, "is a vote for Stalin." In 1947, ex-New Dealers like Hubert Humphrey and Eleanor Roosevelt, labor leaders like Walter Reuther and David Dubinsky, and writers and intellectuals like economist John Kenneth Galbraith and theologian Reinhold Niebuhr announced their opposition to Wallace's politics with the formation of Americans for Democratic Action (ADA), an organization that combined liberal reformism in domestic policy with an unremitting anticommunism at home and abroad. Based on an acceptance of the cold war, their decision to abandon Wallace for Truman's modest reformism signaled the death knell of postwar radicalism and marked the emergence of a new breed of cautious, quiescent liberal that would remain dominant until the mid-1960s.[18]

Cultural signs of the new, more conservative and individualistic perspective were everywhere: in the postwar vogue of psychiatry and psychoanalysis; in the novels of Raymond Chandler and Mickey Spillane, with their isolated, private-eye ("I") heroes, calculating survivors in a corrupt and dangerous world; in the genre of film noir, whose existential protagonists could seldom do more than attribute their downfall to a bizarre contingency; in the bursts of enthusiasm for entrepreneurship and a creative avant-garde; in the comic strips, where "Steve Canyon" debuted on 13 January 1947 as a worldwide, free-lance troubleshooter; and in the paintings of the abstract expressionists, who abandoned the social realism of the 1930s for a focus and reliance on the self.[19]

Consistent with their declining enthusiasm for wartime values, postwar Americans threw aside the group-based culture of production—of assembly lines, factories, coworkers, and union activity—for a culture of consumption whose central activities could be pursued by individuals or, at most, by families. But this is not to say that everyone ran for the stores the moment the war ended. Hundreds of thousands of rank-and-file workers went on strike in 1946 and 1947, not simply for higher wages that would allow greater access to consumer goods, but over a variety of producer issues: better working conditions, control of the work process, independence on the job, and fellowship with coworkers. Only after 1947, when the Taft-Hartley Act brought militant workers under the control of management, and when the United Auto Workers (UAW) and other major unions agreed to trade off production demands for pensions and increased wages, did the movement toward a consumption-based economy approach full stride. Irreconcilable differences between workers and owners over production were displaced into the realm of consumption, where issues of ownership and class were softened and attenuated. Postwar elites, disturbed by class divisions, new political parties, and other signs of a divided and confused society that together threatened to prevent the creation of a "national political economy," used consumption as a cultural "cement."[20]

One sign of the emergence of a culture of consumption was the disappearance of those wartime advertisements that featured the workplace; most postwar advertisements hardly recognized that a production process existed. Instead, Coca-Cola became a product to be consumed while consuming—one postwar advertisement pictures two women with packages stopping at a soda fountain, along with the slogan: "Shop Refreshed . . . Have a Coca-Cola." A 1949 advertisement for Chevrolet commingled the idea of purchasing with the automobile as an irresistible spectacle: "Look . . . Ride . . . Decide . . . it's the most Beautiful BUY of all!"[21]

The mass media also helped to sell the idea of consumption with programs such as "Queen for a Day": the desperate women who participated competed for a cornucopia of consumer goods by describing the conditions of poverty, ill health, and misfortune under which they and their families lived. Television missed nary a beat during its first full season in 1948, conjoining consumption and entertainment in "Kelvinator Kitchen" and "Missus Goes A-Shopping," the latter a customer participation program broadcast from supermarkets. Postwar situation comedies such as "The Honeymooners" and dramas such as "I Remember Mama" often revolved around the purchase of consumer goods for the home, encouraging Americans to spend rather than save and presenting consumerism as a mechanism of assimilation in a classless and family-centered way of life.[22]

By midcentury, Americans were weighing the costs and benefits of a society that seemed on the verge of eliminating hard and serious work altogether. Such was the world of the comic strip "Pogo," where a surplus of goods and leisure made possible poetry contests, baseball games, and the regular celebration of holidays. In "Pogo," the situation rankles Bun Rabbit, who announces his readiness to take his complaint to the Oval Office: "Put down that piano! An' fix our holiday situation. Every time a man wants to work he got a vacation staring him in the face." Even the depression-era world of "Li'l Abner" yielded to postwar consumerism, captured by cartoonist Al Capp in a white bottle-shaped creature called a Shmoo. Introduced in 1948, the Shmoo is consumer utopia incarnate, capable of bypassing the factory and the production process by laying cartoned eggs and giving bottled milk. Depending on how one cooks it, the Shmoo tastes like steak, chicken, or pork. As a popular recording put it, succinctly summarizing postwar consumerism, "A Shmoo can do most anything." The Shmoo mentality was apparent in late-1940s home design: the phrase "home of tomorrow" had ceased to connote avant-garde style or mass production and had come to refer only to a container for consumer goods and gadgets.[23]

The high consumerism of the postwar years was more than an economic phenomenon; it influenced and shaped questions of morality. In two Hollywood films of the mid and late forties—*Good Sam* (1948) and *Miracle on 34th Street* (1946)—moral inquiries were launched from the consumer Elysium of the department store. In both films, store employees engage in what are presented as acts of high morality by sending customers elsewhere to locate a particular product, but it is a morality grounded only in the consumer's right of access to the entire marketplace. *Miracle on 34th Street* narrates the journey of a little girl from cynicism to faith; her breakthrough to true religion is achieved in a final, heart-rending scene in which she, her mother, and her mother's fiancé happen upon a house in the suburbs that is for sale and ready for immediate occupancy. In short, she can believe in Santa Claus

11

(and, in a larger sense, in God, progress, and the goodness of man) only when he can deliver the ultimate postwar consumer good. The willingness of Mom—an anal-retentive personnel manager at Macy's—to go along with the big purchase represents her decision to shed a veneer of production-based (wartime) values and to acclimate to a new, consumer-based (postwar) domesticity. In the terms of feminist theory, acquiescence in consumption of a product (the house) signifies the woman's acquiescence in her own objectification; in the act of consuming, she agrees to become a commodity.[24]

Consumerism also helped disguise the strongly capitalist, elitist, and patriarchal dimensions of postwar society. The central argument was contained in a 1947 *March of Time* segment on the fashion industry, whose title "Fashion Means Business" implied that "fashion" was the cause of "business," rather than the reverse. Denying the power of the fashion industry and capitalism to influence style and shape social patterns, the newsreel program described fashion as the product of a perfect female democracy—of "fifty million determined consumers," each entirely independent of all but personal desire ("What every woman wants, no one in the business can foretell with certainty"). As *The March of Time* conceptualized the process, these female desires are translated into high fashion, and then into mass-produced garments suitable for ordinary people, a point at which "fashion becomes big business." Thus, women were held responsible not only for the "New Look" designs of the late 1940s that accompanied their return to the domesticity of the kitchen and boudoir; they were also the first link in the chain of mass production. The ideology of consumerism elevated women into veritable captains of industry.

Because consuming was the essential act of the good citizen, to save—let alone hoard one's money—was at best anachronistic, at worst an invitation to social upheaval. Scrooge McDuck, who first appeared in Disney comic books in 1947, was for the most part a throwback to an earlier capitalism of acquisition and hard work, a fowl willing to forgo consumption for the accumulation of money itself—mountains of greenbacks and gold coins, stored in an enormous vault—and the sensuous pleasure of rolling around in it. Radio comedian Jack Benny was another famous miser. He, too, had a vault—the site of an annual pilgrimage—as well as a pay phone and a cigarette machine, should friends drop by. Amid the automobile craze of the late 1940s, Benny denied himself the quintessential postwar commodity—a new car—refusing to part with an ancient Maxwell.[25]

By 1948 American society had entered a postproduction phase of consumption and abstract wealth and, under pressure, was beginning to come apart. The perils of hoarding and the pitfalls of consumerism were explored, along with other aspects of conduct in a hyperconsumer society, in *The Treasure of Sierra Madre* (1948), which earned John Huston Academy Awards for writing and directing. The film starred Walter Huston (John's father), Tim

Holt, and Humphrey Bogart as western adventurers who discover and pan a rich lode of gold dust, only to have it vanish in the wind after a disastrous falling out on the trip back to civilization. On one level the film is a parable of unrequited consumerism, about the consumption that never takes place and to which all else is secondary. Postwar audiences, itching to see how the protagonists would spend their winnings, must have found the film enormously frustrating. On another level, it is a parable of a society that has given up production for the burden of abstract wealth (a raw material to which no value has been added, a wealth that bears no relation to any product or real system of production and whose only use is the potential one of consumption). In this sense, the film is related to the pyramid friendship clubs that were so popular in the winter of 1948–49: thousands of people engaged in chain letter schemes, desperately trying to make instant fortunes. On still another level, the film found the postwar money mania responsible for the destruction of the wartime world of male companionship; under the influence of the gold and what it will buy, Bogart descends to a hysterical paranoia, denying the values of friendship and trust and the existence of human decency. By the same token, *The Treasure of Sierra Madre* would seem to argue for the moral superiority of the wartime world, when the requirements of production served as a kind of social glue; as long as the miners maintain some marginal relationship with production (as long as they labor at the mining process) they—and by implication the society—remain intact as a social unit.[26]

As Huston's film reveals, the emergence of an economy and culture of consumption brought anxieties and doubts. Perhaps, after a decade and a half of economic depression and war, Americans were too accustomed to thinking in terms of production and saving to feel entirely secure in their new roles as consumers and spenders. Despite their newfound access to automobiles, television, and a panoply of other consumer wonders, Americans were—as *Time* and *Life* seemed to relish pointing out—unhappy. Postwar affluence was a key ingredient in the guilt felt by the surviving son in *All My Sons:* "I felt wrong to be alive, to open the bank-book, to drive the new car, to see the new refrigerator." The exasperation of the moment was captured by Far Westerner Richard L. Neuberger in an essay in *Harper's* on Americans' uncomfortable relationship with the wilderness: "Our patron saints are no longer Lewis and Clark, but Abercrombie & Fitch."[27]

Just as the mentality of production gave way to the postwar culture of consumption, so the wartime culture of separation and sentimentality yielded to one of reunification and domesticity. According to the standard postwar mythology, weary GIs trudged home to the accepting arms of wives and girlfriends, went to college on the GI Bill and took out a VA home mortgage, moved the new baby-boom family to the suburbs, and, of course, lived happily ever after.

There is no doubt that the culture of the late 1940s was profoundly shaped by domesticity, or that Americans were, in the title of historian Elaine Tyler May's recent book, *Homeward Bound*. Yet differences of opinion exist over the meaning of the turn to domesticity. According to May, the "family-centered culture" of postwar America signified neither a simple return to familiar prewar social patterns nor an optimistic celebration of the end of conflict. For May, the postwar family was a mechanism of "containment" in an age of profound insecurity—a fortress protecting its members from the potential decadence of consumer capitalism, from the anxieties of the atomic age, from an unpredictable economy, from perverse and promiscuous sexuality, from the freedom and rootlessness of modern life, and, most of all, from cold war communism, which intensified every other threat. Obsessed with security from the middle of the war years through the 1950s, Americans—both men and women—willingly surrendered independence and autonomy for the certitude of a stable future. From this perspective, domesticity was pessimistic rather than optimistic, defensive rather than forward-looking.[28]

While granting this perspective on the family, the 1940s should also be understood as a relatively unstable period in the long history of domesticity. It was a time when domesticity could still be feared, resisted, and deflected. That is the theme of Todd Webb's "Welcome Home" series of postwar photographs. Following his discharge from the Navy in November 1945, Webb took to the streets of New York City, training his camera on doorways and the signs that beckoned to returning servicemen: "Welcome Home, Leo," "Welcome Home, Jim & Henry," "Welcome Home, G.I. Joe." Reviewing a 1946 exhibition of these and other Webb photographs at the Museum of the City of New York, critic Beaumont Newhall praised Webb for his "warmth of appreciation" and for bringing out "the human quality even when people are absent." The photographs, however, suggest something quite different. Not only are they peopleless, but they present the home as a black hole, an abyss of darkness guarded by the sort of doorway that threatens detective Philip Marlowe in the film noir production, *The Lady in the Lake* (1947). Similarly, the best known of Hollywood's postwar films about returning veterans depict the moment of homecoming—that is, the founding moment of postwar domesticity—as awkward, traumatic, or disappointing. In *Till the End of Time* (1946), Cliff Harper (Guy Madison) arrives home to an empty house; his father is out playing golf. In *The Best Years of Our Lives* (1946), Al Stephenson's distance from the domestic is confirmed when his daughter reveals that she has taken a course in "domestic science"; as a site of expertism, Al feels the home moving beyond his old-fashioned ways.[29]

These and other films also suggest that the culture of domesticity was in its own way imperial, forged over and against a surprisingly powerful male subculture produced by the war. In both *The Best Years of Our Lives* and *Till the End of Time*, the male-female bond of the new domesticity is rendered problematic by a preexisting male bonding. Indeed, in contrast to the dynamic, natural, and familiar interaction of the male subcultures that open these films, domesticity is usually presented as a self-conscious experience in which real men only reluctantly participate. *The Men* (1950), a late entry in the genre, starred Marlon Brando (in his first film) as Ken, a moody, introspective, paraplegic veteran, and Teresa Wright as Ellie, his pre-injury girlfriend, who still loves the guy and wants to marry him. After an initial bout of deep and general disillusionment, Ken settles into the hospital routine of male camaraderie, group sports, and determined (upper) body building. He eventually agrees to see Ellie, and then, after considerable coaxing, to marry her. But Ken and Ellie have only to cross the threshold of their marital abode to find themselves locked in a paired isolation so intense that their fragile relationship breaks down. That same night, Ken returns to the male world of the hospital, determined to stay. When, for his own good, a committee of the "self-governing" Paraplegic Veterans Association votes to require his discharge, Ken, having now given up all illusions about his physical condition (as well as the possibility of his remaining in a male world), and having come to grips with "reality" (the reality of his body and of the necessity of hearth and home), appears as the supplicant before the shrine of domesticity, a single-family, suburban house. As he drags his broken body (and soul) up the walk, the ever-helpful Ellie appears. "Do you want me to help you up the steps?" she asks. And Ken replies, "Please." If one interprets the paraplegic theme as a metaphor, and Ken's reluctance as the reluctance of all veterans—or even of all postwar men—one can see postwar domesticity as a fear-inducing experience of isolation and confinement, an ideology of contentment screening an arena of discord.

Postwar domesticity was a powerful social and cultural force from which few Americans were completely free. Yet despite its strength, it was also depicted in the 1940s as a fragile frame, as vulnerable and besieged as the cold war–engaged nation itself. One source of that vulnerability was the desire and sexuality of the female, usually signaled in film by scenes in which the female protagonist appropriates the gaze—that is, looks too long and hard at the male protagonist, thus committing the primal sin of turning him into an emasculated subject. In *Humoresque* (1946), it is the gaze of wealthy society woman Helen Wright (Joan Crawford)—a gaze signaled by Wright's eyeglasses—that tempts working-class violinist John Boray (John Garfield) to deny the values of his own community and family, represented by his mother and a sign, "Home Sweet Home," in the stairwell of the family homestead. From *Rebecca* (1940) to *Caught* (1949), the forties was also the period of female gothic or paranoid women's films in which the home—the woman's space of domesticity—becomes the site of suspense, dread, and horror, usually as the result of some exterior menace.[30] The threat from without is especially obvious in a film such as *Sorry, Wrong Number* (1948): a bedridden Leona

Stevenson (Barbara Stanwyck), linked to the world beyond her apartment only by a bedside telephone, gradually discovers that the city outside her open window is hatching a plot that will result in her murder that very evening.

The incipient hegemony of the domestic was threatened by another sort of invasion in 1948, when television arrived in the American home. Like cigarette smoking in the 1960s, television in the late forties was the subject of studies and counterstudies, each heightening or allaying anxieties over the new technology's impact. While research carried out in southern California presented television viewing as an activity that monopolized energies and decreased time spent on everything from pleasure driving to family conversation, a 1948 CBS–Rutgers University survey emphasized the "new family interests" that developed in TV homes after six months of ownership, including 32 percent of respondents who reported "new interest in each other" (half of whom said that the new interest in each other revolved around "television itself"). In his important book, *Radio, Television, and Society* (1950), Charles A. Siepmann lamented the decline of privacy in a "gregarious" and "noisy" world too often given over to collective, mass experiences, yet found television a "more private, intimate, and personal" medium than radio or cinema, and one ideally suited to the exploration of psychological themes.[31]

Early advertisements for television reveal the society's need to conceptualize television as a social instrument consistent with domesticity and to otherwise contain its disruptive potential. In one advertisement a mirror was pointedly used to multiply the number of people pictured, apparently to emphasize that television was compatible with, and even encouraged, social activity; in another, to optimistically emphasize television's ability to function in the traditional home, the set was placed in a colonial-style room beneath a collection of mounted antique plates; in others—in which television's role in generating images of spectacle with enormous mass appeal seemed to be denied—the intruding technology was surrounded with encyclopedias, books, framed art, potted plants, and other signs of civilization, culture, learning, and elitism. Still another approach, designed to assuage concerns about the medium's hypnotic qualities as well as its impact on sociability and activity, was to present at least one viewer turned partially or completely away from the instrument, sharing with others some television-inspired thought or, in the case of children, acting out an image displayed on the screen.[32]

The separation of the forties into half-decades—the first half characterized by World War II, the group, democracy, sentimentality, and production, the second half by the cold war, the individual, freedom, domesticity, and consumption—provides the most basic sort of outline for understanding some of the era's major themes and developments. But the differences between the first and second halves of the decade were neither complete nor unqualified. In contrast to the "we" imperative of the war years, popular song of the time rang with a litany of "I," "I," "I," and the frequent mention of "slackers" in wartime films and newsreel serials such as *The March of Time* belied the assumption that the war had produced an easy consensus on the value of productivity.[33] Granting the far-reaching domesticity of the postwar years, the culture of domesticity was, as we have seen, a contentious one whose ability to absorb postwar social tensions and fissures was something less than complete. As the mass strikes of 1946 revealed, the production-centered culture of the war years did not yield at once or fully to the imperative of consumption. One might interpret the Taft-Hartley Act, which contained several measures to discourage strikes, as an effort to redirect the energies of workers away from the still-vital arena of the workplace and toward the developing ideology of consumption.

Nor do other data fit as neatly as one might wish into the wartime-peacetime framework. Although the arrival of commercial television, the Polaroid Land camera (a commercial success in 1949), and xerography (the Xerox copier appeared in 1950) would seem to make a strong case for the late 1940s as a newly visual culture, other elements of the period's heightened visual sensibility, including *Life* magazine and *The March of Time* newsreels, date to the mid-1930s. If one demarcates the decade by the wide and wild ties worn by men of all ages, then the forties began in late 1943, when the bold cravat was first introduced, and ended in 1951, when the Red Scare, the Korean War, and concern about the Soviet acquisition of the atomic bomb (1949) led to a more sober and conservative male look.[34] Similarly, the creative spark that produced the excitement, energy, and individual virtuosity of bebop jazz was struck in 1939, two years before the United States entered the war against Japan and Germany. While hard-boiled detectives seem a perfect representation of the decade, Raymond Chandler's famous protagonist, Philip Marlowe, was introduced in 1939, and Dashiell Hammett's Sam Spade dates to the late 1920s. Scholars have most thoroughly studied the intellectual life of the forties through the prism of politics, focusing on the death rattle of Marxism and the decline of ideology as the decade's most salient themes; yet disaffection with radicalism was under way in the mid-1930s—when word of Stalin's purge of his political opponents reached the United States—and had taken another step forward in 1939 with the Nazi-Soviet nonaggression pact. If one used cinematic trends to mark major turning points, the forties might begin rather sensibly in 1941, with Orson Welles's exploration in *Citizen Kane* of multiple narrators, the flashback, chiaroscuro cinematography, and other techniques that would characterize the new genre of film noir. But the end of that era would not arrive until 1958 when another Welles film, *Touch of Evil*, proved to be the last contribution to the genre.

Divided the forties surely were, but the decade just as surely had its own essence: doubt. This doubt was rooted in the forebodings of an age that had witnessed a war that left sixty million persons dead; the murder of six million Jews in the Holocaust; the development and use of the atomic bomb; the Great Depression, which seemed always on the verge of reappearing; and the cold war, which ironically matched the nation against the Soviet Union, its wartime ally. Against the backdrop of these events, Americans questioned the central assumptions of their culture: the essential goodness of man; the immutability of progress; the worthiness of democracy; the feasibility of freedom; the beneficence of science. Although this questioning continued into the next decade—fueled by the fall of China to communism in 1949, the beginning of the Korean War in 1950, and the fervor of Sen. Joseph McCarthy's campaign against internal subversion—by the mid-1950s Americans had repressed, modulated, or put to rest most of the concerns over which they had agonized just a few years before.

The asking of fundamental questions in the forties produced a culture that was more pessimistic and cynical than before, but it did not—at least not at the time—create anything resembling a new, more negative cultural consensus. Instead, ambivalence held sway. Culture took the form of disparate and conflicting responses to the central problems of forties existence. At the deepest level of their culture, Americans simply did not know whether to smother their anxieties with pension plans and the security of domesticity or celebrate chance as a way of transcending the controlling structures and institutions of modern society. They could not decide whether to embrace the science that had produced wonder drugs and radar or deny the cold rationalism that had brought forth the bomb and engulfed the emotional side of the human psyche. They could not be sure whether the hope of the future lay in the international arena of Wendell Willkie's "one world" and the United Nations or—on the other side of the spectrum, bypassing the sphere of politics and society—in the unconscious mind of the individual self. Americans of the forties lived their lives in a present that was every bit as uncertain as the depression-ridden past they were fleeing and the atomic-age future they feared.

two

The Culture of Contingency

In the years after 1945, Americans moved to the suburbs by the millions, enrolled in thousands of newly created pension plans, and gave their support to massive federal expenditures for armaments. These activities, and many others, were evidence of a deep desire for security—security from urban chaos, from the anxieties of old age, and from the unemployment lines that had been a part of life in the 1930s. While cities, old age, and fears of job-lessness were hardly new to the 1940s, events unique to that decade—Pearl Harbor, World War II, the Holocaust, the dropping of the atomic bomb, the cold war—produced a culture of profound contingency, in which virtually everything, one's employment, one's values, one's very life, seemed dependent on the vagaries of chance. The sense of contingency that hung over the forties, then, was more than the contingency of capitalism—more, that is, than worries about the state of the economy, inflation, the stability of the banks, or the job market.

Aside from the economic, two sorts of contingency affected the mood of Americans during the decade. One was the contingency of existence, a contingency that flowed from being drafted and shot at, from witnessing the murder of the Jews, and from subjecting others—the populations of Dresden and Hiroshima, to start with—to the possibility of sudden, undeserved death. The other, a moral and ethical contingency, was characterized by the growing sense that it was now more difficult than ever before to ground one's conduct in a stable system of values. Although moral contingency was a matter of general concern as early as the Darwinian revolution of the mid nineteenth century, the seminal events of the forties seemed to confirm that humanity had, indeed, been set adrift from its ethical moorings. Like life itself, values seemed to come and go, without pattern or reason.

The new sense of contingency was initially, and perhaps primarily, a product of World War II—of how it began, how it ended, and how it was fought.[1] For Americans, the war had begun, of course, at the remote Pacific naval base of Pearl Harbor, when the Japanese air force shattered whatever remained of the belief that the country could through sheer force of will control its destiny. This loss of control was reflected in the ordinary language in which soldiers described the military situation on Hawaii after the surprise attack. "I don't believe we will have another major attack in the near future," wrote Lt. Col. Herbert Blackwell, "since now we are completely on guard. However, since what happened Sunday I am not placing much weight on expectations." In the days that followed, understandably wary guards fired their guns at animal sounds and swaying bushes—the first signs of the neurotic sensibility, itself the child of contingency, that would wash over the decade of war and cold war and ultimately produce the UFO scare of 1947 and the anticommunist witch hunts of Harry Truman and Joe McCarthy.

Contingency inheres in combat, and, as one might expect, the letters of American servicemen reflect their immersion in a roulettelike military culture. "Everyone intends to do just as much as he can to get himself home," wrote a Marine Corps dive-bomber pilot in 1943, "and everyone has an equal chance."[2] Yet the contingency of combat directly affected only the minority of soldiers who were actual combatants and, except for the traumatic nightmares of returning veterans, was for the most part erased or shelved with the return to peacetime conditions.

In contrast, the contingency brought about by the end of the war—the contingency of the atomic bomb—was of a different order altogether. An unemployed man could understand his joblessness in the context of business cycles, and even a dying soldier could find a meaning for death in the enduring struggles of nation-states and ideologies. But the instant incineration of one hundred thousand civilians by an atomic bomb offered up a new kind of death for which there could be no adequate preparation, that seemed perversely designed for urban, civilian populations, and whose source—the atom—seemed at once simple and incomprehensible. Writing for *Saturday Review* following the explosions at Hiroshima and Nagasaki, Norman Cousins described what he called "a primitive fear, the fear of the unknown, the fear of forces man can neither channel nor comprehend. This fear is not new; in its classical form it is the fear of irrational death. But overnight it has become intensified, magnified. It has burst out of the subconscious and into the conscious, filling the mind with primordial apprehensions."[3]

Although until 1949 the bomb was an exclusive possession of the United States, the feelings of indeterminacy created by the mere existence of the new weapon were remarkably vivid and concrete among Americans. The bomb's enormous destructive power was not lost on ordinary citizens, among them a western New York woman who penned these diary entries for 6 August (the day of Truman's announcement) and 9 August: "The atomic bomb was dropped on Hiroshima and killed everything."/"An automatic bomb was let loos on Hirijima a city size of Rochester and it obliterated the whole population." In 1946 Edward C. Condon, the head of the National Bureau of Standards, described the anxiety generated by a device whose very nature had created a climate resembling terrorism: "In any room where a file case can be stored, in any district of a great city, near any key building or installation, a determined effort can secrete a bomb capable of killing a hundred thousand people. . . . Will you look equally at the great sea of roofs around your house in the city? Any one of them may conceal the bomb. . . . We may never know who did it, who planted or smuggled or shipped the bombs." Some social analysts predicted that the uncertainty built into a nuclear world would result in a presentist culture given over to fashion, spectator sports, sensuality, and other examples or products of the fleeting and trivial.[4] Having learned of the bombing of Hiroshima and Nagasaki as she was writing a sequel to *And Keep Your Powder Dry*, anthropologist Margaret Mead "tore up the manuscript. Once we knew that it was possible for a people to destroy the enemy, themselves, and all bystanders, the world itself was changed. And no sentence written with that knowledge of man's new capacity could be meshed into any sentence written the week before."[5]

The UFO scare of mid-1947, a product of foreign policy frustrations, fears of attack, and the developing cold war, was one expression of the culture of contingency. The first sighting occurred on 25 June 1947, when the pilot of a private plane flying between Mounts Ranier and Adams claimed to have seen nine "saucerlike" objects. Only days before, *Pravda* had rejected Soviet participation in the Marshall Plan program for European reconstruction, and the United Nations was proving incapable of resolving a crisis in the Balkans. In early July, Eisenhower raised the possibility of an "insane attack on those who work for peace" and said the United States did not "exclude the possibility" of war within one year.

In this atmosphere of anxiety, Americans began seeing things. By mid-July, "flying saucers" had been reported in thirty-five states and Canada—from a Texas woman who reported a disk "as big as a washtub" to a United Air Lines pilot and copilot who claimed to have seen "four or five 'somethings.'" When the Veterans of Foreign Wars (VFW) national commander in chief wired Washington for an explanation and received no answer, he announced that "too little is being told to the people of this country." Scientists and public officials described the saucer scare in naturalistic and psychological terms, arguing that UFO sightings amounted to a "mass hysteria" triggered by visual observations related to rocket testing in White

Sands, New Mexico. Assigned the task of analyzing the UFO sightings for the readers of *Life* magazine, cartoonist Boris Artzybasheff explained that "residents of the planet Neptune, having attained a civilization far in advance of that now enjoyed on earth, are shelling the universe with crockery." "More favored planets," he added, had been bombarded with "teapots and dinner plates."[6]

By generating the anxiety that danger lay behind any and every door, the cold war exacerbated the feelings of contingency and fostered a second panic, similar in timing to the saucer scare but not so harmless in its consequences. The "sex crime" panic that began in the late 1940s focused on the rape and sexual murder of women and especially children. The tenor of public concern may be gleaned from a photograph that appeared in the July 1947 (the month of the UFO panic) *American Magazine*. Accompanied by the query of the Federal Bureau of Investigation (FBI) director, J. Edgar Hoover, "How Safe Is Your Daughter?" the photograph featured three little girls fleeing an enormous hand that threatened to grab them from behind. A battered garbage can served to remind readers that the problem was an urban one. A caption, set within the photograph against a black background, announced that "the nation's women and children will never be secure . . . so long as degenerates run wild." Although crime reports reveal rising incidents of sexual offenses throughout the two decades after 1935, they also reveal no epidemic of the violent and sensational crimes described in the media;[7] the sex crime panic appears to have been nearly as independent of social reality as its UFO counterpart.

Despite evidence that most sexual contacts between children and adults involved an adult known to the child (i.e., the incidents were not contingent), the sex crime literature encouraged feelings of contingency by focusing on strangers as the source of the problem. The popular press also played up indeterminacy by insisting on the unpredictability of the crime. "Who knows," asked a *Collier's* essay as the panic was nearing its peak in the summer of 1949, "where or when the next psychopath or hoodlum will strike? In your town? In your street?"[8] Indeed, contingency was embedded in the concept of a sexual psychopath, defined by psychiatrists as someone with an "utter lack of power to control his sexual impulses" and thus "likely to attack . . . the objects of his uncontrolled and uncontrollable desires."[9] Although the timing of the panic suggests that it followed rather than overlapped the problems of adjustment facing returning soldiers, concerns over the social stability of war veterans suggest that related anxieties about sexuality and violence may have shaped the public's image of the sexual psychopath. At the very least, newspaper headlines such as "Veteran Beheads Wife with Jungle Machete," "Ex-Marine Held in Rape Murder," and "Sailor Son Shoots Father" marked the veteran as a threat even to the family unit, contributing to the atmosphere of uncertainty that was so much a part of the late 1940s.[10]

The war, the use of the atomic bomb, and the murder of six million European Jews contributed to the other contingency—the moral and ethical contingency, which made itself felt as a worldwide failure to conceptualize and act upon reasonable standards of human conduct. Even in a decade clarified by war and cold war, Americans had some difficulty distinguishing right from wrong and friend from enemy. *Mister Roberts* (1946), Thomas Heggen's best-selling novel about a Navy cargo ship plying the South Pacific in the last days of World War II, describes a wartime America bereft of idealism. The war in Europe hardly exists (Lieutenant Langston observes V-E Day "by retiring at nine instead of ten, and by sleeping a little more soundly than usual"), and the Japanese are nowhere to be seen; instead, the crew members focus their hostility on the bumbling and authoritarian captain of the *Reluctant*. The only "moral" person in the book is Lieutenant Roberts, whose repeated requests for reassignment to the "real" war are denied. Yet even Roberts questions the truth of phrases such as "our honored dead" and wonders aloud if the conflict in Europe served any moral purpose. "If you had asked me four years ago," he tells the ship's doctor, "I could have told you to hell and back what this war was about. I would have overwhelmed you with moral superiority. I would have used terms like 'war against fascism,' 'holy war,' 'crusade,' and so forth. . . . And perhaps, Doc, there was a lot of justice in that sort of talk. Perhaps there still is: I don't know. It seems to me that causes are hellishly elusive things."[11] In the end, Roberts is reduced to the symbolic (though possibly existential) act of throwing the captain's potted palm overboard. Heggen committed suicide in 1949.[12]

While Heggen seemed to be mourning the loss of something important to believe in, Sidney Kingsley's play *Detective Story* (1949) criticizes excessive moralism and suggests the need for understanding the contingent nature of things. The protagonist is detective James McLeod, a hard-nosed, messianic moralist whose relentless efforts to punish the guilty will brook no opposition. The immediate object of McLeod's passion is illegal abortionist Kurt Schneider, whose latest "ice-tong job" has resulted in the death of a young woman and whose guilt is, for McLeod, beyond question. A very different position is articulated by the reporter Joe Feinson, who in response to McLeod's injunction to "print the truth for once" says, "Which truth?—Yours, his, theirs, mine?"

Gradually, Kingsley undermines McLeod's moralism. We learn that McLeod's sense of conviction has its origins not in reason but in a traumatic childhood; his hostility toward Schneider is displaced hostility toward his father, who abused and tormented his mother ("Every time I look at one of these babies, I see my father's face"). We learn, too, what McLeod at first does not know—that his wife, Mary, had long ago been the beneficiary of one of Schneider's abortions. In a world in which truth is complex and guilt problematic, McLeod's rigid moralism is literally psychopathic. As Joe puts it, "Why must you always make everything so black and white? Remember, we're all of us falling down all the time."[13] Yet beyond the conviction that passion and reason are inadequate guides to conduct, and that the truth is a mosaic in gray, Kingsley offers his audience little help in constructing a convincing ethics. The road to moral decisions is largely intuitive, dependent on something as vague as a feeling about people, the "sixth sense" that Joe mentions.

In the cold war universe of the late 1940s, it was all too easy for Americans to see the world in the black-and-white terms of a James McLeod, with peace, freedom, individualism, and democracy on one side and war, dictatorship, tyranny, and collectivism on the other, irrevocably separated by an "iron curtain." There were, to be sure, real and significant differences between the Soviet Union and the United States, and between the Eastern and Western bloc powers. But the simplifications of cold war thinking distorted nation-state relations and contributed to the paranoid sensibility that underpinned Truman's loyalty program (1947) and McCarthy's anticommunist crusade.

Without entirely dispensing with the us-versus-them point of view, the influential theologian Reinhold Niebuhr used the concept of contingency to develop a perspective on foreign relations far removed from the rigid anticommunist moralism of the Truman administration. His reflections, written for the most part in 1949 and 1950, were published in *The Irony of American History* (1952). Just as Joe had brought McLeod to question whether his way of seeing the world was "true," Niebuhr cautioned Americans to be aware of the "contingent elements" in our deepest ideals, even when those ideals seemed to be "universally valid." Just as McLeod needed to understand that he and Kurt Schneider were part of a larger network of relationships (including McLeod's wife) that made simple judgments inappropriate, so had American strength "interwoven our destiny with the destiny of many peoples and brought us into a vast web of history in which other wills, running in oblique or contrasting directions to our own, inevitably hinder or contradict what we most fervently desire." The "irony" of recent American history, then, was that the reasonable, proper, and "innocent" exercise of world responsibility in defeating Japan and holding back communism had brought the nation into a situation of enormous complexity and mystery in which innocence was inevitably lost and responsibility could be exercised only by "courting the prospective guilt of the atomic bomb."

A contingent, unpredictable world, governed by the "illogical and contradictory patterns of the historic drama," was no place for grand ideological systems (of whatever political hue) or the idealistic, universalistic nostrums of an Arthur Miller; nor could blame be fixed in any significant way in such a world. Just as Kingsley virtually eliminates McLeod's responsibility by interpreting his vision and conduct as the inevitable product of childhood experiences, so did Niebuhr understand the problems of the American nation as the product of "illusions which were derived both from the experiences and the ideologies of its childhood." His use of irony (which he defined as a "responsibility [that] is not due to a conscious choice but to an unconscious weakness") bypassed issues of agency and treated foreign policy as a matter distinct from economics and politics. Niebuhr's America had no great corporations seeking foreign markets and no hack politicians making political capital of anticommunism—only idealistic citizens unquestioningly accepting the nation's innocence and failing to appreciate "the fragmentariness of all human wisdom, the precariousness of all historic configurations of power, and the mixture of good and evil in all human virtue."[14] Just as McLeod must learn to love his wife Mary as someone other than the Virgin Mother, Americans needed to see their country through the prism of the Christian doctrine of original sin, and hence not as a fount of objectivity but as a nation affected by the ambitions and passions that affect all human relations. To the extent that Niebuhr assigned blame, it was leveled not at ambition or passion, or the mistaken policies they produce, but at the more abstract failure to understand and appreciate the absurdity of absolute innocence in a contingent world.

Film noir, the most important new film genre of the decade, was a conspicuous vehicle for the dissemination of the idea of contingency in both its basic forms: contingency experienced as chance event, and contingency experienced as a chaos that denied moral absolutes. Film noir protagonists were often ordinary, middle-class people whose lives—reflecting French existentialist philosopher Albert Camus's dictum that "at any street corner the absurd may strike a man in the face"—were suddenly altered by some unpredictable, even quirky event. For example, an accountant's trauma in *D.O.A.* (1950) begins when he is fatally poisoned for the altogether innocent act of notarizing a bill of sale; car trouble on the wrong stretch of Sunset Boulevard sets writer Joseph C. Gillis (William Holden) on the path to a bloody death in a Hollywood pool (*Sunset Boulevard* [1950]); and in *He Walked by Night* (1949), the protagonist is shot down by police when a car parked on a manhole cover prevents his escape.

Those who pridefully claim to be able to control contingency inevitably reap the whirlwind. In *Double Indemnity* (1944), the genial and competent Walter Neff (Fred MacMurray), salesman for the Pacific All-Risk Insurance Company, is fatefully tempted to commit murder for the love of a woman. The scheme fails not just because Neff has chosen an immoral course of action, nor even (though this is certainly a factor) because he has been somehow trapped by the opposite sex. Neff's sin is to believe that he can shape the future to his will, that he can bring events under his control in the most precise and sure way ("I'm the guy to do it"). Neff's plan begins to break down when he makes his way to the rear platform of a train to set the stage for a faked suicide, only to discover that it is occupied by another passenger (bad luck!). Neff carries on, but in the days that follow, his story and nerves are shredded by the mathematical probabilities (science) and hunches (intuition) offered up by his curious and determined supervisor, Keyes, and by a face-to-face meeting with the stranger on the train (who, in another twist, turns out to be of no consequence in the case). For Neff at least, the universe is at once too irregular, too unpredictable, and ultimately too perverse, to be mastered.

Film noir also captured the moral ambiguity of the age. Unlike the Bogart hero of *Casablanca* (1943), whose struggle to remain aloof from commitment is destined to fail under the pressures of nationalism and personal integrity, film noir's nonheroic hero has nothing to offer save an essential vulnerability and a basic decency that often is irredeemably compromised (Walter Neff commits murder, Joseph Gillis becomes a gigolo). Rather than articulate a set of responsible values, most film noir heroes, at best, only survive in their contests with unseen or amorphous enemies. "I feel all dead inside," says detective Bradford Galt in *The Dark Corner* (1946). "I'm backed up in a dark corner and I don't know who's hitting me!"[15] Other heroes of the genre, such as Neff, invite identification (it is difficult to desire Neff's fall) but not emulation (essentially a technocrat, and not the best one at that, he lacks a moral code that goes beyond competence in the workplace). Occasionally a film made explicit the contingent nature of morality. In *The Big Carnival* (1951), the editor of the *Albuquerque Sun-Bulletin* displays the paper's motto, "Tell the Truth," above his desk. Yet the film centers on reporter Chuck Tatum's efforts to create and manage any "truth" that might be told, thus casting doubt on the basic idea of an objective, exterior truth.[16]

In a world dominated by a sense of the contingent, writers increasingly dispensed with the kinds of social and economic explanations for conduct that had made perfect sense only a decade before. The new explanations were psychological, and often they were hardly explanations at all, laced as they were with idiosyncrasy, mystery, and indeterminacy. Among the writers whose work reflected this change was Richard Wright, a black novelist and Communist party member who achieved widespread recognition with the publication of *Native Son* in 1940. In this book, as well as in work published after his break with the party in 1944, Wright explored the problem of responsibility for criminal acts. Partly through his association with psychiatrists—including Dr. Frederick Wertham, who campaigned tirelessly against violence and sadism in comic books—Wright's quest for the source of the homicidal impulse came to settle on a combination of social and psychological factors. In the short story "The Man Who Killed a Shadow" (1946), based on the case of Julius Fisher, a black janitor who killed a white librarian at the National Cathedral in Washington, D.C., in 1944, the murder turns on the complexities of the victim's scream—a scream that for the fearful perpetrator resonates with accusations of rape, the sounds of police cars, and the ritual hunting down of the black man. Thus Wright merged traditional categories of analysis, including race and gender, with something—represented by the librarian's scream and the unpredictable and complex response to it—that was more mysterious and less rational.[17]

Shorn of the self-confident moralism the decade opened with, the popularity of traditional movie heroes like John Wayne had begun to give way by the end of the forties to a preference for tortured, suffering, and unpretentious antiheroes who made no claim to a universal code—as represented by Montgomery Clift's symbolic thrashing of Wayne in *Red River* (1948). Villains changed, too. Two-Face, a Batman nemesis created in the 1940s, was a good man turned bad when one side of his face was disfigured by acid. Two-Face established his ethical stance randomly, actually flipping a coin to determine whether he would be a force for good or evil.[18]

For some, contingency served as a lever of creativity against a dominant culture that sought to control every expression; for others, it also operated as a quixotic antidote to the regularity and boredom of mainstream middle-class life. But most Americans of the 1940s had had enough of both physical and moral contingency and looked instead for ways to make their lives more predictable, to ground and anchor values, or at least to function more effectively within the milieu of contingency.

Critics of the sort of ethical relativism articulated by Lieutenant Roberts and Two-Face attacked the persons and movements most often linked to its spread. Philosophic pragmatism and its offspring, progressive education and permissive child-rearing, increasingly came under censure for having contributed to a confused and spiritually adrift culture. Typical was the criticism offered at the 1948 *Life* roundtable on the "pursuit of happiness"; Betsey Barton, the youngest participant in the Rye, New York, conference and daughter of the famed advertising executive Bruce Barton, took the popular position that modern pragmatic philosophy had produced "moral anarchy" for a postwar generation that had "no inner authority that they can trust."[19] In 1950, opponents of pragmatic methods forced the resignation of Willard E. Goslin, the superintendent of schools in Pasadena, California, who had earned the wrath of right-wing critics by inviting the renowned progressive educator William Heard Kilpatrick to participate in a teacher training workshop.[20]

Progressive education was a convenient, accessible, and highly visible opponent. Its critics did not really care about classroom methods; they were expounding their belief that society had lost its moral roots and succumbed to a rampant relativism. No doubt there was some truth in the claim. In postwar eras, survivors inevitably rethink the past conflict, find the carnage less justified and less defensible than it had seemed at the time, and often become estranged from the moral certainties of wartime. Two popular books, published in 1949 and representative of the growing movement criticizing progressive education that would peak in the mid-1950s, mark the reaction to post–World War II relativism and reveal the movement's abiding concern with morality and moral standards. Mortimer Smith, in *And Madly Teach: A Layman Looks at Public School Education*, found Dewey and other advocates of progressive methods guilty of having emphasized action, process, and "self-realization" at the expense of morality, values, rigorous intellectual training in the basic disciplines, and "the traditional knowledge of the race" (a phrase that apparently meant great Western traditions). As an antidote to the relativism he found among teachers and students, Smith called for renewed attention to drill and memorization of fundamentals and for more focus on "intellectual or moral standards of knowledge." Bernard Iddings Bell, in *Crisis in Education: A Challenge to American Complacency*, echoed Smith's concerns and described Western civilization as "in crisis" and in need of "morally sound guidance." Arguing that "free love" and a "politics based on force" were the inevitable results of amorality, Smith advocated a more prominent role for religion in the home and schools.[21]

The critique of progressive methods also pointed back to the Munich Pact of 1938: British and French leaders had agreed to allow the transfer of the Sudetenland of Czechoslovakia to Germany in return for a guarantee that the remainder of the country would be protected from aggression. When the agreement failed to stop Hitler, its underlying mechanism of "appeasement" was severely criticized. Throughout the forties, its authors were held responsible for having failed to draw the line—in effect, to insist on moral standards of conduct—against the German dictator.

In film, hostility to the policy of appeasement, and to the pragmatic, valueless order it represented, was a theme explored in the realm of child-rearing in *Mildred Pierce*. The film opens with a cold-blooded murder, which the audience is led to believe was committed by Mildred (Joan Crawford). Later we learn that Mildred has been protecting the real killer, her incredibly self-indulgent daughter, Veda (Ann Blyth). Though Mildred does not pull the trigger, the film makes it clear that she is not without ultimate responsibility for her daughter's act. When Veda begs her mother's help in the coverup of the crime, her argument—"It's your fault I'm the way I am"—rings true. Although Mildred is not a bad woman, she fails to provide Veda with the most elemental of standards: the sense of what makes a good life. In an early scene, for example, Mildred fails to challenge Veda's vicious, materialist criticism of a dress that Mildred has just bought for her. Indeed, not long thereafter Mildred dedicates herself to indulging Veda's penchant for luxury. "I want you to have nice things," she tells her, "and you will have. Wait and see. I'll get you everything, anything you want. I promise." Another act of self-denying indulgence—marriage to a man she does not love in order to secure a mansion that will satisfy Veda's cravings—puts the murderess and victim in the same household and sets the stage for the crime. Although

Crawford's Mildred is in many ways a woman of enormous strength, purpose, and will, these qualities emerge from a drive for security so strong that she loses the ability and desire to appreciate and mark appropriate limits to Veda's materialism. Only when the police have proven Veda's guilt, and when Veda herself has been tricked into confession, does Mildred's permissiveness reach the end of its tether—and even then the issue is in doubt.

The quest for moral standards found another enemy in the social sciences, whose reliance on scientific method and mathematics seemed to remove its practitioners from moral concerns. At the center of controversy was one of the postwar decade's outstanding scientific achievements, Alfred C. Kinsey's *Sexual Behavior in the Human Male* (1948) and *Sexual Behavior in the Human Female* (1953), known collectively and familiarly as the Kinsey Report. A biologist and insect taxonomist by training, Kinsey had turned to research on human sexual behavior in the late 1930s, organizing his extensive interviews with the same methods and the same cold precision he had once used to study the gall wasp. The Kinsey Report measured sexual activity largely in terms of orgasms, and it treated orgasms—whether through masturbation, sexual activity, or animal contacts—as equivalent "outlets." Determined to "accumulate an objectively determined body of fact about sex which strictly avoids social or moral interpretations," Kinsey presented much of his data through hundreds of charts and graphs, many of which emphasized the wide range of sexual practices. The great discrepancy between the behavior revealed in the variation studies and the society's mores (an estimated 95 percent of American men were guilty of some "illegal" sexual activity) led Kinsey to conclude that "our conceptions of right and wrong, normal and abnormal, are seriously challenged."[22]

Kinsey's methods, implications, and conclusions provoked a chorus of hostile reactions from moralists who interpreted the reports as another heavy dose of relativism. Barnard College dean Millicent Cary McIntosh wrote in *Time* of "insistent voices . . . analyzing behavior as 'normal' which in the past we were accustomed to associate with the gutter." Describing the current standardless generation as "born in confusion" and "suckled in tumult," she called on educators to employ "freedom of inquiry and discussion" to produce a "moral synthesis."[23] The editors of *Reader's Digest* introduced a June 1948 collection of essays on sexuality with its own plea for a body of science that would hold "fast and firm to the long accepted ideals and ways of virtue. . . . Because of newly published polls and cold, detached, scientific surveys, many people have come to fear that old anchors are being swept away, old foundations destroyed. They have just been told," continued the *Digest*, "that practices long held in abhorrence must now be regarded as acceptable. . . . Pretty much anything is all right."[24]

Americans of the 1940s wanted to establish some controls over the contingencies of their lives. But they were also deeply apprehensive about those instruments and devices that might yield a less contingent environment.

Hence, the jubilation that greeted Harry Truman's 1948 victory over the public opinion polls that had predicted his defeat should be seen as the kind of response that could occur only in a culture increasingly given to taking its own pulse in order to measure the condition (and predictability) of the democratic body politic. By the same token, Kinsey's monumental effort to provide a statistical framework within which virtually any sexual practice might be understood (if not appreciated) and hence rendered less deviant (i.e., less contingent), was resented by some as an attempt to illuminate what they felt should remain mysterious.

Because the atomic bomb was the most significant source of the contingent in the postwar world, efforts to control contingency necessarily involved recasting the bomb in familiar images and within familiar contexts. The transmutation of the bomb from the killer of Japanese civilians into a peacetime scientific wonder began with Truman's 6 August 1945 announcement of the use of the bomb at Hiroshima. Truman described the bomb as an instrument of nature, an expression of the "basic power of the universe" that contained (in an ironic implied reference to the Japanese Empire of the Sun) "the force from which the sun draws its power." Truman waxed eloquent on the bomb as "the greatest achievement of organized science in history," and, in the last four paragraphs of the address, he discussed not the bomb but the role of "atomic energy," converting the contingency of destruction into the knowledge-based security of a "new era in man's understanding of nature's forces." Truman's address concluded with his promise to pursue "how atomic power can become a powerful and forceful influence towards the maintenance of world peace."[25]

Throughout the 1940s, the idea of the nuclear as a force of deadly contingency was contested in a torrent of nuclear utopianism that hugged the line between predictive science and fantasy. Among the most prominent visionaries was science writer R. M. Langer, who in 1941 forecast an age of "universal comfort," "free transportation," and "unlimited supplies of materials," all produced with typewriter-size nuclear reactors. After the use of the bomb against Japan, such images only increased in number and intensity, prompting the *New Republic* to suggest that these "roseate dreams of the future" were Americans' way of placing the destruction of Hiroshima and Nagasaki within a national moral context. Leading the way were mass-market magazines such as *Science Illustrated* and *Popular Mechanics*, whose William McDermott painted nuclear fission as "the greatest magic carpet of all ages." A writer for *Harper's* magazine envisioned Americans seeing the U.S.A. not in a Chevrolet (as a popular commercial had it) but in "Nuclear-8 sedans." Others offered dreams of nuclear-powered planes, weather modification through artificial suns mounted on towers ("No baseball game will be called off on account of rain in the Era of Atomic Energy"), nuclear excavation, nuclear farming leading to a worldwide classless and poverty-free society, and—

the one dream that stayed alive and panned out—the medical use of radio-active isotopes.[26]

Although the U.S. government applauded every construct of the nuclear future that might assist in reimagining the bomb, ordinary Americans seemed to have little quarrel with the process or the goal. The bomb was almost immediately incorporated into the iconography of mass consumption. A Fifth Avenue jeweler advertised "new fields to conquer with Atomic jewelry. . . . As daring to wear as it was to drop the first atom bomb." In 1946, fifteen cents and a Kix cereal box top would buy an "Atomic 'Bomb' Ring." In one of numerous references commingling the destructive and the erotic—and, unknowingly, raising the serious and complex issue of the relationship between death and sensuality—*Life* labeled starlet Linda Christians, "The Anatomic Bomb." And a strait-laced Louisville collection agency used an image of the exploding bomb to represent the "Atomic Force" its three teams were applying in an effort to "Wipe Out Delinquent Accounts."[27] The cumulative impact of such ephemera was to cheapen the atomic bomb's essence as an agent of deadly contingency. To suggest even in jest that the bomb's force was somehow equivalent to the personal courage required to wear the latest fashion, or to the energy required to reach quota, was to suggest that the bomb was just another force that could be absorbed and contained.

In the same way, efforts were made to assimilate the robot, the foremost symbol of the contingent nature of modern technology. Not only were the fictional robot creations of the day prone to inexplicably turn against their creators, but the very idea of a robot—a heartless, mechanical man—seemed an affront to the foundations of morality. Science fiction writer Isaac Asimov's solution to robotic contingency—mechanical and moral—was to program his robots with a system of ethics known as the Three Laws of Robotics:

1. A robot may not injure a human being nor, through inaction, allow a human being to come to harm.
2. A robot must obey the orders given it by human beings except where such orders would conflict with the First Law.
3. A robot must protect its own existence as long as such protection does not conflict with the First or Second law.

In essence, the Three Laws of Robotics made robots, if not moral, then at least incapable of immorality—incapable, as Asimov's scientist heroine Susan Calvin explained, "of harming humans, incapable of tyranny, of corruption, or stupidity, or prejudice"—incapable, that is, of the essential human cruelties of the 1940s.[28]

The search for a new measure of predictability enhanced the prestige of authorities and experts—in fields as diverse as child-rearing, poetry, public works, and psychiatry—who could decipher, read, and order the contingent. Since the mid nineteenth century, the expert had gradually but inevitably replaced tradition and the community as the locus of social authority. By the mid-1940s, having observed the havoc that "experts" could produce in the name of science and reason, many Americans developed a healthy skepticism toward "expertism." Nonetheless, so great was the sense of contingency in the 1940s that Americans succumbed, often and willingly, to the expert's promise of a more predictable and more normative world.[29]

The quintessential wartime expert was, of course, a military leader. In selecting Gen. George C. Marshall as its 1943 Man of the Year, *Time* described the chief of staff of the American armed forces as a man "worshipped—not with the rapture evoked by 'born' leaders, but with the happy admiration of experts for the most expert." Marshall's particular contribution was not simply to have supervised the arming of the republic but to have done so in the midst of a crisis of contingency "so deep that the very street signs were submerged; men wandered in an unfamiliar waste of circumstance, scanning the horizons for some marker, some direction point." At this moment, "when no man [by implication, not even Marshall] could both comprehend the vastness and dissect the particular," Americans "clung" to Marshall for his honesty and competence.[30] In response to a similar sense of urgency brought about by the use of the atomic bomb, atomic scientists were not only celebrated for their knowledge and technical skills but expected to translate their expertise into the arena of international politics.[31]

During the sex crime panic, another kind of expert—the psychiatrist—was called upon to "read" the social terrain for whatever street signs and markers it might yield. Because sexual criminality was in some basic sense indeterminant (the it-could-be-the-fellow-next-door syndrome), and given the prevalent assumption of a correlation between sexual deviancy (e.g., homosexuality or window-peeping) and criminal sexual conduct, it seemed essential to secure expert assistance in determining whether a particular minor deviate was likely to "degenerate" into more dangerous activity. Although many psychiatrists disputed the claim that sex crimes could actually be predicted, the press treated psychiatrists as sex crime experts. The authority granted psychiatry also ensured that psychiatrists would play a major role in the more than fifteen state commissions set up to study the problem.[32]

Despite an obvious commitment to depicting the contingent world, even film noir produced its share of experts—mostly law enforcement figures—whose role was to cut against the isolation and fragmentation at the core of experience, to "comprehend the vastness and dissect the particular," in the words *Time* had used to explain what Americans wanted from George Marshall. Amid the chaos and flashbacks of *Crossfire* (1947), the amiable but efficient detective Finlay (Robert Young) was there to "collect all the facts possible" and, in the end, make them cohere for the audience. If the inspector in *Mildred Pierce* seems to contribute to the Kafkaesque atmosphere of his bureau and to exacerbate the contingent with his apparent lack of either direction or perspicacity, his curious behavior ultimately proves to have been goal-directed and altogether reasonable. *Quicksand* (1950)—strictly speaking, a film beyond the noir genre—also depends for its conclusion on a figure outside the action of the film. In the final scene, the victimized Danny Brady (Mickey Rooney), driven to a binge of crime by a series of bizarre events and circumstances, is comforted by a venerable attorney who, in his role as an expert in legal matters, is able in a matter of seconds to reduce a long list of crimes that threaten to bring the protagonist to the gallows to a couple of first offenses warranting as little as a year in jail.

Another strategy for dealing with contingency was to establish some basis on which distinctions and judgments of all kinds might be made. One approach, popular with "traditionalists" both in and out of academe, was to ground the present not in a linear, historical narrative but in certain intellectual and cultural moments of the past, moments that seemed to offer a body of established truths about human nature, ethics, and values. "The West," wrote University of Chicago president Robert Maynard Hutchins, "needs an education that draws out our common humanity rather than our individuality." The traditionalists attacked John Dewey, progressive educators, and other advocates of an experimental, specialized, scientific approach to understanding human affairs. They championed a "humanistic" approach that included certain constant aspects of human nature and universal principles of conduct that they claimed to have identified. To reestablish the sense of commonality between past and present, Hutchins and the psychologist and philosopher Mortimer Adler developed the Great Books curriculum, which consisted of adult education discussion seminars covering some 130 classic works. Founded in the mid-1930s, Great Books' significant growth began in 1943 and continued through the decade. Besides Hutchins, the traditionalist group included Catholic prelate Fulton Sheen and poet and critic Mark Van Doren, who, in his influential *Liberal Education* (1945) lamented the virtual suspension of college liberal arts and humanities programs during the war and argued for a revitalized curriculum, steeped in history and the classics and giving renewed attention to humans as rational, conceptual, moral beings. Literature, wrote Van Doren, "makes the world available to us as chance and appetite do not."[33]

Against the burgeoning relativism of the age, many writers and intellectuals struggled, often without much success, to locate the ground on which a firm foundation of morality might be laid. Among them was Arthur Miller, whose plays capture the desperation of an age anxious to locate a source of the moral imperative. Miller's *All My Sons* exemplifies the attempt. The play is set after the war in the backyard of the home of Joe Keller, whose son

Larry has been missing in action for three years. During the war, Joe's company had manufactured and shipped cracked cylinder heads to the army air force, resulting in the deaths of the occupants of twenty-one P-40s. Joe is briefly jailed, then cleared, but we learn that he is guilty and, indeed, that Larry has killed himself because of his father's involvement in the incident.

Miller shapes the problem of morality as a conflict between Joe's particularism and the universalism articulated by other characters. Joe's world is a "forty-foot front" that ends "at the building line"; he explains his conduct as a function of his deep investment in family ("Nothin' is bigger!"). Speaking through Joe's other son, Chris, Miller tells us that there is indeed something bigger: "What the hell do you mean, you did it for me? Don't you have a country? Don't you live in the world? What the hell are you? You're not even an animal, no animal kills his own, what are you?" Finally acknowledging his error, Joe admits that, to Larry, "they were all my sons. And I guess they were, I guess they were."[34]

As this narrative reveals, Joe's conversion from the particular to the universal, from one son to "all my sons," is accomplished all too easily and in the absence of sustained and effective argumentation. Although Miller bemoaned the absence of universal morality, he was unable to establish the ground on which such a morality might be based. As Tom Driver has written, "Miller's strident moralism is a good example of what happens when ideals must be maintained in an atmosphere of humanistic relativism. There being no objective good and evil, and no imperative other than conscience, man himself must be made to bear the full burden of creating his values and living up to them."[35]

If absolutes proved hard to justify or establish, one could find a standard of a sort in the views of the majority as determined—with a finality that functioned as a kind of objectivity—by a public opinion poll (the Gallup Poll began in 1936), or a survey of the Kinsey variety. That Americans were increasingly prone to employ the public opinion standard in place of individual judgment was the charge of the Russian-born philosopher and novelist Ayn Rand, whose books argued the virtues of a creative, selfish individualism and denounced bureaucracy, government, altruism, and any form of collectivity. In *The Fountainhead* (1943), a best-seller that established Rand's reputation in the United States, the fountainhead (the source) of progress is the brilliant and principled architect Howard Roark, who prefers to dynamite his work rather than see it ruined by other hands. "I do not recognize," he announces, "anyone's right to one minute of my life. Nor to any part of my energy. Nor to any achievement of mine. . . . The world is perishing from an orgy of self-sacrificing." The highly individualistic Rand was opposed to the idea that a survey of public opinion could yield a reasonable standard of judgment.[36] In the film version of *The Fountainhead* (1948), her point of view is articulated by the heroine Dominique Francon, who, at the opening of Roark's visionary Enright House, has this brief conversation with Peter Keating, another architect, whose monetary success is matched only by his lack of talent, creativity, and integrity.

KEATING: Tell me, what do you think of this building? I've been trying to take a poll among the guests, but . . .

FRANCON: A what?

KEATING: A poll of opinion about it.

FRANCON: What for? In order to find out what you think of it yourself?

KEATING: We have to consider public opinion, don't we?

Instruction in manners, a staple of the forties, grew in direct proportion to the difficulties people experienced in defining and articulating a moral code; that is, manners (good behavior) replaced morals (good values) as a way of getting along in a shifting and transient world. High school students bore the brunt of the instructional onslaught, as principals assembled their student bodies for films such as *Everyday Courtesy* (1948), which enjoined students to do "the simple things—being friendly, thinking of the other person, and showing respect—that make up everyday courtesy." Helen Sprackling, in *Courtesy: A Book of Modern Manners* (1944), characterized etiquette as the behavior of the majority at a moment in time (the public opinion standard that Francon detested) but insisted that it was also based on "a certain amount of logic and common sense" (that is, on a very nearly, but not quite, absolute standard). The need for rules of etiquette was obvious in a world changing with "panoramic swiftness." One's eating techniques, for instance, had to be responsive to changing environments—a cafeteria, a lunch counter, a college dining room: "Life in a democracy being what it is, neither you nor I can tell where we are going to be eating next. One's table manners must be prepared for anything." Mary Beery, director of social conduct at a Lima, Ohio, high school and author of *Manners Made Easy* (1949), grounded her standards only in pragmatic concerns; good manners helped a person "fit himself into a society in which people must get along together," avoiding "personal tragedies" and obviating "antisocial behavior." Again, the only standard was a social one. Manners were good or bad depending on the "motives they revealed," and good manners revealed "consideration for the rights and feelings of others."[37] Guidebooks for a pragmatic culture lacking ethical moorings, these tracts offered advice without moral substance, advice set in a mortar at once social and transient.

The effort to locate a bedrock for problematic values also produced a deep appreciation for those persons, real and fictional, whose reckless, combative, and even belligerent self-confidence—sometimes coupled with archaic moralism—seemed to belie doubt, ambiguity, and the centrality of contingency.

These men (and they were always men, for women who possessed these qualities were invariably destructive) were not experts of the usual sort, for they lacked the polish that one associates with expertism. Yet they somehow managed to move through history with a margin of comfort not available to ordinary beings.

A prime example of the type is the character of Stanley Kowalski in *A Streetcar Named Desire* (1947). Described by playwright Tennessee Williams as a man whose life is centered on "pleasure with women, the giving and taking of it, not with weak indulgence, dependently, but with the power and pride of a richly feathered male bird among hens," Stanley's self-possession emanates from a strong working-class culture that puts him in touch with his most basic drives and allows him the sense, at least, of control. During a game of poker (what else?), Stanley explains how he survived the great contingency of the 1940s—the war—and applies that lesson to his current life as a factory worker: "You know what luck is? Luck is believing you're lucky. Take at Salerno. I believed I was lucky. I figured that four out of five would not come through but I would . . . and I did. I put that down as a result. To hold front position in this rat-race you've got to believe you are lucky."[38] In short, while Stanley cannot ignore contingency and cannot deny its impact, he does deny its ability to penetrate his own being. Put another way, Stanley describes himself as being able to work with the "numbers" provided by a contingent universe, to achieve predictability (a "result") within a larger— but not necessarily all-encompassing—contingency. This enormous self-confidence, translated into a swaggering and intimidating style, is Stanley's great strength.

The same could be said of Mickey Spillane's fictional hero, Mike Hammer, who first appeared in the best-seller *I, the Jury* in 1947. Though Hammer has all the skills and savvy of a good detective and respects the more "scientific" expertise of the police department, his character is defined by a combination of brute force and moral vision. A lone vigilante, Hammer strides through *I, the Jury* spitting on, pummeling, and disfiguring his adversaries. ("I took the side of my free hand and smashed it across his nose. The bone shattered and blood poured out. That guy probably was a lady killer in Harlem, but them days were gone forever.")

Hammer's approach stems in part from his frustration with and distrust of the legal system and its institutions. But it is also fueled by a streak of moral indignation rooted in the recent past and revealed in the first scene of *I, the Jury*, when Hammer and the captain of homicide, Pat Chambers, investigate the scene of a murder. The victim, Jack Williams, had served with Hammer in "the stinking slime of the jungle" and had lost an arm in the act of stopping "a bastard of a Jap from slitting me in two."[39] Like Kowalski's swaggering masculinity, Hammer's moral purposefulness is derived from the male bonding of World War II and seems to exist in part as a response to the contingency of war: but for Jack Williams, Hammer would be dead; Hammer can defy death only because he has already died.

It is possible, then, to tease a moral dimension and argument from Spillane's work. But there is no doubt that Hammer's appeal as a protagonist stemmed primarily from the aggressive and physical way in which he managed a contingent universe of punks, drug dealers, and mobsters, dispatching one thug after another as if the fury of violence itself would inevitably yield the truth. Among Hammer's real-life counterparts were "tail-gunner Joe" McCarthy, the irascible senator from Wisconsin who waged war on "Communists" with methods not unlike those of Spillane's hero; McCarthy once threatened to "kick the brains out" of the secretary of the army, and he relished the thought of using a "slippery-elm club" to make liberal Democrat Adlai Stevenson a "good American." Indeed, the columnists Joseph and Stewart Alsop once wrote that the heavy-shouldered McCarthy was "reasonably well cast as the Hollywood version of a strong-jawed private eye."[40] Another politician cast in the Hammer mold was Harry Truman, whose tough vetoes, combative liberalism, and ability to present himself as the "symbol of the real virility of his party" won him the 1948 election.[41] When music critic Paul Hume wrote disparagingly of a vocal performance by Truman's daughter Margaret at Constitution Hall in 1950, the president promised Hume that if they ever met, "you'll need a new nose and plenty of beefsteak and perhaps a supporter below."[42]

Acceptance of contingency as a starting point for thinking about the problem of living with it yielded two rather abstruse contributions to a solution: existentialism, a philosophy that at once recognized and transcended the contingent; and a theory of games that claimed the ability to guarantee triumph within a contingent context.

"Nothing is more certain, nothing more humbling, nothing less effaceable," wrote Ralph Harper in his 1948 study of existentialism, "than the impress of one's own contingency." Mike Hammer had come face to face with the contingency of his existence in a foxhole in the Pacific, when only his best friend's arm kept his body from being fatally penetrated by a Japanese bayonet. Hammer's decision—a decision also made by millions of ordinary Americans who had fought in the war, witnessed Hiroshima, or shuddered at the Holocaust, and a decision chronicled in the popular fiction and film of the day—was the decision, as Harper explains it, of the existentialist: to "continue to live uniquely as long as one can, to make no compromises with the enemies of existence in all its fullness."[43] Despite potentially debilitating self-knowledge, and operating within a world so absurd that the murderer is perforce a woman to whom he has committed his passion and love, Hammer pursues the existential solution and takes on the tragic stature that Arthur Miller described in a 1949 essay, "Tragedy and the Common Man," remaining resolutely fixed—even fanatical—in his determination to find and execute the killer.[44]

Perhaps the purest example from the popular culture of the behavior of an existential hero in a contingent world is *D.O.A.*'s Frank Bigelow, played by Edmund O'Brien. Faced with the indisputable medical evidence that he has been fatally poisoned and has less than forty-eight hours to live, Bigelow emerges from the hospital and begins a headlong run of fear through the streets of San Francisco. Gasping for breath against a newspaper stand, a series of events—the glow of a brilliant sun, a child chasing her ball to his feet, a couple embracing—work a miraculous transformation. Fortified by the (nonexistential) knowledge that life does, indeed, have meaning, Bigelow gathers himself and, to the martial strains of the music of Dmitri Tiomkin, strides forward grimly and purposefully, determined to solve the crime and seek retribution for his own murder. Like Hammer's, Bigelow's gritty courage taps the wellspring of his own contingency; because he is dead he knows no fear. "He's not afraid, Chester," comments one of his adversaries. "You can tell from a man's eyes when he's afraid. Look at his eyes."

While Hammer tried to pummel the contingent into submission, a very different approach to the problem, called "games theory," accepted contingency as a working premise that could be neither finessed nor transcended and constructed around it a theoretical and yet practical strategy for generating a predictable environment. A theory of games was apparently first devised during World War II, when the Navy's Anti-Submarine Warfare Operations Research Group took up the hypercontingencies involved in the interplay of a submarine and an airplane engaged in a deadly search for each other. Fully developed by two Europeans—mathematician John von Neumann, a participant in the development of the atomic bomb, and economist Oskar Morgenstern—the theory was popularized for the American audience by John McDonald in articles appearing in *Fortune* magazine in 1948–49 and in a book, *Strategy in Poker, Business, and War* (1950).

Games theory was developed as a strategy of survival in the contingent world of the 1940s. According to von Neumann and Morgenstern, that contingency was one of "imperfect information"; it was generated by "interdependence," not unlike that faced by players in a poker game (or by nations at war), who must act in the context of the moves and anticipated (though hardly predictable) deceptions and counterdeceptions of other players. The genius of games theory was to find a way for a player in any game—poker, big business, or national defense—to guarantee himself some sort of victory regardless of the actions of the other players. Using what von Neumann and Morgenstern call a "minimax" strategy, a player proceeds along two lines. First, he or she assumes that any strategy pursued will be known to the opponent. Second, the player adopts a random strategy, thus neutralizing any advantage the opponent may have in gaining knowledge of it. In return, the player gives up any hope of maximum gain in return for a guaranteed, statistically determined, minimum gain. When more than two players are involved, as in economics and international relations, players inevitably form coalitions (mergers, alliances) that allow games theory to function.

By midcentury games theory had been linked not only to atomic war ("War is chance," wrote McDonald, "and minimax must be its modern philosophy") but to economics: developing theories of monopolistic competition and oligopoly were built on concepts of interdependence and indeterminacy not unlike those at the heart of games theory.[45] However, games theory was important not for its everyday uses but for representing the degree to which contingency suffused the 1940s—the decade finally yielded a theory specifically designed to deal with the problematic nature of the new culture.

The search for an antidote to contingency was contrived, desperate, and ultimately futile. Hammer could level his .45 at his adversary's abdomen and pull the trigger, but not even a bullet through a female reproductive system would make the new woman go away, or give Hammer back the sense of invulnerability that he had lost in the Pacific. *Crossfire's* Finlay could reconstruct a crime from the fragments of experience and even generate a motive for it, but he dared not attempt to explain why hatred existed or even what it was. School officials could show films about courtesy in auditoriums overflowing with students, but they could not honorably or convincingly present good manners as a significant step toward a world without conflict. Nostrums such as these could not make a war in which sixty million had died into an ordinary war, nor convert the use of the atomic bomb into an ordinary act of war, nor turn the attempted extermination of European Jewry into something that could be conventionally understood. Against these events, reasonable persons would fear for their lives, question their moral heritage, and look about for ways of living in and shoring up a contingent world.

three

The March of Time

After the war was over, there was a lot of talk among Americans about how good the times were. A typical late-1940s advertisement, for New England Mutual, featured photos of a field representative as a toddler (1902), a college freshman (1919), an employee (1935), and a family man, complete with son in the service (1946), the last photo labeled, "The best year of my life." The titles of two of the most widely acclaimed films of the decade were *It's a Wonderful Life* and *The Best Years of Our Lives*, the latter of which won nine Academy Awards in 1946 and featured an amateur actor, Harold Russell. Despite having lost both hands in the war, Russell would later claim that the postwar years "truly *were* 'the best years.' . . . We felt the day had come when the wars were all over, we were going to break down the bonds that separated people."[1]

One can understand why so many people felt this way, especially in the year or two after 1945. The Allies had won the war, vanquished their enemies, and created the United Nations, which held out the hope for a new kind of world order. Alone among the major powers of the world, the United States had not been physically devastated by the conflict. Although tensions with the Soviet Union, a wartime ally, were present even during the conflict (and former British prime minister Winston Churchill would coin the phrase "iron curtain" in the spring of 1946), the seriousness of the coming cold war was not yet fully apparent. The Great Depression—a decade of desperation, worries, and lost opportunities for a generation of Americans—lay in the past. For Harold Russell and millions of others, it seemed altogether reasonable that this would be, as *Time* publisher Henry Luce had predicted in 1941, the "American Century."[2]

While some individuals may have experienced the forties as an era of unqualified optimism, the culture of the 1940s presents a more mixed and complex picture. Even the most significant expressions of the optimism of the age were tempered and tainted with ambiguity, cynicism, and doubt. The effusive title of *It's a Wonderful Life* belied the potentially suicidal frustration of protagonist George Bailey at being a banker in Bedford Falls, an oppressive small town that could not help but thwart his aspirations and deny his dreams. *The Best Years of Our Lives* presents the return of three veterans to civilian life as a study in humiliation and rejection. Fred Derry (Dana Andrews) comes home to a woman who can appreciate him only in uniform ("Now," she says as he puts it on once more, "you look like yourself"); he is reduced to the infantilizing and feminine work of selling cosmetics in the drugstore where he had once been a teenage soda jerk. Al Stevenson (Frederic March) returns to his bank as a loan officer, a position in which he can survive only by refusing loans to veterans who have no collateral. Handless Homer Parrish (Russell) expects people to treat him like "everyone else," but unlike "everyone else," Homer is by definition dependent—without aid from another person, he cannot even put on the harness that holds and allows him to operate his mechanical hands. In the film's penultimate scene, Derry wanders a field of engineless bombers, castrated wrecks like himself, and takes a job dismantling for junk the very planes that once brought him place and respect.

Full of dreams that neither science nor postwar prosperity—nor the kind touch of a gentle woman—could fulfill, and bearing the scars and carrying the emotional burdens of a dislocating, frightening, and deadly war, Americans in the forties wondered aloud about their innocence, jettisoned revered notions of progress for an increasingly pragmatic and even dystopian perspective on the future, and took flight from a past that had long ago ceased to offer comfort and security.

The World's Fair of 1933 celebrated the "Century of Progress," and the theme of the 1939 fair was "Building the World of Tomorrow." Despite the very real and remarkable technological developments of the 1940s, the decade would generate no fair to house them. Yet something of the spirit of inevitable progress was carried through into the 1940s in the twenty-minute film newsreels known as *The March of Time*. Introduced in 1935, *The March of Time* was a regular feature at neighborhood theaters throughout the forties, bowing out to television early in the 1950s. The newsreel captured the idea of progress in an opening sequence that featured ranks of flag-bearing marchers; in the spirited line "Time Marches On!" that closed each segment; and in the content of individual segments, which might recognize the dramatic achievements of science, technology, and a consumer-driven, free-enterprise capitalism, praise the "slow progress toward perfection" that characterized

American ethnic and racial problems, or hold out the promise of the rapid modernization of "Tomorrow's Mexico."[3]

For many Americans, the core notion of a "march of time"—of a consistent, dependable, linear progress—seemed increasingly unrealistic, even deeply flawed. After a decade of depression, many economists were exploring a new theory of "stagnation," which postulated a mature economy characterized by the absence of economic growth. Talcott Parsons and other sociologists described normal social relations in terms of stasis, with society tending toward equilibrium, a "state of rest," and change being possible only at moments of severe disturbance. In "90 North" (1941), poet Randall Jarrell concluded that what he had once understood as the acquisition of knowledge was just so much ignorance and pain. And in December 1946, Sidney Fay used his position as president of the American Historical Association to dismiss progress as "logically meaningless."[4] Neither "progress" nor "stasis" were in the vocabulary of drummer Frankie Machine, the heroine addict, hustler, and would-be Gene Krupa of Nelson Algren's novel, *The Man with the Golden Arm* (1949), but Frankie knew all the same that the world was not open to a "regular guy" like himself, even one with "the touch." As Algren put it for Frankie, "being regular got you in about as often as being off balanced on one side. That was the way things were because that was how things had always been. Which was why they could never be any different. Neither God, war, nor the ward super work any deep change on West Division Street."[5]

The very thought that change itself might have gone by the wayside sent shudders through the fashion industry, where making money depended on convincing the public that change was progress, that new was better. Dior's New Look, introduced in April 1947, was greeted as the savior of haute couture and, in a certain sense, of capitalism. While *Time* bluntly charged the fashion industry with seeking to "make all the present styles unwearable," *Harper's Bazaar* issued a clarion call to "get yourself a new shape." Promoting nothing less than a return to the halcyon days of linear progress, the magazine counseled its readers to avoid the humiliation of being "a last-year girl. You *can* let the clock stop, of course, if you want to ally yourself with women who hold off until a new fashion is on everyone else's back."[6]

Titles such as *The Best Years of Our Lives* might best be understood, therefore, not as literal pronouncements but as the residue of the dream world of deferred gratification that was one response of a generation trapped by depression and war. As we have seen, many Americans lived the war as a series of dreams—dreams of idyllic reunions with loved ones long absent, of a world so productive as to abolish need altogether and open the way to a limitless leisure, of plentiful and meaningful work, of a blissful and harmonious domesticity, of an "American Century." No real present could measure up to these grandiose expectations, but the dreams did not simply disappear

42

at the first brush with bureaucracy, inflation, the cold war, domestic quarrels, and other realities of the postwar world.

What happened to the collective "dream" in the late 1940s may be gleaned from the cinema, where two genres popular with postwar audiences—boxing films and films about alcoholism—showcased the ongoing disintegration of the idea of progress in the American mind. The boxing films are essentially mobility studies, stories of men who start with nothing and end up champions, or, as in the case of Stoker Thompson (Robert Ryan) in *The Set Up* (1949), spend years toiling in the ring with only their integrity to show for it. All the boxers are dreamers. In *Champion* (1949), boxing itself eclipses Midge Kelly's (Kirk Douglas) dream of teaming up with his buddies in a Los Angeles diner; in *Body and Soul* (1947), Charlie Davis (John Garfield) wants to escape from the penny-candy store run by his Jewish parents, "to be a success." And Thompson, over the hill at thirty-five, fights his last fight at the Paradise City A.C. (next door to Dreamland), believing not only that he can "take this kid" but that he is "one punch away" from "the top spot" (on the boxing card). Indeed, all three boxers achieve success within their relative frameworks: Kelly and Davis win the championship, and Thompson is victorious in what proves to be his final bout.

However, this success is tempered and compromised in each film by the "fix"—the match whose outcome is determined in advance by a promoter, gambler, or racketeer. After three years of hard work and plaudits, the "fat bellies with the big cigars" inform Kelly that he must take a dive in his first title fight. Though Kelly naively disregards the instructions and wins the championship, he can remain in boxing only by firing his longtime friend and manager (i.e., by severing his roots in the community) and handing his career over to a big-time promoter. Davis wins the title with his savage and ultimately fatal beating of black champion Ben Chaplain, who, despite a blood clot on the brain, agrees to fight after having been assured by Roberts, the promoter, that the "fix" was "in"—that Davis would go easy on him. When Davis explains to his sweetheart, Peg, that quitting is out of the question because "I'm the champ," she replies, "You mean Roberts is." Thompson's situation seems all the sadder for there being no championship on the line. Asked to relinquish the opportunity to demonstrate his skills and courage by defeating a younger man in a fair fight (he is informed of the fix in the fourth round), he can have integrity only at the cost of his career. In an alley behind the arena where Thompson has made his choice and knocked out Little Boy Nelson in the fifteenth round, a vengeful gambler and his henchmen break the boxer's hand.

While these stories described the sordid reality of boxing's domination by "fixers, grafters, tin-horns, and racketeers," to quote a 1948 presentation of *The March of Time*, they also functioned as social parables for a culture unsure of its ability to provide the most basic form of access and opportunity.[7] Despite talent, determination, and, in the beginning at least, integrity, Kelly, Davis, and Thompson inevitably come up against a device—the fix—that makes victory and defeat problematic, success and failure irrelevant, talent and skill unimportant. It is not so much that the fix denies the appearance of success to those who seek it; after all, Kelly and Davis win the championship. What it denies are the standards necessary to validate that success and give it objective meaning. Because the fix is indeterminate, because it is "in" sometimes and not others, or "in" for one fighter and not another, the results of any fight (and by extension, of any life endeavor) will also be indeterminate. One cannot say who won or lost, who fought well or poorly, or who, in the end, has made admirable progress, whether through boxing's ranks or life's thickets. Indeed, in a culture of the fix, all forms of success become completely irrelevant, save one: moral success. The only stance worthy of approbation is the stance against the fix itself. To be unaware of the fix (as is Davis in one of his fights, and Thompson through a portion of his) is to have no important attitude at all, since the fix is everything; yet to acquire knowledge of it (if sure knowledge can really be had) is to face a range of options so narrow as to deny to man many of his basic drives and needs.

Like the fix, the compulsion of alcoholism threatened the dream. A problem that received increasing attention throughout the 1940s, especially after 1945, alcoholism was both a real-life barrier to achievement and happiness and a metaphor for the culture's growing anxiety about progress. *Time* put its finger on an important aspect of the problem when it described an alcoholic as a person whose drinking was such that "it takes him out of one or more of the traffic lanes of life."[8] That is, alcoholism interfered with *linearity* (the traffic lane metaphor)—with progress along identified and sanctioned paths—an especially significant social objective in an age when directionless returning veterans and working women seemed to stand in the way of a smooth transition to postwar normalcy.

The traffic lane argument is central to the decade's most important films about alcoholism: *Smash-Up: The Story of a Woman* (1946) and *The Lost Weekend* (1945). *Smash-Up* explores the role of alcoholism in short-circuiting one of the decade's important social progressions: the transition from working woman to wife and mother. Talented night-club singer Angelica Evans (Susan Hayward) marries songwriter/crooner Ken Conway (Lee Bowman), and they have a daughter. As Ken becomes a star with the money to hire maids and nurses, an increasingly functionless Angelica takes to the bottle. Although Angelica's mothering instincts are sound enough and for a time overpower her desire to drink, her bouts with alcohol continue, and eventually Ken leaves, taking the child. Vowing to "get my baby back," she returns to singing, but this time her maternal impulses prove powerless. Now drinking constantly, she kidnaps her daughter and lovingly puts her to bed, only to leave a cigarette smoldering on the blanket. In the ensuing blaze she rescues the child but is severely burned. Lying in a hospital bed bandaged and virtually incoherent, she cries, "My baby, my baby." Though ambivalent on the question of woman's relationship to the workplace, the film clearly makes the point that mothering is central to womanhood (a postwar "traffic lane").

The Lost Weekend uses the subject of alcoholism to explore the postwar concern with commitment and purpose. The film's protagonist, Don Birnam (Ray Milland), is a well-meaning, genial writer whose efforts to put words on paper are thwarted by a maniacal fondness for booze. The inverse relationship beween career and alcoholism can be seen in his understanding of himself as two Don Birnams—Don the drunk and Don the writer—as well as in his efforts to pawn his typewriter for the money to purchase a quart of rye. The film appropriately ends with Birnam determined to get to work on a novel about his struggle against the bottle. What we have here in civilian garb is the familiar saga of the returning veteran (and, perhaps, of the nation)—glad to be home from the war but curiously lacking in resolve and direction, that is, pausing for a moment on the shoulder of one of those traffic lanes. When Helen St. James (Jane Wyman) argues that "other people have stopped [drinking]," Birnam can only reply, "People with a purpose, with something to do." Of course, Birnam does ostensibly have something to do—a novel to write—but rather than plunge ahead and get it done (the linear approach), it's down the hatch with that "one little jigger of dreams." As the bartender reaches out to wipe away the ring of moisture left by the glass, Birnam entertains him with a bit of philosophy that denies the linear: "Don't wipe it away, Nat. Let me have my little vicious circle. The circle is the perfect geometric figure. No end, no beginning."

Even if one managed to break the circle, there was growing doubt within the culture that humanity was capable of acting with a moral purpose consistent with progress. The Stalinist purges, Nazism, the Holocaust, Hiroshima—these emblems of humanity's problematic morality led to endless speculation about its desire and ability to construct a just world. A case in point is *All About Eve*, a film that received the Motion Picture Academy's Best Picture Award for 1950. Eve Harrington (Anne Baxter) first appears in the film as the young victim of a tragic past, humble, selfless, and altruistic, seemingly interested only in being near the object of her admiration, actress Margo Channing (Bette Davis). As we learn "all about Eve," her flawless, innocent exterior is peeled away to reveal a cold, deeply ambitious, and calculating person, driven by desire for the applause and celebrity of the theater. Thanks to Addison DeWitt (George Sanders), the drama critic whose rational faculties allow him to decipher Eve's character (and who represents the rational side of all of us), we come to see Eve's history as a fraud and to understand her "contempt for humanity" and "inability to love and be loved" as critical and irreparable faults. As if to say that the problem will not go away, the final moments of the film find Eve accepting an acting award with a speech packed with lies and delivered with trademarked false piety and feigned humility, then later that evening coming face to face with a high school girl whose calculation and ambition mark her as a second-generation Eve Harrington.

The possibility that events of the late 1930s and early 1940s might have uncovered some ugly truth about the essential nature of modern humanity permeated the work of writers whose subject matter was ostensibly far removed from such speculation. Two books of the naturalist Rachel Carson, *Under the Sea-Wind* and the best-seller *The Sea around Us*, mark the beginning and the end of the decade. Although neither book presents humans as entirely innocent, the first book integrates them into the world of the ocean in a way that the second does not. The curious creatures of *Under the Sea-Wind* are invested with an array of thoughts, feelings, and observational skills, which they employ in a natural, organic, rhythmic, interdependent, and sometimes brutal world:

The ghost crab, still at his hunting of beach fleas, was alarmed by the turmoil of birds overhead, by the many racing shadows that sped over the sand. By now he was far from his own burrow. When he saw the fisherman walking across the beach he dashed into the surf, preferring this refuge to flight. But a large channel bass was lurking nearby, and in a twinkling the crab was seized and eaten. Later in the same day, the bass was attacked by sharks and what was left of it was cast up by the tide onto the sand. There the beach fleas, scavengers of the shore, swarmed over it and devoured it.

In this Darwinian world of weak and strong, humans exist in two very different ways. On the one hand, they appear as the thoughtless and violent midnight intruder, torturing the migrating shad with needless gill nets. On the other hand, another kind of fisherman, confident in lore and skills passed "from one generation to the next," has a rightful place within the natural order of the sea. Dispense with the gill nets, Carson implies, and we will be in harmony with nature.[9]

A decade later, in *The Sea around Us*, the intimate, personal, and knowable ocean of 1941 has become a removed ocean of "shadowy" origins, a midcentury "changeless eternity" that dominates the planet and mocks our meager efforts at understanding it. The subjective tone of the earlier book has been replaced by the objective language of science. The artisan-fisherman, the flawed but perfectible creature of *Under the Sea-Wind*, has been replaced by the plunderer, who is forgetful of the planet's history, ignorant of the insignificance and finiteness of humans, and lusting for control of a "water world" that must forever remain beyond reach. Carson's picture of humanity in 1941 was essentially a reflection of European power politics: some people were bad (the Nazis and the gill fishermen) and some good (the democracies, the artisan-fishermen); the good were expected to triumph in the end. By 1951 the problem was not some people but *all* people, and the result was a book in which a powerful ocean took on heroic status and stood alone in its own defense.[10]

Among the most widely read and controversial of the allegorical attempts to describe and explain humanity's fall from innocence was Shirley Jackson's short story "The Lottery." Written on a sunny morning in the spring of 1948, the story appeared in the June issue of the *New Yorker*, where it provoked a storm of reaction from readers who found it "gruesome," "nauseating," "in incredibly bad taste," and the sign of "a new low in human viciousness."[11] Set in a village like New Bennington, Vermont, where Jackson lived, the story described a fictional community of some three hundred men, women, and children that annually selected one of its members to be ritually stoned to death. It was also about the Holocaust.

Like Carson's *The Sea around Us*, "The Lottery" found humankind to be coldly and mindlessly united in wrongdoing; no villager expressed remorse or grief, nor did any step forward to question the efficacy or propriety of the lottery. Just as Carson had questioned the viability of custom and tradition in her second book, Jackson described a people who had long ago forfeited any meaningful understanding of their deadly custom. Much of the ritual had been "lost or discarded," the paraphernalia "lost long ago"; it was sufficient, as Old Man Warner said, that "there's *always* been a lottery." And like Carson, Jackson had given up as futile any effort to locate the source of evil in an understandable political or economic framework. Jackson's villagers were evil in the most thoughtless and banal ways. One "clean forgot what day it was"; another urged that the process be conducted expeditiously, "so's we can go back to work." In careful prose, Jackson linked the ordinal of death to square dances, the Halloween program, and other "civic activities." And, as if to suggest her own culpability, Jackson's opening paragraph fused the lottery with her writing of the story, which, like the lottery, took two hours and was completed by noon.

Shirley Jackson described a humankind that had failed to resist evil and had somehow found itself committing the most heinous of acts; her perspective was far removed from the notion of human perfectibility that was part of the larger idea of progress. But even those who seemed not to have done anything really wrong did not always escape from the forties unscathed. Another kind of guilt—no less damaging to one's sense of innocence and almost as prejudicial to ideas of linear progress—was the guilt of those cursed with survival. Survivor guilt and its impact are the subject of Darryl F. Zanuck's production of *The Razor's Edge* (1946), based on a novel by W. Somerset Maugham. Set in the wake of World War I, the film features Tyrone Power as Larry Darrell, an idealistic, young American who veers off the "traffic lanes" of life to search for truth in the garrets of Paris's Left Bank and the temples of India. Throughout the film, Larry's explanation for what strikes his first love, Isabelle, as absurd behavior remains the same. He has not only seen death but was saved from it on the last day of the war, a quirk of fate that causes him to question the idea of purpose itself, to wonder if he owes his very being to "a stupid blunder." A decade later, when knuckleheaded Isabelle still cannot understand why Larry would rather take a tramp steamer to America than sell stocks and bonds, he explains again. "Do you know what it means," Larry asks, "to see another man give up his life for you," to know that "you're walking in another man's shoes?" Larry Darrell's survivor guilt is consistent with an idealistic conception of progress, but he lives outside life's mainstream. For Mickey Spillane's Mike Hammer, who was miraculously spared from a death by Japanese bayonet, survivor guilt leads to a life of violent retribution.[12]

The fall from innocence that was the message of works as disparate as *All About Eve*, Carson's *The Sea around Us*, and Jackson's "The Lottery" was not entirely inconsistent with ideas of progress; one could recoup some of the old optimism by accepting the fall—indeed, insisting upon such acceptance as a precondition for any larger movement in the direction of moral progress. To pursue the problem in this way was to call for a new recognition of "reality," or, as Leslie Fiedler did in a series of essays published in the late 1940s and early 1950s, to challenge the American people to part with myths of their own innocence. Fiedler charged Alger Hiss, accused of turning classified documents over to the Communists, with failure to undertake "the qualifying act of moral adulthood," that is, "admission of responsibility for the past and its consequences." According to Fiedler, liberals in key positions, among them Dean Acheson, Eleanor Roosevelt, and members of the House Un-American Activities Committee (HUAC), had similarly failed, so committed were they to the innocence of liberalism itself. In another essay, he found Montanans "unconfessed" over the treatment of the Indians, and in a third, he called for a frank acknowledgment of the male homosexuality that Fiedler claimed was at the heart of *Moby-Dick*, *The Adventures of Huckleberry Finn*, and the white man's treatment of the black man, his "dark-skinned beloved."[13] Hannah Arendt, the political theorist whose important study of totalitarianism and the Holocaust, *The Origins of Totalitarianism* (1951), was completed in 1949, wrote from much the same realist perspective as Feidler. Warning that "Progress" and "Doom" are both forms of superstition, Arendt counseled her readers to come to grips with the most sordid and concrete realities and experiences of life. "Comprehension," she wrote, "means . . . examining and bearing consciously the burden which our century has placed on us—neither denying its existence nor submitting meekly to its weight. Comprehension, in short, means the unpremeditated, attentive facing up to, and resisting of, reality—whatever it may be."[14]

The insistence on "reality" that marked the work of Fiedler and Arendt was necessary and valuable precisely because so many Americans—and not just scholars—did not want to face the past head-on. Although some scholars continued to find sustenance in history, for the vast majority of social analysts history had not only lost its power to reassure but had become unsuitable, useless, or even damaging, less a rational working out of benign processes than a trap for the helpless and unsuspecting. In response, Americans abandoned history for utopian primitivism, myth and symbol, abstraction, and a variety of other cultural expressions that seemed to offer some relief from an uncooperative and oppressive past.

Curiously enough, among some professional historians this growing unease with history had much to do with the increasing loss of faith in Marxism as an explanatory framework. Although Marxist historians were undeniably critical of the American historical experience, they believed in the efficacy of the historical process; whether through science, conflict between social classes, or the agency of the working class, in the Marxist worldview history moved inexorably and predictably along a linear path toward a better, revolutionary future.

The flight from Marxism occurred within every discipline and intellectual community in the two decades after 1935; historians responded by finding new ways to understand and use the past. In place of the Marxist dialectic and the linear progress it forecast, many historians moved toward a view of history that emphasized the core values and ideals that united Americans of every social class and era. One can see the change in the work of Arthur Schlesinger, Jr. Schlesinger's early work, including *The Age of Jackson* (1945), had posed historical issues in the traditional progressive framework of the "people" versus the "interests": Jacksonian democracy emerged as a movement of noncapitalist farmers and laboring men to control the power of Eastern capitalists. By 1949, however, Schlesinger was writing as if classes and sections no longer existed. He urged Americans to reject such conflicts and to meet the challenge of fascism and communism by investing themselves in a "vital" center defined by freedom and democracy.[15] Similarly, in *The American Political Tradition*, Richard Hofstadter downplayed conflict as an aspect of American political and social life, emphasizing instead the extent to which political figures as diverse as Thomas Jefferson, Andrew Jackson, William Jennings Bryan, Woodrow Wilson, and Herbert Hoover shared certain core values, such as the "sanctity of private property" and the "value of opportunity."[16] Proponents of this "consensus" perspective, as it was soon labeled, not only denied that the American past had been a ground of dissidence and conflict; by finessing differences between historical actors, they denied historical change itself. Americans were asked to forgo a meaningful historical past and the possibilities of an unknown future for a new and oddly static view of U.S. history that featured Americans locked in an ideological deep freeze.

Building on the theoretical foundations laid by the German philosopher of science Karl Popper, historians also rejected systems that promised to predict the future. For Schlesinger, such systems were the province of the misguided (and totalitarian) ideologist, who "contends that the mysteries of history can be understood in terms of a clear-cut, absolute, social creed which explains the past and forecasts the future. . . . The history of the twentieth century is a record of the manifold ways in which humanity has been betrayed by ideology." The search for a nonideological history brought growing numbers of historians to the doors of the social sciences, some in the belief that an empirical approach would yield the "objective" history that seemed to be the birthright of the "free world," others having lost confidence in the power and utility of the narrative form. A few of the new arrivals, including the business historian Thomas Cochran, were not without self-doubt. Responding in 1951 to a letter from fellow historian Merle Curti that commented on the difficulties of doing history in an age of reaction, Cochran wrote of his own disinclination to "swim against the overwhelming current. I guess what I've done is to build an ivory tower called the Social Science Approach to History where I can live wrapped up in social roles, and protected from reality by sanctions, basic personalities and cultural themes."[17]

Fearful and distrustful of the past, and unwilling to countenance the most negative readings it might yield, Americans embraced Arnold J. Toynbee, a celebrated English historian whose vision, though realistic and pessimistic, held out hope of a reasonable future. In *Civilization on Trial*, a book of postwar essays published in 1948, in *A Study of History*, an abridgement of his multivolume study and a 1947 best-seller in the American market, and in a series of sold-out lectures delivered at Bryn Mawr College in March 1947, Toynbee delivered a message of ambivalence that *Time* succinctly summarized beneath a picture of him that graced its cover: "Our civilization is not inexorably doomed."[18]

Although Toynbee saw in the history of nineteen previous civilizations a "pattern of decline and fall," he stopped short of drawing the conclusion that modern civilization would experience a similar fate. Toynbee found much that was negative and suggestive of decline in modern Western civilization, including a tendency toward standardization and uniformity; the existence of sharply defined social classes in an age of relative abundance; and the achievement of a level of technological prowess and war-making capability that made possible the destruction of "the entire human race." But Toynbee thought the "one world" enthusiasm (see Chapter 4) was a hopeful sign, and he continued to reject determinism, insisting (with some obvious equivocation) that "man is master of his own destiny, at least to some extent in some respects," and "with God's help." Though the age-old observation that "history repeats itself" suggested that Western civilization would follow the rest in decline, Toynbee rather stubbornly claimed that repetition could also serve as an "instrument for freedom"—by providing sufficient materials (i.e., civilizations) for the sort of social experimentation necessary to eventually produce a society immune to decline. Because past failures were failures of experimentation, of trial and error, the prognosis for modern civilization, whatever its failings, was not necessarily fatal. For *Time*, Toynbee's lesson was that the American Century—the moment of American empire—had arrived: it was time for the United States to "take over from Britain the job of trying to solve the problem of contemporary history," to become "the champion of the remnant of Christian civilization against the forces that [threaten] it."[19]

For many Americans, history seemed just so much excess baggage—a system of inquiry that did not appear to have much to do with what people wanted out of life. Margaret Mead, turning in the 1940s from the study of Samoans to examining the American people, applauded the geographical and social mobility of her new subjects. "Nostalgia for the past," she argued in *Male and Female* (1948), "is out of place among a people who must always be moving, to a better job, a better house, a new way of life." Mead used a recently published novel, *White Fawn*—which featured a love match between an Irish physician of working-class heritage and his Boston blue-blood sweetheart—to illustrate Americans' propensity to choose their lives and fates from "out of the future, either unrelated to or definitely contradictory of the past."[20]

History also suffered in comparison with science. The argument went something like this: radar, atomic fission, and other examples of pure and applied science had won the war. To the extent that science had also outrun humanity's ability to control the fruits of knowledge, what was required was more science, not less—specifically, a more rigorous, scientific approach to human relations (i.e., the social sciences). History, in contrast, was unscientific, nostalgic, and therefore useless.

The most severe indictment of this sort was issued by T. E. Frazier, the leader and spokesman for Walden Two, the fictional utopian community created in 1948 by Harvard University psychologist B. F. Skinner. According to Frazier, history was an altogether "spurious science" that lacked predictive powers and had nothing to offer either mainstream political reformers seeking a basis for policy formation or Waldenites engaged in the search for an experimental ethics. Worse still, history was easily adapted to false, "emotive" purposes. "Your Hitlers are the men who use history to real advantage," claimed Frazier. "It obfuscates every attempt to get a clear appreciation of the present. . . . The present is the thing. It's the only thing we can deal with, anyway, in a scientific way."[21]

There were also those who believed that the use of the atomic bomb had rendered history irrelevant and even absurd—as if the explosions over Hiroshima and Nagasaki had severed all links with the past. This, at least, is one theme of George R. Stewart's *Earth Abides*, a popular science fiction novel published in 1949. As the book opens, graduate student Isherwood Williams emerges from a field expedition in the California hills to find the nation, and perhaps the world, devastated by a disease (a surrogate for a nuclear device), leaving only a few survivors. After many months on his own, Ish finds an acceptable mate and settles down in the vicinity of San Francisco, raising a family and taking on the role of community patriarch and teacher. At first, he sees his proper function as that of educating the others about the past. He wants to keep track of time. "After all," Ish reflects, "time was history, and history was tradition, and tradition was civilization." For a while the community responds, monitoring time by remembering each year for some significant event: the Year of the Lions, the Year of the Deaths, and so on. Eventually, however, even this simple system of record-keeping falls into abeyance as history and the progressive, linear, planning-oriented culture it presupposes are gradually displaced by the community's more primitive, more practical, and essentially presentist culture, in which civilization comes to be represented in the icon of Ish's hammer. Ish, too, begins to see the irrelevance of historical knowledge (knowledge of street names and state boundaries) to a world in which survival depends on a practical sort of earth-knowledge (knowledge of the location of streambeds, and of how to "read" the appearance of sagebrush for signs of increasing aridity). Ish dismisses school "forever" and later dies not only resigned to the new ways but convinced that "earth abides."[22]

The reaction against history had another, more important source than the concern with scientific objectivity raised by Skinner's Frazier, or the feeling that the bomb had left the world beyond the realm of history. By the end of 1945, the past was the repository of the most frightening memories—of desperate joblessness and totalitarianism, of separation and death in war, of the mass murder of the Jews, of the bombs dropped on Hiroshima and Nagasaki—and these memories were shared by millions of Americans. Though postwar Americans would throw themselves into a frenzy of consumption and familial bliss in an effort to locate themselves in a timeless present, the past proved difficult to shed. The failed effort of Joe Keller's family to avoid or transcend the past is the subject of Arthur Miller's *All My Sons*. Joe's son Larry is dead, killed years ago in the war. Unable to accept the fact or the circumstances of that death, the Kellers live as if frozen in time. "We never took up our lives again," explains Chris, whose desire to marry Larry's old girlfriend is thwarted by the lingering possibility that his brother may still be alive. "We're like at a railroad station waiting for a train that never comes in."[23]

When the trains of the forties did come in—and, despite Chris's statement, they inevitably did—they were invariably loaded with a lethal message from the past. The Kellers learn that Larry *is* dead, but that he killed himself upon discovering that his father had manufactured and knowingly forwarded faulty engine parts that caused the deaths of numerous pilots. In Kingsley's *Detective Story*, the train that will run over Detective McLeod carries the word that his wife, Mary, whose innocence and purity had served as a wellspring of moral stability in a world of chaos and vice, had years before suffered an unwanted pregnancy and undergone an illegal abortion. Overcome by the "dirty pictures" that cloud his brain and unable to accept Mary's explanations, McLeod rejects his once "immaculate wife," insisting that he would "sooner go to jail for twenty years—than find out this way that my wife was a whore." For McLeod as for Joe Keller, there is a steep price to be paid for coming face to face with the past; both men die, Keller by suicide, McLeod in the aftermath of a redeeming act of heroism. While McLeod's experience brings with it a measure of self-knowledge previously denied him, it is not at all clear that the past is worth probing or that one ought to trifle with one mechanism for doing so—that is, history. When Detective Brody of *Detective Story* asks the beleaguered Arthur (charged with stealing from his boss) about his college course of study, the following exchange ensues:

ARTHUR: Majored in History.

BRODY: History? What for?

ARTHUR: To teach. I wanted to be a teacher.

BRODY: Much of a career in that?

ARTHUR: I used to think so.[24]

The most powerful cultural representation of this dark and dangerous past was the flashback, a device regularly employed in film throughout the 1940s. Far from denying the past, the flashback insisted upon it, interrupting the narrative for a look backward at a moment or series of moments that might help illuminate the present. But the past revealed by the flashback was not intended to be comfortable, pleasurable, nostalgic, or even entirely clarifying. On the contrary, the function of the flashback was usually to offer an explanation for the current and often desperate plight of the protagonist/hero. A lengthy flashback in *Double Indemnity* reveals the path that brought nice-guy insurance salesman Walter Neff to a confession of murder. *Sorry, Wrong Number* opens with invalid Leona Stevenson's accidental discovery of a murder plot, then cuts to a series of flashbacks that offer differences in social background as an explanation for the murder—her own—that will take place that very evening. In *Crossfire*, the detective uses a series of flashback narratives provided by witnesses to find an anti-Semitic murderer. *Body and Soul* opens on the night of champion Charlie Davis's last fight, a fight that he has agreed to throw; the flashback begins with Davis waiting alone in his locker room for the call to the ring, muttering, "Everything down the drain." *D.O.A.* begins with the determined but funereal march of poisoned businessman Frank Bigelow into a Los Angeles police station, where he reconstructs (in flashback, of course) the events that have brought him to the brink of death. Finally, the flashback that serves as almost the entire content of *Sunset Boulevard* is narrated by writer Joseph C. Gillis while his body floats face down in a swimming pool.

By interrupting a traditional, linear narrative, the flashback challenged the form strongly identified with progress: the story with a beginning, a middle, and an end, and open to all possibilities. The flashback film often began with the ending, which thus became known and fixed, impervious to the strength, guile, or moral purity of the protagonist. Gillis is dead as the film begins. Bigelow is fatally ill ("You've been murdered," he is told). Neff has committed murder. Stevenson's fate is not entirely sealed as the film opens, but the flashbacks show her lacking the time necessary to digest what she hears and to save herself. Of these characters, only Stevenson can shape her future in any important way, but her deeply flawed personality prevents one from caring much whether she survives or not.[25]

The device of the flashback invited exploration not of an open-ended present, replete with possibilities and options, but of closure, impasse, and limits. Within this framework, the films focused on two questions, each of them central to the 1940s. The first was the existential question: how would a person react when confronted with a condition of virtual hopelessness? The second, of greater relevance here, was the historical question of origins and causation: how had such a condition been generated? How, asked *Body and Soul*, had Charlie Davis, celebrated by the Iroquois Democratic Club as "our own neighborhood champ" and blessed with an intelligent and charming girlfriend, ended up killing a fighter with a blood clot on his brain, destroying his best friend, and agreeing to take a dive in his last fight? How, asked *Sunset Boulevard*, did a talented, handsome, cordial Hollywood writer who had "always wanted a pool" end up dead in one? And how, asked *Double Indemnity*, had a competent and comfortable salesman like Walter Neff found himself pumping bullets into his lady friend?

Although movie audiences enjoyed the films on just this level, the stories they told were parables of the fall from innocence, and the specific questions they asked pointed to the larger ones that troubled Americans in the forties: How had the civilized Western world generated a war that killed sixty million persons? How had the German people, known for their refined sensibilities, welcomed Hitler, given rise to the Nazis, and tolerated the murder of six million Jews? How had right-thinking Americans rationalized the killing of civilians at Hiroshima and Nagasaki? And how had the isolationist America of the 1930s found itself a decade later the leader of the Western world, charged with the containment of world communism?

Although each film's flashback offered a variety of answers to its own specific question, as a group the films of the forties provided a sympathetic response to these larger questions. This response featured the past and its exploration as a baited trap; the films held out the possibility that an answer might be found in a narrative of events, but they were ultimately incapable of generating any truly satisfying explanation for the troubles of their protagonists (i.e., the American people). The dead narrator of *Sunset Boulevard* promises us "the facts, the whole truth," but the flashback that follows locates the beginning of Gillis's downfall in nothing more significant than a flat tire in a driving rain that forces him off the road and into the life of the aging star of silent film, Norma Desmond (Gloria Swanson). Walter Neff describes the events that enfolded his life in a series of mechanical metaphors of "gears" that "meshed" and "machinery [that] had started to move and nothing would stop it," depicting the narrated past as an inexorable and exogenous force. *Out of the Past* (1947) features Robert Mitchum as Jeff Bailey/Jeff Markham, a man whose search for happiness is more than once violated by the untimely appearance of some portion of his past life. "There wasn't one chance in a million we'd bump into our past," Bailey explains, but bump into his past he did, with dire consequences.

In short, the flashback film understood the past as hostile and, ultimately, impenetrably murky, full of twists and turns that defied both logic and the odds and mocked the very idea of a reasoned and understandable causation. Peg said as much when she urged Charlie Davis to quit boxing: "If one could only see, Charlie, that it started here or there. . . . We're in something horrible and we've got to get out. . . . It was all inevitable."

Nonlinear explorations were also common in the literature, poetry, and visual arts of the 1940s. Among those who took umbrage with American "linear consciousness" was William Faulkner, whose climb to literary prominence began in 1946 with the publication of Malcolm Cowley's edited collection, *The Portable Faulkner*. According to the literary scholar Jean Kellogg, Faulkner's opposition to the "linear thinking of the West" and to the vision of technological and scientific progress that it encapsulated led the Southern writer to explore nonlinear modes of consciousness in which past and present existed simultaneously.[26] Similarly, one critic described Nelson Algren's *The Man with the Golden Arm* as a series of "stills," a succession of "timeless moments" stitched together in a mosaic.[27] Dance choreographers, including Martha Graham, George Balanchine, and Merce Cunningham, rejected the "rhetoric of civilization"—the narrative—for the plotless, abstract, visual spectacle; their figures moved, but the space they moved in was purely physical, rather than historical or social.[28]

The growing importance of the new non-narrative techniques can also be observed in poet Ezra Pound's *The Pisan Cantos*, published in 1948 and the controversial winner of the prestigious Bollingen Prize. While in certain respects *The Pisan Cantos* resembled an epic along the lines of Dante's *Divine Comedy*, the lengthy and complex poem lacked a beginning-to-end narrative. Indeed, Pound purposefully and consistently avoided the chronology of history. By choosing to order facts, events, and documents capriciously—often in the order in which they came to him—Pound denied history and causality and sought to transcend, as one writer has put it, "the mindless flux of time."[29]

The forties, then, were a time of disruption, when the narrative had lost its power to persuade the reader that the world was sensible and would yield in appropriate ways to his or her efforts. To employ a conventional narrative in this context was to risk failure and disapproval; doing so to describe the use of the atomic bomb at Hiroshima—the event that more than any other had shattered the narrative illusion—was nothing less than foolhardy. But this was precisely what John Hersey did in *Hiroshima* (1946), originally published in the *New Yorker* magazine and reissued as a Book-of-the-Month-Club selection.[30]

Hersey presented the Hiroshima experience through the lives of six residents of the city—a personnel clerk, a physician, a tailor's widow, a German priest, a surgeon, and a Methodist pastor. Although Hersey was aware that the use of the bomb had made the printed word itself problematic ("I started to bring my books along," says the priest, Father Cieslik, "and then I thought 'This is no time for books'"), in *Hiroshima* he employed a traditional frame, describing the activities of its protagonists before, during, and after the explosion and doing so in an uninflected narrative not all that different from Ernie Pyle's war dispatches or novelist Erskine Caldwell's social realism. The book opens in this precise, narrative vein: "At exactly fifteen minutes past eight in the morning, on August 6, 1945, Japanese time, at the moment when the atomic bomb flashed above Hiroshima, Miss Toshiko Sasaki, a clerk in the personnel department of the East Asia Tin Works, had just sat down at her place in the plant office and was turning her head to speak to the girl at the next desk."[31]

A few reviewers and literary critics wrote harshly of Hersey's effort, most on the grounds that the author had failed to invest his account with sufficient emotion. Dwight Macdonald, editor of the journal *Politics*, suggested that Hersey's "antiseptic" prose might be more suited to a description of "white mice" than the flesh-and-blood humanity of Hiroshima and speculated on naturalism's moral and esthetic incapacity "to cope with the modern horrors." (Writing in *Sewanee Review* in 1947, Frederick Morgan criticized Eugene O'Neill's new play, *The Iceman Cometh*, for "its flatness of dramatic conception and deadness of language.") Novelist Mary McCarthy suggested the absurdity of attempting to capture the horror of the bomb by describing the activities of survivors, and she traced Hersey's failure to the magazine in which the account had first appeared. "Since the *New Yorker* has not," she wrote, "so far as we know, had a rupture with the government . . . it can only assimilate the atomic bomb to itself, to Westchester County, to smoked turkey, and the Hotel Carlyle."[32]

Yet most readers applauded and celebrated Hersey's achievement—for reasons that may have had much to do with the book's form and structure. By employing a narrative form that had arguably been rendered meaningless by an event that seemed to have stopped history in its tracks, Hersey was engaged in a comforting defense of the immutability of history. The book's tripartite structure, with the bomb in the middle, located the bomb *in history*, rather than at the beginning of some new epoch in which the past had been reduced to the rubble of Hiroshima. *Hiroshima's* narrative core seemed to suggest that for all its tragic and grizzly horrors, the experience was not incapable of being framed, like other experiences, as a story; though clearly different in degree, it was not so different in kind. Hersey's six survivors were compelling for Americans precisely because they responded to the bomb with such resolute linearity, losing nary a beat in getting on with the tasks of life. The central message of *Hiroshima* was that for all the devastation the bomb had caused, we had remained firmly within history, grounded by memories of the past, working resolutely in the present, and projecting our lives into a difficult but hardly intolerable future. We would muddle through.

When a narrative of the past failed to provide reassurance or even to ground the present in some satisfying way, scholars and writers in many fields turned to other modes of understanding. Economists gradually renounced the traditional concern with social policy and social theory for a new interest in mathematics.[33] Beginning in the late 1930s, the literary critic John Crowe Ransom pioneered New Criticism, which abandoned ideology and history as systems of explanation and instead featured intensive, technical analysis of the individual poem as an isolated and distinct unit.[34] Anxious mothers thumbing the pages of Dr. Benjamin Spock's 1946 best-seller, *The Common Sense Book of Baby and Child Care*, would find that Spock's "common sense" was indebted not so much to history as to some notion of the primitive. *Baby and Child Care* evoked a simpler, older, less complex culture than that to which Americans were accustomed. "In civilizations that are simpler than ours," writes Spock, "children and grownups too go to sleep curled up together," helping the young ones to relax and fall asleep. Counseling mothers to adopt a flexible, "natural" schedule, Spock asked his readers to "think of a mother, far away in an 'uncivilized' land, who has never heard of a schedule, or a pediatrician. . . . The rhythm of the baby's digestive system is what sets the schedule."[35] Erik H. Erikson's analysis of adolescence, *Childhood and Society* (1950), displayed much the same antipathy toward modernization and historical change, applauding the Sioux Indians for maintaining methods of child-rearing that allowed for resistance to the "ambitious strivings" and "boundless discontent" of Western civilization.[36] The turn away from history was also apparent in the theater. When Thornton Wilder's *The Skin of Our Teeth* opened at New York's Plymouth Theater in November 1942, audiences must have wondered just where, or when, the action was taking place. Protagonist George Antrobus is introduced as the "inventor of the wheel" and yet lives "right handy to an A. and P." George's suburban household is threatened by an enormous, southward-migrating wall of ice, whose presence has thrust the family into a prehistoric anthropological dream world. As the character Sabina remarks, "The author hasn't made up his silly mind as to whether we're all living back in caves or in New Jersey today, and that's the way it is all the way through."[37] The popularity of such nonhistorical approaches prompted critic Philip Rahv to attack the growing number of writers whose work utilized timeless myths and symbols for their desire to escape from the "flux of temporality," and he proclaimed the continued relevance of historical, ideological, and social frameworks to an understanding of literature.[38]

For the most part, then, Americans of the 1940s found the historical past either not very useful or downright frightening. But there was another sort of past, accessible to those willing to make an imaginative leap backward in time, that was comfortable and dependable. This past was rooted in mythic recreations of the countryside and the small towns and in the nation's colonial heritage and frontier experience.

The desire to reside in this mythic past was a commonplace one in the 1940s, a product of the links forged during the war between patriotism and rural life, of a certain wariness of technology, and, most importantly, of a long-term American hostility to the city, exacerbated by the mass urban migrations required by a burgeoning wartime economy. The nightmares of film noir were invariably urban tales, set amid the alleys, night clubs, and rain-slicked streets of the city. Bigelow's poisoning in *D.O.A.* is closely linked to his journey to Los Angeles (at once America's city of the future and the source of darkness) and occurs in a city bar as a black bebop band plays urban "jive"; the message is that he should have stayed home. The woman who tempts the auto mechanic Danny Brady into crime in *Quicksand* is a victim of life in a steel-town boardinghouse; "I never saw a star until I was sixteen," she confides. *Sorry, Wrong Number* contrasts the urban shrew Leona Stevenson, confined to bed in a room overlooking Manhattan, with the other woman Henry might have married, a simple woman of integrity named Sally Hunt, from his own small town of Grassville. Though not strictly within the film noir genre, *The Asphalt Jungle* (1950) carries a similar message. It stars Sterling Hayden as Dix Handley, a "hooligan" with good looks, intelligence, and integrity who signs on with a gang planning a jewel heist. As the film ends, a wounded Dix retreats from the "asphalt jungle" to his home town, there to die in a pasture on the farm where he grew up.

Consistent with this bleak perception of the city, Americans of the forties imagined an existence that was, at the very least, simpler, more bucolic, and more uplifting than that offered by contemporary urban America. One version of the past located Elysium in rural life. During the war, the regional Americanism of the 1930s was easily transmuted into the theme of rural patriotism. Aaron Copland's "Appalachian Spring" (1944) used variations on Shaker songs and country fiddle tunes to capture Pennsylvania rural life; Ross Lee Finney was inspired by colonial music in his choral work "Pilgrim Psalms" (1945); and Virgil Thomson drew on the Cajun songs of the bayou for his score to the documentary film *Louisiana Story* (1948).[39] Hollywood "backstage" musicals of the 1940s generally combined a central urban backstage plot with rural, folk elements such as a hoedown (*Babes on Broadway* [1941]) or a show put on in a barn (*Summer Stock* [1950])—all, according to the film scholar Jane Feuer, to soften and deny the economic relations underlying mass entertainment. "Remember neighbors," sing Gene Kelly and Judy Garland in *Summer Stock*, "when you work for Mother Nature you get paid by Father Time."[40] The mass-market magazines were in the vanguard of the ruralism movement, tempting the subdebs of 1943 with gingham plaids and ruffled blouses and calling on their parents to adopt an "indigenous," "honest, straightforward, functional architecture" based on nothing more than farm buildings.[41]

One of the purest expressions of antiurban ruralism was Virginia Lee Burton's *The Little House*, the winner of the Caldecott Medal for the best children's book of 1942. The story is about a little house that is solidly built and supremely happy in its country surroundings, a fond observer of the change in seasons. As the children in the area grow up and leave the countryside for the city, the burgeoning suburbs and then the city itself reach out and encircle the little house, until it is surrounded by dark tenements and looks out upon that icon of urbanization, the elevated train. "Now she couldn't tell when Spring came, or Summer or Fall, or Winter. It all seemed about the same." As the shadows of skyscrapers blot out the sun and a subway rumbles underground, the great-great-granddaughter of the man who built the little house recognizes the suffering building, puts it on wheels, and moves it to the country, where, of course, it lives happily ever after.[42]

A second model for an alternative way of life was the historical West, a region explored in the late 1940s in the films of Howard Hawkes and John Ford and in Western magazines such as *Western Story Annual* and *Avon Western Reader*, which vied with their detective counterparts for the consumer dollar at the corner newsstand. Indicative of the postwar Western revival was the popularity of the ranch house. Derived from Frank Lloyd Wright's turn-of-the-century "prairie style," the ranch house hugged the ground, enabled its occupants to move easily from room to room, and had a close relationship with the outdoors, where (after 1951) the man of the house might "rustle up" some "chow" on his Weber grill.[43] Dude ranches—Western spas for the well-to-do—were also doing a "land-office" business. So strong was midcentury interest in the West that the Pulitzer Prize committee passed over distinguished work by William Faulkner to bestow the award on two ordinary books about the frontier: *The Way West* by A. B. Guthrie, Jr. (the 1950 winner) and *The Town* by Conrad Richter (the 1951 winner), the latter a detailed and moralistic recollection of mid-nineteenth century life and costume. Also appearing in 1950 was Henry Nash Smith's *Virgin Land: The American West as Symbol and Myth*, perhaps the twentieth century's most significant reinterpretation of the region.[44]

The Jefferson National Expansion Memorial Association followed the American imagination west in 1948, when it awarded architect Eero Saarinen first prize in a contest for a St. Louis memorial to commemorate Thomas Jefferson, the Louisiana Purchase, the opening of the West, and, as the name of the awarding agency suggested, national expansion. To make room for whatever entry won the prize, the city and the National Park Service had razed all but a few buildings on a Mississippi river front site previously occupied mostly by old warehouses—or what was referred to in some circles as a "slum." The architectural and design community applauded the winner for incorporating the warehouse of fur trader Manuel Lisa (one of the few buildings remaining on the site) into his project, whose centerpiece was an enormous parabolic arch, and for capturing the spirit of St. Louis as the "Gateway to the West." Although the project was clearly intended to assist in the revitalization of St. Louis, it did so not only by tearing down eighty acres of buildings in a historically significant area of the city (an antiurban and antihistorical process known even then as "urban renewal").[45]

The effort to relocate the American consciousness in a more congenial place and time found a third locus: the small town, vintage 1910, complete with steepled churches, gabled roofs, and streets blissfully free (or almost free) of automobiles. In 1946 the editors of *Architectural Forum* acknowledged the strength of this small-town mythology. The collective American "dream house" was "a quaint little white cottage, shyly nestled in a grove of old elms or maples, bathed in the perfume of lilacs, and equipped with at least one vine-covered wall. . . . The eaves come down so low that one can almost touch them. Tiny dormers on one side poke themselves through the old roof and let in light through tiny-paned windows to the upstairs bedrooms. In front of the house there is invariably a picket fence, with day lilies poking their heads between the white palings."[46]

This was Norman Rockwell's America, an America of the extended family and the involved community, where the butcher was a friend, the postman a helpmate, and the worst thing in life was the embarrassment of a bad hair-cut. Such was the setting for composer Samuel Barber's "Knoxville: Summer of 1915," opus 24 (1948), a "nostalgic, misty, and dreamlike" musical accom-paniment to James Agee's rendering of the thoughts, feelings, musings, and yearnings of a child lying with his mother, father, uncle, and aunt on quilts spread over the wet grass of a backyard in a small town in Tennessee.[47]

Many Americans encountered these images in the mass culture, and es-pecially through the small-town pastoral musical, a film genre that flourished between 1944 and 1948 and included *Meet Me in St. Louis* (1944), *State Fair* (1945), *The Harvey Girls* (1946), and *Summer Holiday* (1948). These musicals offered viewers the illusion of stasis: a family-centered and largely traditional world frozen in time, poised on the brink of the assembly line, the Great War, and other developments that would sweep the small town into the twentieth century. The mid-1940s enthusiasm for the sentimental, pastoral musical was a response to wartime separations and disruptions. (Later, in the cold war context, the continuing popularity of these movies was a form of resistance to the Soviet challenge to American power.) Moreover, these mu-sicals were far from being simple, unadulterated expressions of the pastoral mythos. *Summer Holiday*, for example, offered pastoral images that were so starkly idealized that audiences were tempted to see them as somehow ironic. *Meet Me in St. Louis* broke through its nostalgic reverie to a dark and windy Halloween night alive with the primitive and potentially disruptive forces that lay beneath the surface of the community.[48] Americans could question the dream, even as they valued and consumed its basic content.

America in the 1940s was no longer the determined social-reformist nation of the 1930s, but not yet the self-assured, even complacent, world power of the 1950s. Fears and anxieties—about the end of progress and the decline of civilization, about economic stagnation and social stasis, about a historical past that was at best irrelevant to the present and at worst the source of present predicaments—dominated intellectual and cultural expression. Yet against this backdrop of gloom and doom there were those who imagined, even proclaimed, a revitalized culture. This revitalization movement (if in-deed these disparate and unconnected phenomena can be labeled a "move-ment") had two motifs: renewal (spiritual, economic, and social), often under the aegis of a charismatic leader; and speed, motion, and action.

The most obvious sign of the desire for renewal was the emergence of a national religious revival. The revival had begun during the war for reasons other than renewal: growing numbers of Americans turned to religion to deal with the anxieties of mobilization, distended families, and combat. After 1945 interest in religion surged again as the special uncertainties of a nuclear age and the perils of a new era of affluence brought forth a spate of "reassur-ance" tracts, beginning in 1946 with Joshua Liebman's *Peace of Mind* and in-cluding Norman Vincent Peale's *Guide to Confident Living* (1948). The Red

Scare of the late 1940s also contributed to the revival, since going to church was one way of demonstrating one's commitment to the "American way of life" in the cold war against the communist, atheistic foe. In 1948 nine of every ten Americans said they believed in God, and by 1950 church affiliation had increased to 55 percent from 49 percent a decade earlier. Because midcentury mainstream religion was by and large so practical—so oriented toward helping people deal with their problems and insecurities—doctrinal controversies were few. One result was that the Protestant denominations were able to move toward greater unity, consolidating their educational and missionary activities in the National Council of Churches (1950).[49]

The religious reawakening of the 1940s had another, more rigorous side, rooted in theology. Among the theologians, two stand out as exceedingly influential and representative of the age. One was Reinhold Niebuhr, the "crisis" theologian whose writings were important to figures as diverse as W. H. Auden and Arthur Schlesinger, Jr. Under the banner of "realism," Niebuhr called on Americans to recognize their unremitting sinfulness and moral inadequacy that made all their activities, including those in the political and international realms, inevitably corrupted and flawed. Yet against this message of inescapable imperfection, Niebuhr insisted on the need for a life of political involvement and commitment. Just as important was Paul Tillich, the German-born professor of philosophical theology at Union Seminary in New York City (1933–1955), who introduced many Americans to European existentialism. Like Niebuhr, Tillich spoke the language of realism; spiritual renewal could only come through direct confrontation with the most chilling truths: that being contained within it nonbeing, and that existence was meaningless. Applauding Auden, modern artists, and playwrights Arthur Miller and Tennessee Williams for probing the terrain of meaninglessness, Tillich explained how the acceptance of nonbeing might yield faith rather than cynicism. In a paradox typical of the age, Tillich confirmed the relationship between despair and faith: "The act of accepting meaninglessness," he wrote in *The Power of Being*, "is in itself a meaningful act. It is an act of faith." At the end of the process was "*re*-conciliation, *re*-union, and *re*-surrection": in sum, a "New Being" brought forth from the corrupted and distorted old being.[50]

Spearheading the religious revival was a resurgent fundamentalism, which was strengthened by the formation of the National Association of Evangelicals (1942) and Youth for Christ (1943) and, by midcentury, the leadership of Billy Graham. An evangelist since 1945, Graham gained the attention of the media while putting on his show in a tent in downtown Los Angeles in the fall of 1949. In the months that followed, Graham took his revival across the country, drawing forty thousand spectators in Columbia, South Carolina, and fifty thousand on Boston Common, where he invoked George Whitefield's 1740 text: "Shall God reign in New England?"

Although Graham's message was largely a traditional one of heaven and hell, sin and repentance, it was delivered through a lapel microphone and a public address system and was embellished with up-to-date metaphors. Graham claimed that on Judgment Day, God would call on his flock to "start up the projector! Because from the cradle to the grave God has had His television cameras on you. God has every sinful word on His recording."[51] Graham was also adept at merging his message of personal salvation with current social issues and national and international problems, an indication that his revival was in some measure a response to perceptions of national decline and to the cold war. The alcoholic culture of forties America was a regular target of his invective, as was a "sinful America" mired in the Korean War, terrorized by atomic and hydrogen bombs, vulnerable to cancer and heart disease, and headed for the apocalypse.[52] In pursuit of a fusion of the personal and political, Graham managed a brief meeting with Harry Truman, during which he asked the president to call a national day of repentance, humiliation, and prayer. "I prayed loud," Graham told the *New York Times*, "and the President stood with his head bowed. I just prayed to the Lord, and asked God to give him wisdom." Unfortunately for Graham's proposal, God's wisdom had to hurdle the counsel offered by the president's grandfather, who had told him that "whenever you heard someone praying conspicuously loudly, 'you'd better go home and lock your smokehouse.'"[53]

On 9 February 1950, as Billy Graham was gearing up for his South Carolina meetings, a revival of a different sort was launched in Wheeling, West Virginia. The speaker was Sen. Joseph McCarthy, the Wisconsin Republican who had hatched the anticommunist theme of his senatorial campaign a month earlier during a dinner meeting with fellow Catholics, among them Father Edmund A. Walsh, regent of the School of Foreign Service at Georgetown University.[54] While the address is deservedly notorious as the opening salvo in McCarthy's anticommunist crusade, little attention has been paid to the movement as a *crusade*. In fact, the Wheeling speech is a document in cultural revitalization. McCarthy began by establishing the context in which revitalization was necessary: "Five years after a world war has been won, men's hearts should anticipate a long peace, and men's minds should be free from the heavy weight that comes with war." Instead, the nation was embroiled in a "cold war," a condition that McCarthy proceeded to define in religious and even apocalyptic terms—as a "final, all-out battle between communistic atheism and Christianity." McCarthy accused Alger Hiss of having "sold out the Christian world to the atheistic world," and he attacked the secretary of state for having committed "blasphemy" by proclaiming "to the American people that Christ on the Mount endorsed communism." Numbed into moral apathy by wartime destruction and mass murder, the American people needed only a "spark" to "rekindle" their moral sensibilities and launch a "moral uprising" that would yield a "new birth" of governmental honesty and decency.[55] Employing the language of the revival, McCarthy would use his Senate seat to bring the gospel of anticommunism into the heart of American politics.

Renewal could also mean *economic* renewal. The most significant postwar contribution in this area came in the theory and history of entrepreneurship. Entrepreneurship was first proposed as a modern field of study by the Committee for Research in Economic History, an organization created and funded by the Rockefeller Foundation in 1940. When interest revived following the war, and was subsequently given institutional expression with the founding of the Research Center for Entrepreneurial Studies at Harvard in 1948, debate among theorists focused on the role of the entrepreneur in generating new, creative ideas within systems that tended to limit such responses. Oxford University professor of social and political theory G. D. H. Cole set the tone for the debate in a 1946 address in which he emphasized the importance of "disruptive, innovating energy" (a phrase possibly derived from the use of the atomic bomb) in business and economic activity, although he also described entrepreneurship as an activity involving the making of "rational" decisions.[56]

In contrast, economist Joseph A. Schumpeter depicted entrepreneurship as a nonrational, intuitive, almost mystical (one is tempted to say religious) force for social change. At its core was what Schumpeter called the "creative response": essentially an act—usually undertaken by one or a few persons—that could not be "predicted by applying the ordinary rules of inference from the pre-existing facts." Clearly concerned about the problem of social stasis, Schumpeter saw entrepreneurship as a "bursting" of barriers, an action-based approach capable of overcoming "resistances" and avoiding the "ruts of established practice."[57]

Although most entrepreneurial historians eschewed the dynamics of the narrative for the relatively static methodology of sociological role theory, they were also in flight from economic theory, an explanatory system that seemed to deny any role to "human creativity and effort." Thomas Cochran, whose *Railroad Leaders, 1845–1900: The Business Mind in Action* would be the first product of the entrepreneurial school to utilize role theory, defended the theory of roles as an approach that "provides a nondeterministic explanation of historical change." Like Schumpeter, Cochran's explorations in entrepreneurship were designed to suggest ways of overcoming the traditions, habits, patterns, and sanctions that served as "anchors of social stability" in an age of stasis. According to Cochran, change occurred in conjunction with "personal idiosyncracies" or in relation to behavior that was sufficiently deviant to significantly alter the field of action.[58] Thus Schumpeter, Cochran, and other theorists and historians of entrepreneurship were not so different from Billy Graham and Joe McCarthy. All were midcentury revivalists committed to disruptive processes in an effort to break through or transcend barriers to change—in an age in which barriers seemed to be everywhere and change seemed impossible.

The second set of motifs for revitalization were speed, movement, and action. At every level of the culture, Americans of the late 1940s valued the doer over the thinker, the object in motion over the fixed and immobile, the hare over the tortoise. While these priorities were natural enough in a society that had been peopled through intercontinental migration and had expanded across a moving frontier, they were also one aspect of the midcentury effort to locate a source of forward-moving energy that would lift the culture out of its postwar doldrums.

The phenomenon emerged full-blown in 1948, the year when the fast-paced and aggressive music of bebop seemed finally to have replaced big band swing as the dominant jazz form, and when *Time* named a racehorse, Citation, athlete of the year.[59] It was also the year when the voters rejected the tidy, well-financed, and efficient campaign of Republican Thomas E. Dewey for the whistle-stop tours of the "Truman Special."[60] The spectacle of Truman's cross-country movement had its countercultural equivalent in the equally frenetic travels of Jack Kerouac and Neal Cassady, manic journeys undertaken in 1947 and 1948 and memorialized in Kerouac's appropriately titled Beat classic *On the Road*. "We were all delighted," Kerouac wrote, "we all realized we were leaving confusion and nonsense behind and performing our one and noble function of the time, *move*. And we moved! We flashed past the mysterious white signs in the night somewhere in New Jersey that say SOUTH (with an arrow) and WEST (with an arrow) and took the south one. . . ."[61]

It was more than the love of speed, more even than the American male's profound fascination with the automobile that took Kerouac's crowd from New York to San Francisco and back again.[62] Fueling the Beats' peripatetic existence, and underlying the overall culture's fascination with speed and movement, was a belief in the value of action, over and against passivity, contemplation, and reason. So it was that Catherine Drinker Bowen's 1944 biography of Oliver Wendell Holmes absolved the intellectual Supreme Court justice of excessive cerebration by depicting him as a "man of action": "Life is action and passion," Holmes said. "I think it is required of a man he should share the action and passion of his time at peril of being judged not to have lived." Similarly, arts critic Harold Rosenberg labeled the work of Jackson Pollock "action" painting, a comment on the artist's desire and ability to eliminate the censorship that intervenes between inspiration and deed.[63] Tennessee Williams's character Stanley Kowalski is a working-class version of Pollock. (Indeed, Brando's muscular, T-shirted Kowalski in the 1952 film production physically resembles the Pollock that *Life* photographed in 1949.) Though not without a brooding self-knowledge, and intelligent enough to have served as a master sergeant in the engineers' corps during the war, Stanley, like Pollock, is capable of the pure, unmediated, and unpremeditated act. As Stella recalls their wedding night, Stanley had taken her slipper and "rushed about the place smashing the light-bulbs [symbols of contemplative thought] with it."[64]

Americans valued this quality of action as much in real life as on the stage and screen. Among the most compelling figures of the forties were those Eugene Lewis has labeled "public entrepreneurs," people like J. Edgar Hoover, Adm. Hyman Rickover, and Robert Moses, all of whom fused the entrepreneurial role with a penchant for action in the public sphere. Public entrepreneurs were at once technical experts and bureaucratic wizards, people with the expertise, the charisma, and the will to move burgeoning governmental agencies to undertake actions that might otherwise be stalled by democratic politics. Moses, whose highways and bridges changed the face of New York City and New York State throughout the 1940s, understood his role as that of the gifted "uncommon man," whose task it was to impose his progressive vision of automobilization on a reluctant population and a political sphere in which power was fragmented among bureaucrats, elected politicians, and the beneficiaries of party patronage. His crowning achievement, the construction of the Triborough Bridge linking the boroughs of Manhattan, Queens, and the Bronx, has been described as a "monument to 'can-do' industrialization." Writing in 1956, Moses echoed this conclusion while trumpeting the virtues of uninhibited action: "Helpful policies and principles can be adopted without referendums, revolutions or too much palaver. . . . It is time for theories, misconceptions and misguided idealism to give way to common sense and realism."[65]

The public's enthusiasm for action can also be gleaned from *Time,* whose Man of the Year selections reflected the decade's growing appreciation for action. *Time*'s selection for 1945 was Canada's prime minister, William Lyon MacKenzie King, who could have received the award only as a representative of the world's desire to return at once to the fullest measure of boring normalcy. "A steady, colorless man," wrote *Time*'s editors, "with too much honor and intellect to be a demagogue, too little fire to be an orator, [and] too little hair and too few mannerisms to be spectacular." The choice for 1946, Secretary of State James F. Byrnes, was applauded for his "patient, purposeful tinkering" with the satellite treaties and praised as an intensely practical man unlikely to lead "crusades."[66]

The next year, however, *Time*'s nod went to George Marshall, whose plan for aid to Europe represented the U.S. assumption of world leadership in the cold war. In explaining how the nation had undertaken this role, *Time* described an America that was free from violence and rich with goods, yet beset by "vague fears," "lack of confidence," and a deep "uncertainty." Into this arena strode world entrepreneur Marshall, ready to take the "calculated risk," the "vastest gamble in peacetime history" that the United States could undertake, and win the war against "want and oppression" that was the first step in reaping the rewards of world leadership. *Time* understood Marshall's role in this process as less cerebral than somatic, and the magazine presented the story in language replete with connotations of the corporeal. The decision of the American people to take the leadership of the world "upon their shoulders" (a physical act) had been brought about by the push and shove of world events "hammering" against an innate American sense of justice; it "sprang *only partly from the brain*." As America "threw all its physical and moral strength into the fight," Marshall came to symbolize not the Marshall Plan as a concept or approach, but the United States once again in forward motion—"the U.S. *action*."[67] Dale Carnegie's 1948 best-seller *How to Stop Worrying and Start Living* offered readers much the same nostrum. "Our trouble," wrote Carnegie, "is not ignorance, but inaction."[68]

Of all the postwar heroes, none combined so well the cultural motifs of the age as Jack Schaefer's Shane, created in 1949 and made famous by Alan Ladd in the 1953 film. The novel is set in a Wyoming valley in the summer of 1889 and features a conflict between Luke Fletcher, the area's largest landowner and the champion of the open range (the bad guy), and the smaller homesteaders, led by Joe Starrett, who favor modern breeding practices and the fencing they require (the good guys). When this irreconcilable difference threatens to drive the Starrett family and other ranchers from the valley, Shane appears, stands up for the homesteaders, kills Fletcher and the hired gun he has brought into the community, and leaves.

In part because the story is told from the perspective of a small boy, Shane takes on a superhuman form. For Bob Starrett he is an object of faith, "a man like father in whom a boy could believe in the simple knowing that what was beyond comprehension was still clean and solid and right." For the Starrett family he is a revitalizing force, his mere presence in the household sufficient to make Joe and Marian Starrett "more alive, more vibrant, like they wanted to show more what they were, when they were with him." Like the God of the Old Testament, Shane is at once righteous and, for those whose moral failures have earned his wrath, utterly dangerous—"the symbol," for Bob, "of all the dim, formless imaginings of danger and terror in the untested realm of human potentialities beyond my understanding." Complete with gun and holster, Shane takes on his ultimate shape: an avenging angel of technology, a cybernetic God-being. "I would think of him," Bob recalls, in a striking combination of technical and religious imagery, "in each of the moments that revealed [as in divine revelation] him to me. I would think of him most vividly in that single flashing instant when he whirled to shoot Fletcher on the balcony at Grafton's saloon. I would see again the power and grace of a coordinate force beautiful beyond comprehension. I would see the man and the weapon wedded in the one indivisible deadliness. I would see the man and the tool, a good man and a good tool, doing what had to be done."[69]

"I have no childhood memories," wrote Georges Perec of his boyhood in France during the war. It was an extraordinary statement; as Perec explained, he had lost his father at age four, his mother at six. "For years," he wrote, "I took comfort in an absence of history: its objective crispness, its apparent obviousness, its innocence protected me."[70] Many Americans with less to lose than Perec found themselves in flight from a history that offered up too many unpleasant memories and seemed to have lost the ability to inspire faith in the future. With the fading of the linear vision of progress, Americans yielded to the darker imagery and flashbacks of film noir, to the overdetermined world signified by the fix, to a sense of their own corruption, and, finally, to a deep sense of cultural stasis. Desperate for a more comforting perspective on the present, many Americans sought refuge in frontier myths and bucolic reveries, while others explored the ways in which charismatic leadership, entrepreneurship, and a curious kind of social physics generated from speed and action might serve as catalysts for a cultural reawakening.

four

The Culture of the Whole

The most brutal and deadly war in the world's history ended in 1945, only to yield to the age of the atomic bomb, to the anxieties and tensions of the cold war, and to the certain knowledge of what the Nazis had done to the Jews. These events had inevitably produced the enormous bureaucracies (symbolized in the completion of the Pentagon in 1943), the concentrations of economic power and scientific expertise, and the propagandistic focus on the nation-state that were deemed necessary to victory over the Germans and the Japanese and containment of the Soviets. Centralization also took place in the realm of culture; the wartime population migrations required to staff the nation's factories accelerated the decline of regional and folk cultures and fostered a national cultural marketplace.

If the impulse to centralization were a simple, automatic product of wartime politics and economics, it would have no place in a history of thought and culture. But the forties' interest in centralization went well beyond the obvious necessities of war and cold war. Throughout the decade, Americans were virtually obsessed with creating, or affirming the existence of, a "culture of the whole"; in areas as distinct and different as world politics, psychology, and race relations, they labored to construct or imagine intellectual, technological, political, and social systems that would encompass and enfold culture on a nationwide and even worldwide basis. Because they had come face to face with humanity's capacity for violence and destruction—and also because of some amount of national self-interest—Americans experimented with an inclusive vision that made connections and discovered commonalities between subcultures, nations, and peoples previously understood as different. Disdainful of the particular, they praised and desired the general. Consistent with this movement toward the universal, some advocates of the culture of the whole stood for an assimilationist posture that denied the efficacy and viability of distinctions based on race, religion, ethnicity, or class.

Clearly not all elements of the culture of the whole were involved in progress toward the same specific goals; "American character" studies, R. Buckminster Fuller's geodesic dome, the United Nations headquarters in New York, and television, for example, existed in different worlds that seldom, if ever, touched one another—at least not in any obvious way. What their creators shared was the compelling urge to understand or shape some aspect of the world as a unified system. Thus, the authors of the American character studies believed that there *was* an American character; Buckminster Fuller claimed to have revealed and utilized a principle of construction that bound all parts of an edifice together; those who designed the United Nations building wanted it to represent, and to bring together, disparate peoples and nations; television's early advocates understood the device as a technology that would unite its viewers. At bottom, these various visions were joined by the idea, central to the thought and culture of the 1940s, that it was both possible and good to make one out of many, that a culture of the whole was an appropriate object of humanity's striving.

The decade's most widely disseminated statement on the culture of the whole was undoubtedly Wendell Willkie's *One World*, a product of the former presidential candidate's forty-nine-day around-the-world tour in the late summer and fall of 1942. Translated into sixteen languages, *One World* sold over three million copies and finished 1943 as the year's second most popular nonfiction book. An unabashed attempt to persuade a wary American public to conceptualize the future in "world-wide" terms, *One World* had a tone of restrained idealism, evoking real people in concrete settings who were not yet given to profound cynicism. For instance, Willkie reported his conversation in Jerusalem with a self-described "ardent zionist" who nonetheless believed that there was no "necessary antagonism between the hopes of the Jews and the rights of the Arabs."

Despite this surface idealism, Willkie's particular vision of one world also contained a measure of national self-interest. Willkie denied that the American nation had any designs on the world. The central obstacle to the achievement of one world, he assured his readers, was traditional European imperialism, which he roundly denounced. Because, Willkie argued, Americans "do not seek—anywhere, in any region—to impose our rule upon others or to exact special privileges," the nation was ideally situated to utilize its "reservoir of good will" in the pursuit of a new worldwide economic system, based not on landed empire but on the free and open exchange of goods over "the whole world." From this perspective, Willkie's notion of one world was hardly new; indeed, it closely resembled Secretary of State John Hay's turn-of-the-century vision of an "open door" in China. Like Hay, Willkie wanted open world markets that would promote exports and increase the American standard of living.[1]

Willkie's argument was also dependent on the rather extraordinary assumption—given the world war that was raging—that long-standing conflicts between nation-states would prove to be only minor obstacles in the movement toward one world. Children learned something of the same lesson in Golden MacDonald's *The Little Island*, winner of the 1946 Caldecott Medal. At issue is the island's relationship with the mainland, a problem first posed by a visiting kitten who tactlessly asserts that, unlike the island, which is cut off by water "from the land," she is "part of this big world." "So am I," the island replies, its position supported by the testimony of a fish, who informs the kitten "how all land is one land under the sea." Just as Willkie understood that his audience would be skeptical of any too-easy alliance of Americans, Soviets, and Chinese on behalf of free trade, so did MacDonald make it clear to his young readers that, because the land connecting mainland and island could not be seen, the connection would have to be taken "on faith." It is also important to note that MacDonald's notion of one world does not assume the elimination of the smaller worlds that make it up. "It was good to be a little Island," the book concludes, "A part of the world / and a world of its own."[2]

The fate of a proposed Hollywood film based on Willkie's journey illustrates how changing historical conditions weakened the public's interest in the idealistic side of Willkie's brand of universalism. The project was the brainchild of Willkie's close friend Darryl F. Zanuck, the head of production at Twentieth Century Fox. Following Willkie's approach of minimizing differences between peoples and nations, an early script for the film featured strong parallels between an Indiana farm family, headed by one John Adams, and its Soviet counterpart; both farms use machinery manufactured in Chicago. In a final scene, Willkie comforts the widow of John's son Ernie, who was killed in the war, with his universalist message: "We can go back to narrow nationalism, we can become international imperialists—or we can help create a world in which there will be equal opportunity for every race and every nation." "It's got to be a good world," concludes Willkie. "Not just a good world for us, Janie, but for all the babies in the world—because there is one world now."[3]

Yet by the mid-1940s, the circumstances that had made possible Willkie's confident universalism had changed, and so, too, had the script. With the breakup of the Popular Front—a 1930s alliance of liberals and Communists against Hitler's fascism—and growing evidence of a bipolar world capable of generating a third world war, hopes for achieving one world dissipated. "I cannot see that the UN is a hope or a menace," wrote Dwight Macdonald, "just a bore."[4] Thus, the final version of Zanuck's film focused not on the

Soviet Union as an ally in a one-world economy but on fears of Communist subversion and of a possible invasion by the Red armies. The project foundered on the shoals of the emerging cold war, and Zanuck turned his energies to *My Darling Clementine* (1946), in which Wyatt Earp cleans the Clantons (i.e., Commies) out of Tombstone.

The cold war produced another one-world casualty in Garry Davis's world citizenship movement. In May 1948 Davis had renounced his U.S. citizenship, proclaimed himself the first "citizen of the world," and called upon the United Nations to provide immediately for a world state. A twenty-six-year-old ex–World War II bomber pilot, he feared that the rising level of East-West tension would inevitably result in the "annihilation of civilization," a viewpoint that brought his movement a considerable following in France, where Davis had gone to take up residence as a "stateless person." Davis insisted that he loved the United States and wanted only to see its "democratic principles . . . extended to include the whole world," a proposition that seemed to echo Willkie's imperial dreams. But he also had decided that his goal of world peace through world government could not be achieved within existing nationalist channels—hence the renunciation of his citizenship. By early 1949 Davis was receiving some four hundred letters a day, mostly from French admirers, and his movement had the support of luminaries such as André Gide, Albert Camus, Jean-Paul Sartre, Richard Wright, and Albert Einstein, who cabled Davis that "only the unbendable will of the people can free the forces which are necessary for such a radical break with the old and outlived tradition in politics."

In the more idealistic climate of 1945 and 1946, even Davis's rather extreme brand of universalism might have garnered considerable support. Against an international background that included the Communist takeover in Czechoslovakia (1948) and the proclamation of the People's Republic of China under Mao Tse-tung (1949), most Americans found Davis either silly or dangerous—or both. A spokeswoman for the United World Federalists organization claimed the "young man" was "misinformed" about the nature of world citizenship in a "federated world," having failed to understand that one need not dispense with one's national citizenship to take on its world equivalent. The *New Yorker* condescendingly described Davis's renunciation of citizenship as an ". . . ineffective maneuver. A man without a country is not in a good position to embrace the planet; he is too busy answering questions." *Time* played up the specter of Communist infiltration of the Davis movement and characterized Davis's followers as deluded visionaries who had lost both "reason" and "good sense"—meaning they failed to understand that a popular movement could not penetrate "the Soviet fortress," and that "the only way to peace is a stony road which involves constant risk of war." *Life* speculated that the "human urge for peace" could easily be transmuted into "an overwhelming urge for 'peace at any price,' and so give Soviet Russia a mighty weapon in the cold and relentless war that Garry Davis cannot talk away." Unable to make much headway in his native land, and anxious to marry a Hollywood dance instructor, Davis returned to the United States in the spring of 1950 and applied for restoration of his citizenship six months later, effectively ending his role in the movement.[5]

Despite Garry Davis's experience, certain forms of one-world enthusiasm remained alive even in the climate of cold war. Among them was the United Nations, whose New York City headquarters, designed in the late 1940s and constructed early in the 1950s, was for millions of Americans the primary iconographic representation of internationalism. As Gen. Carlos P. Romulo of the Philippines, president of the General Assembly, explained at the laying of the cornerstone in October 1949, the building was intended to express "mankind's need for indivisible unity." To carry out this goal, the ten architects who designed the building opted for a simple and yet spectacular rectangular structure in the style of "strict functionalism," as isolated as possible from other skyscrapers and the city's tenements, and bereft of ornamentation that might signify place or culture. While most comments on the design were favorable, Frank Lloyd Wright described the proposed structure as a "sinister emblem for world power." "Grass the ground," he recommended, "where the proposed U.N. skyscraper would stand." Perhaps Wright simply disliked skyscrapers. But it is also possible that he understood that the building's unremitting functionalism was a form of cultural imperialism; the "indivisible unity" of which Romulo spoke was to be achieved by housing the United Nations in a structure whose very form denied the existence of disparate cultures and social classes. As represented in its headquarters, the unity of the United Nations was a curious entity indeed, not so much a complex unity forged from compromises and negotiations as an imperial one, imposed from above.[6]

High school students (and no doubt many other Americans) experienced the United Nations as both an exemplar of high idealism and a technique of social control. In the 1950s the stolid headquarters building appeared frequently in school yearbooks, a symbol of postwar hopes and fears. Editors of the 1947 Buffalo Technical High School *Techtonian* called on "Tech boys to look with hopeful eyes toward the success of that noble project," while editors of the 1947 *Skipper*, the yearbook of Buffalo's Riverside High School, warned that survival itself was at stake. "If it fails," they wrote, "our civilization must crumble." But the United Nations was also a metaphor for approved behaviors and attitudes, a way of encouraging the existence of one world within the confines of the school. The *Skipper* editors described the school as "truly a miniature 'United Nations,' where people of almost every European nation and religion, find no difficulty living harmoniously." Thus,

Its debut delayed by the war, television became a factor in the lives of Americans only in the late 1940s. This 1949 publicity photograph for Crosley illustrates what Americans wanted to believe about the new technology: that television was consistent with the close, nuclear family. The girl's mimicry of the skater on the screen was designed to dispel the idea that television viewing is a passive experience and instead to promote television as a participatory and educational medium. *Caulfield & Shook Collection. University of Louisville Photographic Archives*

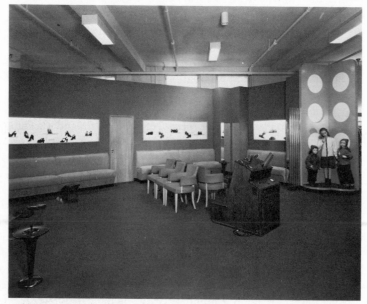

Despite concerns about the ability of science to produce a better world, enthusiasm for what was modern and scientific remained high. Customers of this Louisville, Kentucky, shoestore found a new, modernist shell and a machine (*center*) that used fluoroscopy to provide the perfect fit. 1947–48. *Royal Photo Company Collection, University of Louisville Photographic Archives*

The global imagery of this window display for Sparton Radios ("The radio for every room . . . for everyone, everywhere") is a local and commercial version of the desire of many Americans to understand the world as a single, unified whole. The central place given to the recordings of Bing Crosby illustrates the need of many Americans for the calm reassurance of the most famous "crooner" of the age. 1948–49. *Royal Photo Company Collection, University of Louisville Photographic Archives*

In a wartime culture of separation and potential loss, this Great Falls, Montana, barmaid is already surrounded and victimized by alluring images of what the girl-back-home was supposed to be. 1944. *Standard Oil of New Jersey Collection, University of Louisville Photographic Archives*

Anxiety over the atomic bomb was central to the culture of the 1940s. In this publicity photograph for MGM's *The Beginning or the End* (1946), the film's protagonists confront the threat of nuclear war with heterosexual coupling—the beginning of the "nuclear" families that would smother anxiety in havens of domesticity. *Copyright 1947 Loew's Inc.; renewed © 1974 Metro-Goldwyn-Mayer Inc.*

Traumatized by the cold war, Americans of the late 1940s expressed their fears in the UFO scare of 1947 and in a more long-lasting panic over "sex crimes." This picture from the July 1947 *American Magazine*, with its enormous hand threatening to pluck three young innocents from the city streets, illustrates the power of world events to create an anxious and neurotic culture.

"*The nation's women and children will never be secure . . . so long as degenerates run wild*"

In response to the growing sense that progress was no longer an inevitable part of modern life, artists in many fields repudiated the systems (narrative in film, representation in painting) that had stood for and testified to the surety of progress. None was more famous than Jackson Pollock, photographed in 1950 for *Life Magazine* while creating one of his "drip" paintings. According to Pollock, the drip paintings were an effort to bypass the rational side of the psyche and to tap the unconscious. *Copyright 1950 Hans Namuth*

Willem De Kooning's *Woman* (1949) captured the tortured and confused existence of millions of real women, caught between the new economic opportunities of war and postwar America and a male backlash that demanded obedience to traditional domestic roles. At the National Gallery of Art, on loan from Mr. and Mrs. Boris Leavitt. *Courtesy Boris and Sophie Leavitt*

The quiet intensity of experimental composer John Cage is evident in this 1949 photograph. Like sculptor Alexander Calder and dance choreographer Merce Cunningham, Cage sought to introduce elements of chance into a universe that appeared overrationalized. *Photograph by Naomi Savage*

The Freedom Train, shown here at Jefferson and Main streets in Los Angeles, traveled the length and breadth of the United States in the late 1940s, no doubt boring a generation of students with displays designed to demonstrate the American heritage of "freedom." In *Freedom Train* poet Langston Hughes ironized this propaganda effort, contrasting the implied promises of the Freedom Train with the realities of black life in a racist culture. *Copyright 1947 Los Angeles Daily News Collection, Department of Special Collections, University Research Library, UCLA*

Fred Derry (Dana Andrews) in a scene from *The Best Years of Our Lives* (1946), an epic of male frustration. When the war ends serviceman Derry returns to his hometown and, lacking the skills to perform the genuine producer jobs created by the wartime economy, takes an unsatisfying and even humiliating job in the drugstore (now a part of a chain) where he had worked before the war. Here he is reduced to the women's work of cosmetic sales and locked into the flaccid and feminine world of consumption. In this scene the hapless Derry is tormented by a child's airplane, an ironic reminder of his wartime years as a bombadier, which now seem useless. *Courtesy of the Academy of Motion Picture Arts and Sciences*

The deep shadows of this scene from *Crossfire* (1947) evoke the complex and desperate world that characterized most of the films in the film noir genre. Yet the confident pose of actor Robert Young (*right*) suggests an ongoing faith in the ability of reason and science to sort out a disordered past, account for the most troubling social problems (in this case anti-Semitism), and bring transgressors to justice. *Copyright 1947 RKO Radio Pictures, Inc.; renewed © 1974 RKO General, Inc. Courtesy of the Academy of Motion Picture Arts and Sciences*

The theme of identity was a staple of 1940s film. In *A Double Life* (1947) actor Anthony John's (Ronald Colman) inability to separate his stage persona from his real-life self leads him to commit one murder and, in this scene, attempt another. The avant-garde artworks above the sofa hint at a link between John's insanity and cultural modernism. UCLA Theater Arts Library. *Copyright 1947 by Universal Pictures, a division of Universal City Studios, Inc. Courtesy of MCA Publishing Rights, a division of MCA Inc.*

The most famous photographic image of the meaning of peace featured a sailor and nurse kissing at Times Square. Two rather different images, one dark and mean, the other serious and sad, were captured by Standard Oil of New Jersey photographers.

Schenectady, New York, August 1945. *Standard Oil of New Jersey Collection, University of Louisville Photographic Archives*

A prayer meeting on Main Street. VE-day, Tomball, Texas, May 1945. *Photo by Esther Bubley. Standard Oil of New Jersey Collection, University of Louisville Photographic Archives*

This drawing appeared in a 1946 high school yearbook. It shows graduating seniors marching into a murky postwar world in which the dominant symbol is the tank. It also reveals the prominent role of religion in postwar America; by 1950 the tensions of American life would produce Billy Graham's revivalist crusade. *Riverside High School* Skipper, *Buffalo, New York, 1946*

the United Nations proved a useful device for generating the kind of institutional cohesion believed appropriate and necessary in a properly functioning high school.

The United Nations headquarters was hardly an extraordinary building. Its very simplicity and lack of ornamentation and particularity lent it credence as an icon of the whole; it was a construction that seemed somehow capable of absorbing and containing the multiplicity of races, cultures, and ideologies. The collective identity it achieved—or sought to achieve—might be understood as the product of a stripping away of the particular, so that all peoples and nations could merge their special identities into the transcendent identity of the United Nations. Alternatively, one could argue that the headquarters' international style worked its act of unity by touching a common chord in peoples everywhere, forging a collective identity from some little understood but universal affinity for certain qualities of design.[7]

Interpreted in these terms, as an attempt to arouse certain elemental feelings or desires shared by all peoples, the political iconography of the United Nations building was but one instance of a broad-based effort, characteristic of the 1940s, to explore symbolic and archetypal forms capable of establishing and representing man's collective consciousness. In mythology, Joseph Campbell, in *The Hero with a Thousand Faces* (1949), examined the similarities between Eastern and Western, primitive and modern traditions and myths, hoping to promote the "cause of those forces that are working in the present world for unification, not in the name of some ecclesiastical or political empire, but in the sense of human mutual understanding." For Campbell, the categories of the contemporary world—age, sex, occupation, nationality, income, geography, and so on—were simply trivial, "mere costumes which we wear for a time on the stage of the world," the sorry product of an age that had succumbed to the power-driven machine, scientific method, and the democratic ideal of individual self-determination. Beyond these costumes or "accidents of life" lay a core of being that bound every person to every other person. "The essence of oneself and the essence of the world: these two," wrote Campbell, "are one." It was the function of the modern hero to search for and reveal the existence of this oneness, "to bring to light again the lost Atlantis of the co-ordinated soul."[8]

Within the American artistic community, internationalism became a force early in the decade, its allure heightened by the fall of France in June 1940 and the growing feeling that the United States must take on the mantle of world artistic leadership, just as it was about to assume direction of the struggle against fascism abroad. Expressing a "globalist" ideology resembling that contained in Willkie's *One World*, a 1943 catalog described a New York City exhibition of modern artists as "a first step to free the artist from the stifling control of an outmoded politics. . . . Isolationist art still dominates the

74

American scene. Regionalism still holds the reins of America's artistic future. It is high time we cleared the cultural atmosphere of America."[9]

Like the mythologist Campbell, these artists proclaimed their globalism through reference to the archetypal. Until 1947 American surrealists used mythic titles (e.g., Gottlieb's *Rape of Persephone* [1943]; Newman's *The Slaying of Osiris* [1945]) to comment on the atavistic instincts shared by the primitives and the moderns, or to refer to the timeless struggle between creation and death.[10] Commenting in 1951 on the origins of his painting *Mallarmé's Swan* (1944–47), Robert Motherwell made explicit his universalist goal, ascribing the sustained energy of Mallarmé's poetics to "the secret knowledge that each word was a link in the chain that he was forging to bind himself to the universe."[11]

Many artists and sculptors of the 1940s were influenced by Swiss psychiatrist Carl Gustav Jung, among them, Adolph Gottlieb, Lee Krasner, Willem de Kooning, Barnett Newman, Theodor Roszak, and Jackson Pollock. As opposed to a linear, narrative, and historical approach that emphasized change over time and the differences between historical periods or moments, Jung posited the existence of a collective unconscious that transcended the self and particular historical, national, and cultural circumstances. He argued the need for artists to provide the public with evidence of a humanity linked across culture, time, and space. Roszak's *The Spectre of Kitty Hawk* (1946) was typically Jungian in its melding of phenomena that existed in different time frames: the technology of the aircraft, the dropping of the atomic bomb, and the flight of prehistoric birds. In 1943, reacting to criticism of an exhibition of modern art, Gottlieb, Mark Rothko, and Newman wrote to the *New York Times* critic Edward A. Jewell, explaining their "spiritual kinship with primitive and archaic art." "There is no such thing as good painting about nothing," they argued. "We assert that the subject is crucial and only that subject is valid which is tragic and timeless."[12]

Americans of the forties also explored Jung's interest in a collective consciousness by fusing the Jungian emphasis on the collective with certain early-1940s ideas of nationalism and the "people" to locate, assert, and celebrate a deep interest in "folk identity." Expressions of this Jungian impulse include "Ballad for Americans" (text and music by Earl Hawley Robinson and John Latouche, respectively), a sentimental appeal to the links between Americans of every race, creed, color, and class, performed at the Republican National Convention in 1940 and recorded by Paul Robeson and Frank Sinatra; the stage musical *Oklahoma!* (1943), a far cry from the political and economic problems of Okies migrating from the dust bowl in the 1930s and an almost mystical expression of the vitality of the folk; and "Appalachian Spring" (1944), the Aaron Copland composition with choreography by Martha Graham.[13]

With the war and then the cold war came a concern, natural enough under the circumstances, that American society and culture might prove inadequate to the fascist and communist challenges of the age. In particular, Americans had some doubts that their particularistic, individualistic, and fragmented society would prove capable of survival against their more organized and unified German and Soviet enemies. In response to these anxieties, scholars explored, with an unheard-of confidence and frequency, the social and cultural characteristics common to Americans. The forties was the age of the American character study: anthropologists, journalists, and historians took on the seemingly impossible task of demonstrating that people as different as a Boston banker and a Mississippi sharecropper possessed certain common, "American" traits and values.

The first of the genre, Margaret Mead's *And Keep Your Powder Dry* (1942), conveniently discovered a set of American values that, properly used, could help the country win the war. Americans, she argued, were socially and geographically mobile, ready, if the times required it, to pack up and move on to a new city and a new job. Because they were also "instrumental"—that is, prepared to evaluate themselves and others on the basis of merit rather than family, neighborhood, ethnic, or other personal ties—they were capable of the high level of productive efficiency the war required. Although Mead recognized the existence of an American class structure that had the potential to fragment the nation's war effort, she ignored the danger, emphasizing instead that Americans understood their class structure as a ladder, "up which people are expected to move." "It is possible," she argued, "to describe the American system without mentioning class, to talk instead of the premium on success." Finally, Mead argued that Americans' fondness for democracy ensured that certain indirect, persuasive forms of "social engineering"—the control or management of people—would provide all the direction and motivation necessary for a successful war effort.[14]

The attempt to pin down the American character continued after the war. Readers of *Good Housekeeping* were offered an essay titled "A Vision of the Whole," in which Carl Van Doren lumped the American Civil War with other "temporary and local grievances" that were "few and unimportant compared with the sense of national citizenship that all Americans feel." Fresh from spending six years in the United States, André Maurois was also struck by America's unity. "From New York to Seattle," wrote Maurois in *Reader's Digest*, "most Americans I met spoke the same language, read the same magazines, had about the same standards of living and the same philosophy of life. Public opinion was of continental magnitude."[15]

Englishman Geoffrey Gorer did not dispute the central fact of American unity; indeed, his *The American People* touched on many issues originally raised by Mead. Yet far from sharing Mead's laudatory views, Gorer, writing in a postwar climate of reaction against wartime systems of propaganda and coercion, implied that certain social pathologies existed. While Mead had claimed that Americans' hostility toward certain forms of authority could be overcome through the use of democratic forms of social engineering, Gorer found postwar Americans virtually paranoically suspicious of the authority of professionals, experts, and the state. Where Mead had reveled in Americans' drive for success, Gorer found the nation's children "insatiable for the signs of love" and its adults desperate for social approval to shore up sagging self-esteem.

Finally, Gorer was less taken than Mead with the basic idea that Americans should be unified around certain core values. He believed that Americans' commitment to an "American character" was symptomatic of a profound sense of superiority and self-centeredness. Convinced, as other peoples of the world were not, that "nationality is an act of will," Americans were intolerant of those peoples of the world who lacked the courage to do what Americans had done (and that meant almost everyone). Able to identify with and respect only those nations whose political institutions resembled their own, Americans invested enormous effort in demonstrating that the world's inhabitants were "'really' just like Americans."[16] In short, one could infer from Gorer that the larger American character "project" was not simply so much fact-finding—it was ultimately aggressive and imperial. The very act of looking inward to discover what it meant to be American involved looking outward, with disdain, at what was not.

By midcentury the scholarly consensus was that the American character was rooted in postwar abundance—or what seemed at the time to be abundance. Written by David Riesman, Nathan Glazer, and Reuel Denny in 1948 and 1949, *The Lonely Crowd: A Study of the Changing American Character*, described a change in national "character types" over the previous century. The aggressive, entrepreneurial, self-motivated, "inner-directed" personality characteristic of the nineteenth-century free-market economy was yielding in the twentieth century to a conformist, "other-directed" type more sensitive to peer and social opinion and better suited than his inner-directed predecessor to participation in an economy of pleasure and consumption and to working in modern bureaucracies. The "invisible hand," wrote Riesman with reference to free-market ideas, had become the "glad hand."[17]

Beyond even the idea of an American *character*, some claimed to have observed actual *physical* resemblances. Harvard anthropologist Carleton S. Coon wrote in 1946 of the emergence of a "typical" American physical type: tall, long-legged, with big hands and feet, wide shoulders, a relatively flat chest, and blue eyes and brown hair. Living Americans who for Coon exemplified the type included George Marshall, Dwight Eisenhower, Gary Cooper, and Spencer Tracy. Although Coon's typical American was obviously white, he claimed that 250 years of changes had brought the Negro, too, "well within the white American range" on a variety of dimensions.

"Aside from pigmentation," he wrote in *American Magazine*, "they are the same as other Americans in many features."[18]

Americans were able to envision and desire this larger world, and to imagine its peoples as one, partly because they were witness to remarkable feats of centralization and homogenization in their own country. If one world was indeed within the realm of possibility, "one country" seemed to be happening right then and there, and for many of the same reasons. Of course, this sense of a unified and unifying nation was not new. Depression-era Americans had sought to locate a sense of themselves in an "American" culture; in the process, the phrase "American way of life" was first widely used, George Gallup began taking public opinion polls to determine what Americans thought and believed, and *Life* sent its idealized and unitary conception of the American version of "life" into living rooms across the land. Besides "Ballad for Americans," the most powerful paean to the growing sense of Americanness was Kate Smith's recording of Irving Berlin's "God Bless America," an enormous hit in 1940.[19]

The culture of the whole, then, was more than a set of ideas about what *ought* to be; it was also a description of an encroaching social reality. The day-to-day experience of most Americans was with an increasingly uniform culture. Just as the merger movement at the turn of the century had fostered nationally recognized name brands, and the automobile craze of the 1920s had contributed to the decline of regional differences, the forties brought a new round of cultural homogenization. This one was fueled by the centralizing tendencies of a war economy and advanced industrial capitalism; by the discovery at Auschwitz and Treblinka of the price of hatred based on cultural distinctions; by the specter of a bomb so powerful as to render conflict suicidal; and by the cold war, whose prosecution seemed to require an unparalleled commitment to national unity.

This growing homogenization of culture took place in ways that seem individually trivial yet were cumulatively significant. In contrast to the "yank" who had fought the Great War, World War II produced the "GI"—the "government-issue" soldier who fought in the shadow of that new symbol of system and bureaucracy, the Pentagon. Shaped by national advertising and fashion, Americans dressed more and more alike. In 1949, *Life*, which was typically insensitive to the significant remaining differences among youth yet responsive to basic trends, labeled Levi's part of a national teenage "uniform."[20]

Cultural homogenization was also apparent in popular music; regional forms tied to local subcultures were gradually giving way to national expressions. The most popular black music of the decade was rhythm and blues, an up-tempo, electrified, and urban version of the traditional blues that had been a staple of rural, Southern, black communities since shortly after the turn of the century. Blacks removed from their rural moorings and transplanted to Detroit, Philadelphia, Los Angeles, St. Louis, Kansas City, Memphis, and other cities took to R&B as an expression of their new working conditions and urban ways of life. These migrations also brought R&B to the attention of whites, who could hear the music in clubs and on a growing number of radio stations, including WXLW St. Louis (beginning in 1947), WDIA Memphis (after 1948), and WERD Atlanta (after 1949). As a result, a few black artists "crossed over" and sold records to whites; Louis Jordan's "Choo Choo Ch'Boogie" (1942), "Ain't Nobody Here but Us Chickens" (1947), and "Caledonia Boogie" (1945) all had substantial success in the crossover market. Recognizing that the music of black artists could no longer be categorized as "race music" and consigned to a market tightly circumscribed by color, *Billboard* magazine in 1949 changed the designation of its black chart of popular music from "race" to "rhythm & blues." Although R&B failed to attract the major recording companies and appealed largely to black audiences throughout the 1940s, Jordan's experience and *Billboard's* reclassification foreshadowed the more significant merging of white and black styles in the mid-1950s under the rubric "rock and roll."[21]

The homogenization of styles in country music took place even more rapidly, probably because the World War II military services did not isolate Southern white recruits in their own regiments as they did blacks. For this and other reasons, country music entered the decade a regional music and exited a national one. In the process, Nashville's Grand Ole Opry lost some of the familiar quality of a down-home barn dance, and traditional country singers like Eddy Arnold more closely resembled pop crooners as they lowered their pitch and sang in the fuller, more roundly articulated voice that appealed to a national audience. *Billboard* hastened to adjust its labels, this time from "hillbilly," with its connotation of backwoods isolation, to the more cosmopolitan "country and western." By the late 1940s and early 1950s, popular artists were recording their own versions of country and western favorites for the mass market. Released in November 1950, Patti Page's popular "cover" of "The Tennessee Waltz" became the biggest selling record in modern popular music history; Tony Bennett's pop version of Hank Williams's "Cold, Cold Heart" (1951) was the first of many successful covers of an artist whose seminal contribution had been to bring country music out of the hills and into the American mainstream.[22]

Unlike country and western and R&B, the purest example of the homogenization of music in the forties was not the product of a natural, social evolution. Muzak—"the music that nobody hears"—was really a musical form of social engineering. Although the idea behind Muzak dates to the 1920s, the product achieved no significant market until World War II, when both British and American companies successfully used this musical Velveeta in factories to reduce fatigue and increase production. After the war, Muzak found outlets among dress manufacturers who hoped to put buyers in a receptive mood; in dentists' offices, where the music was designed to relieve the frayed nerves of patients wary of the drill; in banks and photographic studios; in the psychopathic wards of some hospitals; and in countless restaurants and cocktail lounges. In 1940 Muzak had less than eight hundred subscribers, serviced by nine franchises; a decade later the company had over seventy-five hundred subscribers in some two hundred cities, serviced by sixty-nine franchises.

Muzak's contribution to cultural homogeneity was accomplished through a production process that stripped music of its links to particular subcultures. Because Muzak was designed to appeal to the subconscious rather than to entertain, the conversion of a tune from its popular form to Muzak involved rerecording the song using musicians—often celebrities, such as Xavier Cougat—willing to play in the "anonymous" and "other-worldly" Muzak style, stripping the tune of the strong brasses, vocals, pronounced rhythms, and other this-worldly qualities that might attract conscious attention. As one Muzak director explained, "You can't give a drill press operator bebop or a hot lick on a saxophone. Before you know it, he'll be beating time instead of working." To make the music "audible" at low volume and over the competition of a crowded factory floor or restaurant, Muzak was recorded within a fidelity range higher than that normally used for popular music. As the decade ended, Muzak technicians were busy installing basement-to-roof wiring in new office buildings as they were under construction, and company officials were looking forward to the day when its "flat" music would be in every American home. *Nation's Business* closed its 1950 story on Muzak with the observation that the company's ventures into hospitals and funeral parlors had already produced a "womb to the tomb" situation in which Muzak "seems to have covered the whole span of American life."[23] Was such talk simply the harmless musing of capitalists intent on new markets? Or was Muzak a sinister, therapeutic embodiment of Wendell Willkie's one world?

As it happened, the saturation fantasy of Muzak officials was fulfilled not by the company's product but by television, which was destined to come into the nation's living rooms, bedrooms, dens, and kitchens, ultimately through cable technology built into homes during construction. Although television was first developed in the late 1920s, the industry had no meaningful commercial presence until after World War II. In 1946 only six thousand television receivers were available throughout the United States. By 1948, television's first "season," there were 977,000 sets in use, and by 1950 almost ten million.[24]

The arrival of television produced a flood of commentary on the new technology, much of it expressing anxiety over the future of the family and other concerns beyond the theme of this chapter. Directly relevant, however, are the ways in which social analysts and even advertisers conceptualized television's potential role in generating a therapeutic one-world matrix. At the center of these conceptualizations was TV as *unifier*: the power of television to bring people together at every level of social organization. Writing in 1945, an official of the Television Broadcasters Association emphasized the new medium's potential for reassembling distended schools and department stores and corporations with far-flung plants. "There is something about television," he wrote, "that is going to make every city, town, and village in the United States a more democratic, more progressive, more closely knit community than ever before." Other writers emphasized that television would join the American coasts, dissolve remaining barriers between country and city, and bring advice and information "to all." In *Vision in Television*, Hazel Cooley took the argument a step further, suggesting that television should serve as an instrument of "total" peace, reeducating the mass of Americans to understand the responsibilities of democratic social participation, the significance of individual freedom, and the interdependence of nations in the nuclear age. Cooley wanted to use television to break down international barriers. "The 'One World' envisaged by Wendell Willkie," she wrote, "seems far away. Before the kind of world all of us dream about can come into being, the problem of a world divided against itself must be solved." How? Cooley's solution was an "informed and enlightened society," and the medium, of course, was television.[25]

It was only dimly understood at the time that television would contribute to progress toward one world in part by establishing a direct, and thus potentially dangerous, link between the viewer and the telecast event or spectacle. Anticipating Marshall McLuhan's concept of the "global village," *Life* commented on television's "power to annihilate time and space" and hence to "unite everyone everywhere in the immediate experience of events in contemporary life and history." A 1948 advertisement for RCA Victor's "Eye Witness" television called on the reader to "Eye Witness major political conventions!" and "Meet your next President," offering the viewer a pure, unmediated relationship with one of the nation's most important political institutions. Early the following year, *Time* described television's coverage of the Truman inaugural festivities in language that captured the sense of the unprecedented relationship between the new technology and its audience: "At day's end, despite some banal street interviews and the bumbling repetitions of some announcers, TV could boast that it had finally caught a moment of history just as it happened. Ten million televiewers from the Atlantic coast to the Mississippi felt that they had truly been there with Washington's cheering thousands."

Encoded in *Time's* coverage was the one-world fantasy that absolute reality (the "moment of history") actually existed, independent of the networks, a director, or any other narrator, and that television was capable of transmitting that reality intact to millions of viewers, who could not help but feel the power of the presumably unmediated experience (they "felt that they had truly been there"). Yet, as *Time*'s story revealed, television's coverage of the inaugural was far from an objective presentation of what had "happened." Viewers had, instead, been shown carefully selected representations of what *Time* appropriately referred to as the "spectacle": "panoramic sweeps of Washington's long vistas," "dramatic close-ups of top-hatted diplomats," "the wide lawn jammed with humanity," and "the impressive overhead flight of B-36 bombers." Within this spectacle, Truman's speech—a nugget of verbal content in a stream of visual delights—was "the slow movement."[26]

Both television's coverage of the Truman inaugural and *Time*'s story on that coverage suggest that even before 1950 the medium of television had raised ethical problems reminiscent of 1930s European fascism. Just as fascism had reified spectacle and sought to replace political conflict with the unity of technological expertism, so had American television converted a political event into a popular and contentless spectacle. And just as Nazism had labored to eliminate trade federations, clubs, and other social organizations that traditionally mediated between the citizen and the state, so had American media analysts celebrated television's ability to link the masses *directly* with a spectacularized social "reality." (Of course, other aspects of European fascism, including its reliance on single-party rule and its use of terror as a mechanism of social control, had no relation to television.)[27]

In short, as television was presented and interpreted in the late 1940s, the medium took on certain fascistlike characteristics. This was partly a result of the nature of television, which transmitted identical messages to isolated viewers. But it was also a result of conscious desire; *Time* did not have to revel in TV's production of spectacular images from the Truman inaugural. Although some media scholars were aware that German leaders were mindful of radio's power to shape the will of the masses, so compelling was the vision of one world that no such warnings were issued on the American scene.[28]

Though European fascism was by the 1940s thoroughly discredited in the eyes of most Americans, the attachment to the vision of a culture of the whole was so profound that some Americans could not help but embrace expressions of that vision, even when they were tainted by links to fascism. So it was that, in 1949, Americans found themselves in the odd position of having bestowed a national prize on an American poet who in all probability had committed treason against his country in the name of Italian fascism.

The story of Ezra Pound is, in part, the story of Americans' continuing attraction to fascistlike ideas. Born in Idaho in 1885, Pound attended the University of Pennsylvania and Hamilton College. While living and writing books in Rapallo, Italy, in the 1920s, Pound came to appreciate Italian fascism as a viable alternative to democracy, which he believed was fatally flawed by its dependence on a poorly informed and unintelligent mass citizenry. (Pound once colorfully described presidents Wilson, Harding,

Coolidge, and Hoover as "the predominent [*sic*] SHIT chosen by the electorate = 4 barrels of pisss [*sic*].") Convinced of fascism's benefits, Pound broadcast for Rome Radio during World War II, peppering his remarks with anti-Semitic pronouncements and calling on Americans to recognize that "every sane act you commit . . . every reform, every lurch toward the just price, toward the control of a market is an act of homage to Mussolini and Hitler."

After the fall of Mussolini, Pound was captured by U.S. troops and charged with treason. Sequestered in Pisa while awaiting trial, Pound penned *The Pisan Cantos*, for which he was awarded the lucrative Bollingen Prize in Poetry by the Library of Congress the following year. In the meantime, the treason charges had been dropped owing to a finding of insanity, and Pound took up residence at a mental institution in Washington, D.C.[29]

The controversy over Pound's selection by the Bollingen Prize committee first surfaced in *Senior Scholastic* and emerged full-blown in the pages of *Saturday Review*, whose editors labeled *The Pisan Cantos* the "anti-humanitarian ravings of an insane man, the incoherent medley of wild ideas, of symbols that reflect nothing but obscurity." As a glance at *The Pisan Cantos* reveals, such opinions were not as farfetched as they might seem. The work juxtaposed a bewildering variety of autobiographical, mythical, and historical materials; it had no narrative, no beginning or end, no chronological core. Perhaps *The Pisan Cantos* was, as poet Peter Viereck would write, just so much "ugly gibberish."[30]

What, then, had appealed to ten scholars and writers on the Bollingen Prize committee? Far from suggesting a senseless incoherence, *The Pisan Cantos* was Pound's idiosyncratic, elitist, and, arguably, demented version of the culture of the whole—a literary version of Willkie's *One World* and Davis's call for world citizenship. A lifelong internationalist, Pound wrote to generate unity among peoples and cultures separated by geography and time; it was, in fact, this strong attraction to unity that led the poet to advocate fascism and to justify that advocacy as inspired by a vision that transcended the relations of "ordinary people." In *The Piscan Cantos*, Pound rejected traditional Western systems of unification, including narrative, chronology, and causation, for a more subjective approach in which readers were to fuse the bits and pieces of Pound's personal mosaic into a "gestalt"—that is, into a unified whole with a meaning greater than the sum of its parts. As his friend and admirer Buckminster Fuller pointed out, Pound's model for this approach was the Chinese ideogram, a complex "total thought" designed to force its user into patterns of "synergetic thinking" that were in turn essential if users were to perceive and appreciate the commonalities encoded within the ideogram and contained within the cacophony of world cultures. Through *The Pisan Cantos*, Pound was trying to demonstrate the existence of timeless human values and to encourage readers to search out those values within the flux of history. Fuller praised Pound as a "synergist"; poet Conrad Aiken described him as "less traitor than fool," a man charged with treason "for having . . . betrayed a particular society of men for man in the abstract."[31]

Some scholars, dismayed by Pound's fascist leanings, have been unable to appreciate the impulse to social unity that lay at the heart of his thought. Without denying the force of their criticism, it should be said that the foregoing account of Ezra Pound and the Bollingen Prize cuts another way altogether. It can be read not as the story of Pound's moral inadequacy but in two other, more important ways: first, as a sign of the culture's desire for ways of knowing, understanding, and being that partook of one-world universalism; and second, as evidence that some Americans were not beneath exploring the fascist experience for what it might contribute to a revitalized postwar culture.

Among those at once attracted to and repelled by fascism's dynamism was novelist Norman Mailer, whose *The Naked and the Dead* (1948) was one of the most important literary achievements of the decade. Based on Mailer's combat experiences during the war, the novel is set on the fictitious Pacific island of Anopopei, where the protagonists—General Cummings and Sergeant Croft (emblems of totalitarianism) and Lieutenant Hearn and Private Valsen (emblems of a weak and uncommitted liberalism)—play out a struggle around the theme of power. Hearn seems to have all the right values: he stands for personal integrity and "inviolate freedom" and he is repelled by the arbitrary authority that Cummings and Croft possess. Cummings and Croft are in many ways unappealing: Croft is sadistic, loves combat, and detests what he cannot control ("I hate everything which is not in myself"); Cummings is vain, enormously ambitious, paranoid, and enamored of fascism ("There's one thing about power. It can flow only from the top down. When there are little surges of resistance at the middle levels, it merely calls for more power to be directed downward, to burn it out"). While Hearn represents just such a "surge of resistance" (he intentionally drops a cigarette on Cummings's floor), he lacks the courage of his convictions (he picks the cigarette up) and, like Valsen and other liberals, remains subject to a deep and pessimistic fatalism. (In the terms of the next chapter of this book, he "turns inward," seeking from the inadequate self a help it cannot provide.)

Despite their negative qualities, Croft and Cummings are at least committed to something beyond the self—to some version, indeed, of the culture of the whole—even if it is distorted and ugly. They both have faith in the power of the individual to have some impact on the world; and they both have "vision," a sense—twisted and reactionary, to be sure—of how the world might be reconfigured ("There were things," Cummings said, "one could do").[32]

Interest in fascistlike spectacle—in the splendid, wondrous images, for instance, that television had teased from the tedium of an inauguration—could be seen elsewhere in the decade, though observations on the spectacular were not always so positive as those *Time* had rendered. The United Nations headquarters, as we have seen, was clearly designed on a spectacular scale, as if spacious grounds and an intimidating facade could set the building apart from the petty urban and national concerns represented by the surrounding city, yet operate powerfully and directly on individual persons. Eero Saarinen's arch design for the Jefferson National Expansion Memorial competition was quintessentially spectacular. *Progressive Architecture* commented that the monument, though "large in scale . . . does not dwarf other structures"; yet at 590 feet in height (as originally configured), it did precisely that, and no doubt intentionally. During the competition, the supervising commission had pointedly dropped its request for designs of a "living" (i.e., useful, human-scale) memorial in favor of a new requirement that designs be "essentially non-functional," thus opening the way for a structure that would be "practically all-embracing in spirit."[33]

Also searching for the transcendent spectacular were the abstract expressionists, who in 1948 took up painting on the grand scale, working on enormous canvases in an effort, as Mark Rothko described it, to eliminate "all obstacles between the painter and the observer" (note the similarity between Rothko's rhetoric and that used by *Time* to describe television's impact). Director Robert Flaherty's celebrated film documentary *Louisiana Story* (1948) employed stunning cinematography of machinery in the midst of the Louisiana countryside to rationalize Standard Oil's presence in the area and, as one correspondent put it, to refute the "in-human industrial machine philosophy." An official at Metro-Goldwyn-Mayer reported that the audience with whom he saw the film had "burst into spontaneous applause when the picture was over." "Machinery has been photographed often enough," he added, but "never so beautifully."[34]

Yet Americans were not entirely comfortable with the spectacular and the proto-fascist. By the 1940s there were signs of growing disaffection with the sleek, intimidating, people-denying facades of the architecture of spectacle. *Life* could not resist pointing out that Saarinen's design for the St. Louis Arch resembled a 1942 proposal for a monument to Mussolini's fascism. Lewis Mumford described the "unbroken face of brick" of New York's Stuyvesant Town as "the architecture of the POLICE STATE." In films such as *Meet John Doe* (1941) and *State of the Union* (1948), director Frank Capra showed individuals struggling to be heard under conditions of spectacle (press conferences, conventions, and the like) that made effective speech impossible. (Recall that at his own inaugural spectacle, Truman was simply "boring.") Having developed his own systems of social engineering that did not depend on the drama of reification, B. F. Skinner was critical of the spectacular in

Walden Two, a fictional account of a utopian community that had no use for crowds, sporting events, and other aspects of the spectacular. "Matches," announced the manager of Walden Two, "aren't important here. We are not hero-worshipers."[35]

With the exception of Willkie's international realm, the idea of the culture of the whole was perhaps most rigorously pursued in the area of epistemology (a branch of philosophy dealing with the nature of knowledge); scientists, social scientists, and engineers developed new, more unified and synthetic approaches to knowledge that either merged existing disciplines or conceptualized their subjects in more encompassing frameworks. By the end of the decade, one-world epistemology had produced a new approach called "systems theory" and the new field of cybernetics; a boom in "gestalt" psychology; new work in the sociology of organizations; major contributions in music and architecture; and a burst of enthusiasm for interdisciplinary studies. In general, these developments were inspired by the desire to understand the world in holistic terms, as a manageable unit.

The term "general systems theory" was introduced after World War II by Canadian biologist Ludwig von Bertalanffy. Its central premise was that traditionally specialized areas of research and scholarly activity in fact had in common certain structures and functions. Systems theory promoted the development of principles that would apply not just in one field but to any system, whether biological, mechanical, or social. Consistent with this goal, the forties was the heyday of interdisciplinary conferences, many of them held under the auspices of the Josiah Macy, Jr. Foundation and other philanthropic organizations. Similarly, interdisciplinary enthusiasms brought anthropologists, sociologists, and psychologists together in 1946 in Harvard's new Department of Social Relations.

Systems theory was also an effort to soften and humanize the mechanistic side of the modern social sciences. Bertalanffy's interest in systems theory appears to have been motivated by his disdain for the current ideas of man as a programmable machine, a maze-running rat, or a robot. In contrast, Bertalanffy's man was human, an "active personality system," the creator of a symbolic universe in language, thought, science, religion, and art. In much the same way that surrealist and abstract expressionist painters of the mid-1940s were attracted to a timeless symbolism binding man across the ages, systems theory both revived the concept of human nature and recaptured the idea of man as a product of history and culture. "The systems view of man," writes Ervin Laszlo in his treatment of the movement, "links him again with the world he lives in, for he is seen as emerging in that world and reflecting its general character." The structural-functionalist school of sociology, pioneered by Harvard's Talcott Parsons in the late 1940s, used systems theory by attributing human behavior to an interpenetrating and overlapping set of social, culture, and personality systems.[36]

Systems theory was more rigorously applied in the field of cybernetics, defined by its leading practitioner, mathematician Norbert Wiener, as the attempt "to find the common elements in the functioning of automatic machines and of the human nervous system, and to develop a theory that will cover the entire field of control and communication in machines and in living organisms." Although the term "cybernetics" was not used until 1947, the field's origins can be traced to the war, when Wiener and others who were studying machine feedback for the military began to believe that activities of the human nervous system might also be understood as "circular processes." While Wiener and others insisted that they were engaged in the development of a *theory* of communication and control based on observed similarities between machines and animals, it was clear from the beginning that cybernetics could easily lead, on the one hand, toward efforts to conceptualize humans as machines or, on the other hand, toward the development of profit-making mechanical robots. In contrast, Wiener said that cybernetics would find an ideal home in a society "based on human values other than buying or selling." In the absence of such a utopia, he could only suggest that cybernetic research be focused on those areas "most remote from war and exploitation."[37]

Systems theory also made inroads into psychology in the forties, lending new strength and prestige to a field called "gestalt" psychology. The field was founded in 1910 by German scholar Max Wertheimer, whose studies of the "phi phenomenon" produced gestalt's central insight. Wertheimer had found that when vertical and horizontal lines were exposed in rapid succession, the effect was one of smooth movement from the vertical to the horizontal. The point was clear: the unified whole (the gestalt) is greater than the sum of its parts. Like Wiener, gestalt theorists took exception to the narrow, mechanical model of the nervous system then popular among behavioral psychologists, insisting instead that behavior should be studied as a function of the total physical and social situation of the individual—or what social psychologist Kurt Lewin and his numerous followers called the "field." Describing the gestalt approach in 1949, psychologist Rudolf Arnheim focused on the basic gestalt principle of "context," emphasizing that the evaluation of experiences required understanding of one's past experiences and memories (the temporal context) as well as knowledge of the relationship of perceived objects (the spatial context). This insistence on context was in some measure, then, a reaction to approaches to behavior that appeared to reduce human action to statistical averages. "What had disturbed us," recalled Wolfgang Köhler, was "the implication that human life, apparently so colorful and so intensely dynamic, is actually a frightful bore."[38]

Among organizational theorists, applications of systems theory date to the late 1930s and early 1940s, when upheavals within the international polity prompted comparison of the "violent disequilibrium" apparent within the European state system with problems in the realm of the organization (often referred to as the "whole"). Just as the nation-state was unable to exist isolated from its geopolitical environment, the organization, too, was in constant interaction with other organizations and, therefore, could be understood only in relation to its environment, or system. Organizational theorists posited an ideal state of equilibrium in which an organization and its environment were in balance. Yet they also understood that the achievement of such a condition could remain only an ideal, since, as one 1945 essay put it, "the perfect organization would contain everything and organize that everything completely."[39]

Because of the proliferation of large public and private organizations and bureaucracies under the New Deal and during and after World War II, systems theory was often used to study their internal problems. Examining the organization's efforts to eliminate "nonrational" (i.e., personal, and hence dysfunctional) behavior, organizational theorist Phillip Selznick argued that such efforts were doomed to failure because those charged with administering the organization were themselves likely to resist depersonalization, to step outside their assigned roles, and to "participate as *wholes.*" One solution, suggested Selznick, was to study the "totality of interacting groups and individuals," focusing analysis on the "*state of the system.*"[40]

Like Willkie's call to one world, many of the applications of systems theory seemed to partake of a naive and almost desperate optimism, as if the world's most insoluble problems could be magically eliminated. For example, because systems theory had evolved as a response to the existence of disequilibrium, there was considerable scholarly interest in systems that seemed invulnerable to disruption. American physiologist Walter Bradford Cannon's *Wisdom of the Body* (1932) had led the way with its description of the "self-regulating" systems that maintained equilibrium in warm-blooded animals. Wiener examined homeostatic (i.e., internally stabilizing) devices in mechanical, biological, and social systems and concluded his 1948 work, *Cybernetics,* with a plea for a homeostatic society. Selznick was attracted to Parsons's structural-functionalist analysis primarily because it conceptualized the organization in all its complexity as a "stable [i.e., virtually self-regulating] system of needs and mechanisms."[41]

Such ideas also circulated in literary circles. The American New Critics of the late 1930s and 1940s—John Crowe Ransom, Cleanth Brooks, Allen Tate, R. P. Blackmur, and others—understood the poem as just such a system, a whole capable of resolving and integrating the various tensions and ambiguities contained within it. According to literary historian Terry Eagleton, "Just as American functionalist sociology developed a 'conflict-free' model of society, in which every element 'adapted' to every other, so the poem abolished all friction, irregularity and contradiction in the symmetrical cooperation of its various features."[42]

The ultimate triumph of the homeostatic genre was perhaps John Kenneth Galbraith's *American Capitalism*; his theory of "countervailing power" virtually argued away the century-old problem of big business. In contrast to a generation of scholars who had argued that big government was necessary to control the natural rapacity of large corporations, Galbraith postulated an economy held in a state of equilibrium by the competition of big buyers and big sellers. "Given the existence of private market power in the economy," wrote Galbraith, "the growth of countervailing power *strengthens the capacity of the economy for autonomous self-regulation* and thereby lessens the amount of over-all government control or planning that is required or sought" (emphasis added).[43]

The same brazen confidence (or wishful thinking) that Galbraith brought to economics stood behind the decade's most brilliant application of systems theory: Buckminster Fuller's geodesic dome, a spherelike structure composed of lightweight materials set in geometric patterns. The project took shape in 1946 as an attempt to produce a modern version of the cave and vaulted tree branches (i.e., the dome) that Fuller believed had served as man's first dwellings. After two years of planning, a dome was actually constructed in the summer of 1948 at Black Mountain College, an avant-garde institution in the North Carolina foothills where Fuller was part of a small faculty that included artists Willem and Elaine de Kooning, composer John Cage, choreographer Merce Cunningham, and sculptor Richard Lippold. (Fuller's legendary energy, intelligence, and optimism deeply affected Cage, who wrote: "The work and thoughts of Buckminster Fuller are of prime importance to me. He, more than any other to my knowledge, sees the world situation—all of it—clearly.") The dome was finally assembled in a September downpour, only to sag and collapse as the last bolt was set into place and tension applied to the scaffolding. Fuller returned the following summer to erect a more successful version. By the mid-1950s the dome was a commercial success, and the Pentagon was Fuller's best customer.[44]

Fuller conceptualized his geodesic dome as a system. Unlike "parallel structures" (e.g., walls), which "do not help each other" and achieve their strength through "compression"—that is, by piling up huge masses of stone or cement—Fuller's dome features structural members in continuous "tension," reinforcing one another to give the sphere integrity. Fuller called the engineering principle "tensegrity" (tensional integrity). Tensegrity was in turn based on Fuller's own "synergetic geometry," a mathematics derived from the familiar gestalt premise that the whole (the sphere, the dome) is greater than the sum of its parts (its separate structural members). At the base of Fuller's thought was a primary energy system: the finite, knowable, and harmonious universe, governed by scientific laws operating within a "field system of relations." Supremely confident of his ability to penetrate the order and logic that presumably governed all relations, Fuller believed that his plans for the dome—down to the fourteen-sided geometrical forms making up the dome—were simply an application or mirror of certain principles of force that he had derived from an understanding of the universe itself.[45]

Central to the concept of the system was the denial of any independent existence outside the system. For Willkie, the nation-state properly existed only in a family of nations; for Galbraith, corporate prices could be understood only in the context of a determining system of economics; for Parsons, human decisions could be conceptualized only as the product of complex and overlapping systems of interaction; for Fuller, the dome was a structure of interdependent structural members.

The important idea of interdependence was also apparent in the avant-garde music of the "serial" composers. Developed by Jewish composer Arnold Schoenberg in the ideological maelstrom of Weimar Germany in the 1920s, the basic characteristic of serialism was a twelve-tone, "equal-tempered" scale (the white and black keys on the piano) that Schoenberg would later describe as nontheoretical (and by which he may have meant nonideological). The twelve tones were listed in a row or "series," ensuring that each tone would be used as often as any other. Because of this permanent reference to the basic set of tones, Schoenberg claimed that his twelve-tone method produced a coherent "Grundgestalt" (basic form). With the flight from Germany of Schoenberg and other composers in the 1930s, twelve-tone composition became firmly established in the United States. Indeed, by the late 1940s, a majority of younger American classical composers were using the twelve-tone method.[46]

Though his music was seldom performed, Milton Babbitt was among the most influential of the American twelve-tone composers and theoreticians; he helped make the strange-sounding music intellectually respectable. Known for his strict and unremitting application of the twelve-tone system ("the twelve-tone set must absolutely determine *every* aspect of the piece"), Babbitt pushed twelve-tone composition well beyond the boundaries established by Schoenberg. Trained in mathematics as well as music, Babbitt used the serial idea to structure duration and rhythm as well as tones. By the 1940s he had developed a complex method for combining note "aggregates" that he called "combinatoriality," and he employed these advanced ideas in *Three Compositions for Piano* and *Composition for Four Instruments* (both 1947–48). Music historian H. Wiley Hitchcock has described Babbitt's contribution in words that evoke not only the system of Fuller's geodesic dome but the larger vision of the culture of the whole. "Babbitt has created music," writes Hitchcock, "with a staggeringly complex network of inter-relationships. Not only are these relationships complex; they *are* the music; the interlocked components are inseparable; it is no longer meaningful to speak of one, or to hear one, separate from the others; the music, approaching 'total organization,' demands total hearing."[47]

In the hands of a Milton Babbitt or a Buckminster Fuller, one-world thought took the form of high-level investigation of certain ultimate principles. Everyday Americans were much more likely to come across another aspect of the culture of the whole: the decade-long trend toward cultural homogeneity—or, as was often the case, the *appearance* or *ideology* of homogeneity. At times it seemed as if Americans would stop at nothing to eliminate, deny, or assimilate to the culture of the whole every difference of ethnicity, race, or class. As we have seen, some of this homogenization—the gradual decline of hillbilly and the growth of country and western music, for example—was the inevitable product of high wartime levels of geographic mobility. Yet homogenization was not simply the end result of unavoidable economic and social trends; if it were, it would be of only marginal interest in a history of thought and culture.

To the extent that it actually happened—and its story is a curious blend of fire and smoke—homogenization was the tip of an intellectual iceberg. Beneath the surface were rhetorical and ideological banners: toleration, loyalty, democracy, and pluralism—each of them representing a powerful principle capable of motivating great numbers of people. Under these banners, Americans of the 1940s waged campaigns against racial discrimination, anti-Semitism, and the discriminatory selection practices of some high school fraternities and sororities. While each of these campaigns of social reformism was carried out with the promise of ending some grievous wrong and ushering in a more "humane" and "tolerant" society, the intention was more complex than these terms suggest, and the actual social changes they wrought appear to have been of marginal significance. As the decade came to a close, little had been done to change the fundamental realities of American life; class, race, and ethnic distinctions remained. Nor had middle-class Americans learned to respect real blacks, real Jews, or the real poor. What they had learned was that class in America hardly existed; that the black culture needed to be assimilated into white America; and that ethnicity was a shallow veneer that ought properly to be shed.

Throughout the decade, Americans paid lip service to the ideal of toleration but generally remained committed to assimilationist ideas. "Americans All," a *March of Time* program produced in 1941, reflected this ambivalence. The program celebrated the arrival in the United States of scholars, artists, and other European immigrants, citing these new populations as examples of a historical American commitment to cultural pluralism. As the program made clear, however, the commitment did not extend to the largely illiterate first generation of Eastern Europeans, whose presence in the country apparently threatened the social order. Fortunately, with the second generation, "old country customs [including illiteracy] are fast disappearing" as the Eastern Europeans also "become merged into one great people."

The assimilationist fervor of the forties can also be seen in the decade's great intellectual contribution to American race relations, Gunnar Myrdal's *An American Dilemma* (1944). A Swedish economist of liberal persuasion, Myrdal had been hired in 1937 by the Carnegie Corporation to carry out a "Negro study" in the United States. Myrdal's widely praised and influential book described the nation's racial problem as a "moral dilemma" within the heart of every white American. On the one hand, Myrdal argued, whites believed in the "American Creed" of opportunity and democracy; on the other hand, they were full of prejudice against blacks. Although Myrdal seemed to place blame squarely on the shoulders of white America, his admiring focus on the American Creed also suggested that any reasonable solution of the race problem would necessarily mean the assimilation of the inferior black culture, which *An American Dilemma* labeled a "pathology." Having found little of value in black communities in seven years of study, Myrdal called for the "eventual disappearance of black institutions" and expressed surprise that black culture might yield anything worth saving. "After weighing all available evidence carefully," he wrote, "it seems frankly incredible that the Negro people in America should feel inclined to develop any particular race pride at all."

Myrdal's denigration of minority culture and admiration for the American Creed were not simply the product of objective observations of the American scene. As early as 1940, Myrdal had become obsessed by the problem of how to keep his homeland from being swallowed up by the Nazis, a project that for Myrdal required an unheard-of level of national unity. He believed he had found an example of, and model for, such unity in the American Creed, whose ability to produce a united people was limited only by the centrifugal tendencies of the race question. Therefore, the American racial problem became a subproblem of Myrdal's obsession with totalitarianism, and *An American Dilemma* became, according to historian Walter A. Jackson, part of an "ideological defense against fascism." If Americans could handle their racial disorders, then somehow the Swedes would survive their confrontation with the Nazis. No wonder, then, that Myrdal could see black culture only as an obstacle in need of removal.[48]

Of all the decade's minority "problems," none loomed so large or occupied as much public attention as the problem of anti-Semitism. Indeed, it is conceivable that the decade's abiding enthusiasm for the culture of the whole was in some sense a response to the Holocaust and to a "whole view" of reality for which the Holocaust was arguably responsible. Literary critic John W. Aldridge described the "whole view" as the dream of the classless society, the "pathological refusal" to make the simplest "distinctions" for fear of initiating a social chain reaction with another Holocaust as the final consequence. Manners (i.e., customs), wrote Aldridge, "are seen . . . as inseparable from the idea of class; the idea of class is seen as inseparable from the idea of a suppressed minority; the idea of a suppressed minority is seen as inseparable from the idea of the totalitarian state; and the idea of the totalitarian state is seen as inseparable from the idea of totalitarian atrocity." Years later, Alfred Kazin suggested something more prosaic. "Even in death," he wrote, "the Jews were an 'anomaly,' a contradiction to the great 'unifying' tendencies of modern life and revolution. Though prime objects of Hitler's hatred, they were a side issue for everyone else."[49]

Whether Americans were reluctant to recognize Jewishness for fear of engaging the "whole view" of reality, or they simply did not take Jewishness very seriously, their popular presentations of the problem bore the familiar Myrdal-like stamp of assimilationist thinking. Though dozens of Hollywood films had fictional Jewish characters, told the story of Jewish entertainers, or raised the issue of anti-Semitism, few of them dealt in any serious way with the ethnic culture or religion of Judaism or covered the most serious problems facing Jews in the 1940s. Although the state of Israel came into existence in 1948, only one film, *Sword in the Desert* (1949), took up the question of a Jewish homeland. Except for *Sealed Verdict* (1948), the Holocaust was also ignored. Hollywood managed to present the life of George Gershwin (*Rhapsody in Blue* [1945]) while mentioning his Jewish heritage only once, and viewers of Jerome Kern's life story, *Till the Clouds Roll By* (1947), were left completely in the dark about the composer's ethnic background.

Gentleman's Agreement (1947), winner of three Academy Awards and the most famous film of the decade to deal with Jewish issues, illustrates the cinema's tendency to trivialize Judaism. The film stars Gregory Peck as Phil Green, a reporter who pretends to be a Jew in order to experience discrimination firsthand. While Green has numerous encounters with prejudice, the film's message is that Judaism is a set of superficial qualities that one might as easily take on as slough off. "I'll be Jewish," announces Phil. "All I've got to do is say it." Some viewers, like the stagehand described by scriptwriter Moss Hart, took away from the picture a curious but perhaps predictable lesson: "I'll never be rude to a Jew again because he might turn out to be a Gentile."[50]

Arthur Laurents's *Home of the Brave* worked its assimilationist magic on the stage of New York City's Belasco Theater; it opened in the last days of 1945, when most Americans had knowledge of the Holocaust.[51] The play's protagonist is Jewish private Peter Coen/Coney, stationed in the Pacific during World War II and, as the drama opens, undergoing psychiatric treatment at the hands of Capt. Harold Bitterger for paralysis caused by a war-related traumatic shock. Using narcosynthesis (a treatment employing narcotics), Bitterger probes Coney's past for the cause of his affliction. His inquiry settles on the recent mission of Coney and three other engineers, including his Arizona hayseed friend Finch, to a nearby island. At this point in the drama, Laurents leads his audience to believe that Coney's paralysis is somehow related to anti-Semitism, for it is on the island that serious conflict develops over Coney's Jewishness. Another soldier, T. J., calls Coney a "lousy yellow Jew bastard" and Finch a "little kike lover." Later, under Japanese fire, Finch yells at Coney, "I'm not asking you to stay, you lousy yellow————". Because Finch has consistently claimed to be without prejudice, this remark hurts Coney deeply. "He started to say you lousy yellow Jew bastard," Coney later tells Bitterger. "So I knew. I knew."

That is, he thought he knew. Without denying that Coney has been injured by the relevation that Finch, too, is not entirely free of anti-Semitism, Laurents cleverly shifts the ground of his argument, anchoring Coney's paralysis not in the newly discovered *difference* between the two men but in Coney's ongoing affection for and loyalty to Finch, no matter what his transgressions. As Bitterger discovers, Coney's paralysis did not begin with the revelation of Finch's anti-Semitism but rather followed on the heels of another chain of events. Shot, captured by the Japanese, and tortured into crying for help, Finch somehow managed to crawl back to Coney's position, where he died. At some moment in this process, Coney became paralyzed, as Bitterger explains, "because you knew if you couldn't walk, then you couldn't leave Finch. That's it, isn't it?" Finally, Coney must recognize and acknowledge that his deepest feelings—including the guilt he feels as a survivor—are nothing exceptional. "You're the same as anybody else," Bitterger says. "You're no different, son, no different at all." When Coney protests that his Jewishness makes him different, Bitterger describes his ethnic consciousness as a pathology. "This, Peter, this sensitivity has been like a disease in you. It was there before anything happened on that island." A play that begins, then, by purporting to explore the problem of prejudice concludes as an exercise in blaming the victim, locating the source of Coney's problems in his own misplaced and defensive sense of Jewish identity.[52]

Even the rise to prominence of the Jewish intellectual community, so vital a factor in the cultural life of the nation in the 1940s, must be understood in the context of the prevailing idea of the culture of the whole. Prominent Jewish intellectuals did not exactly repudiate their Jewishness or advocate the assimilation of Jews into the larger culture. But neither did they trumpet their Jewishness as the wellspring of their creative endeavors, as a later generation would. Art critic Clement Greenberg claimed that Jewishness not only was of little significance in his own life but was an inappropriate criterion for the evaluation of art. And novelist Lionel Trilling said, "I should resent it if a critic of my work were to discover in it either faults or virtues which he called Jewish." Impatient with any ethnicity, including their own, these and other leading Jewish intellectuals came to a position of intellectual leadership under an ideal of cosmopolitanism. Cosmopolitanism neither celebrated nor denied ethnicity; rather, it took particular subcultures as fuel for the broad-ranging experience thought necessary for achieving a genuinely comprehensive perspective on the world. One might argue that this instrumental view of ethnicity, in which cultural differences were valued not in themselves but for some larger purpose, was in part responsible for the ascendancy of the Jewish intellectual community in the 1940s. Cosmopolitanism was an intellectualized version of the culture of the whole.[53]

No less prominent was the nation's vision in the forties of its own classnessness, an attitude drawn as much or more from wartime egalitarianism as from the affluence of the decade's last years. Just as the American Federation of Labor (AFL) had forgone the right to strike during the war—that is, to exercise the prerogatives of class—so did most Americans give up the very notion of "social class" for the duration, preferring to invest themselves in the spurious notion that they were "all in this together." While surveys reveal that most infantrymen deeply resented the officers' clubs and other classbased privileges of their noncombatant superior officers, Hollywood treaded gingerly on the question of command, preferring to depict leaders who, like John Wayne in *Sands of Iwo Jima* (1949), were ordinary guys willing to die with their mates. Classlessness was also implicit in the plurality of ethnic types that peopled combat units in war films. The motley collection in *Bataan*—six WASPs, a Mexican, a Jew, a Pole, an Irishman, two Filipinos, and a black—deflected attention from the working-class composition of the typical platoon. The most elaborate effort to equate the sacrifices of the working-class soldier with those of more fortunate noncombatants occurred in *Stage Door Canteen* (1943) and *Hollywood Canteen* (1944), films based on successful real-life celebrity canteens (clubs) in New York City and Hollywood. Both films featured ordinary GIs being wined, dined, and otherwise entertained by humble and appreciative luminaries of the silver screen, who were only too glad to bus tables if it meant they could stay out of foxholes. At least in the movies, the soldiers got the message. "Democracy," comments Sergeant Nolan (Dane Clark) in *Hollywood Canteen*, "means that everybody is equal—where all those big shots talk to little shots like me."[54]

The fantasy of classlessness picked up speed as the war ended, propelled, perhaps, by veterans who believed that their sacrifices had earned them an open society that would yield to their ambitions. Hopes for a new level of prosperity, available to all, were also fed by the prospect of an unending supply of inexpensive energy through nuclear fission. Louis Wirth, the respected University of Chicago sociologist, argued that increased agricultural productivity based on nuclear power would significantly reduce the gap between rich and poor. Hollywood contributed in the late forties to the illusion of classlessness with a spate of films suggesting that the problems of middleclass professionals were the only ones worthy of consideration. Among them were *The Hucksters* (1947), based on a best-selling novel by Frederic Wakeman about a troubled advertising executive, and *Cheaper by the Dozen* (1950), which examined the lives of efficiency experts Frank and Lillian Gilbreth. Americans went to see these films because they could relate to the protagonists; in 1948, 80 percent of the population identified itself as middle-class.[55]

By midcentury serious scholars in a variety of fields were arguing that classes had become obsolete, that future social conflicts would feature groups formed by age rather than economics, and that the dramatic postwar migrations to the suburbs were producing the "second great melting pot." Even the iconoclastic sociologist C. Wright Mills joined the debate, with *White Collar: The American Middle Classes*. Although Mills insisted that accountants, purchasing agents, billing clerks, and other midcentury white-collar workers were in fact working-class, he also perceived that a dramatic change in the structure of occupations had eliminated the old, clearer division between entrepreneur and wageworker.[56]

This assimilationist message was by and large an ideological one, a reflection of the *desire* of the dominant culture, but by no means an accurate representation of reality. For example, Hollywood might neglect to put the creation of Israel on celluloid, but it could not prevent thousands of people from packing New York's Madison Square Garden for a "Salute to Israel" rally.[57] Similarly, advocates of a culture of the whole might wish devoutly for the disappearance of categories of race, ethnicity, and class, but the social realities that sustained these categories could not easily be dismissed. One could not simply outlaw ethnicity.

There was, however, one institution—the high school—where the law could and did reach, and where a major, nationwide effort was made to prohibit membership in organizations that discriminated on the basis of race and ethnicity.[58] The offending organizations were the numerous high school fraternities and sororities, many of them informally associated with big-city public high schools. The "secret societies," as they were sometimes called, had been under fire for decades, but in the assimilationist forties they came in for a new round of censure. Under legislation first passed in the progressive era, states and municipalities prohibited interschool clubs and suspended, expelled, or denied extracurricular activities to students who refused to renounce membership. Media criticism grew in the late 1940s, when *Time* and *Ladies' Home Journal* published exposés of fraternity and sorority practices.

The secret societies were attacked not only because their members were not yet adults and hence were vulnerable, but because their existence seemed to mock and threaten the very idea of a culture of the whole. In Buffalo, Cleveland, and other cities, fraternities and sororities were organized by ethnic group, socioeconomic class, race, religion, and gender. In doing so, of course, they were only reflecting the structure and values of the larger society. But, as we have seen, many Americans no longer cared to be reminded of these social realities, preferring to see their culture as on the verge of genuine homogeneity. Because the public school had long been understood as the great engine of social and economic equality, organizations such as the secret societies, which were perceived as interfering with this mission, were deemed outmoded and destructive. According to the *Ladies' Home Journal*, the secret societies promoted class distinctions that might not otherwise exist, especially in a society on the verge of classlessness.

The forties campaign against the secret societies took place at the same time, and often used the same rhetoric, as the more famous assault on domestic communism. In each case, the key word was a cold war favorite—*loyalty*. The new loyalty was evident in Washington, D.C., where Truman's federal government was engaged in determining the loyalty of its employees; in California, where every teacher in the state university system was required to sign a noncommunist loyalty oath; and on the streets of New York City, where in 1948 the traditional Eighth Avenue May Day celebration competed with a Fifth Avenue "affirmation of Americanism" known as the Loyalty Day Parade. Teenagers might have noticed the National Education Association's (NEA) version of loyalty on school bulletin boards. The NEA's "Law of Loyalty" was a pledge of loyalty to family, town, state, country, humanity, civilization and, of course, school.

The high school was one of many institutions charged with producing and defining the culture of the whole. Organizations that challenged this goal—and that included the secret societies—were charged with violating the concept of loyalty. When students wore society jackets rather than school jackets, and when pledging and initiation activities bonded youth to secret, "self-perpetuating" organizations beyond the supervision of teachers and administrators, school officials resolved to eliminate the offending organizations. Because they "divided loyalties within the school," or, worse yet, forged "a greater and stronger loyalty" than that granted the school, the secret societies threatened the centralizing mission of the institution.[59]

Despite the widely held ideal of toleration, the nation's investment in the idea of the whole allowed for only the most limited appreciation of distinct subcultures.[60] Under the doctrine of toleration, racial, ethnic, and class differences not only were to be tolerated but were to be celebrated—for example, in high school assemblies, pageants, and brotherhood weeks. One school claimed to be doing its part to "make the world safe for differences." But Americans were a long way from the sixties perspective that cultural differences were good and right and important in themselves. The high schools were uncomfortable with applying cultural differences in any concrete way. At one Buffalo high school, for example, the Color Guard, selected by the student body, was the most prestigious school organization, held out as a model of harmonious group living under democratic pluralism. Yet the thought that students would actually select the Color Guard on the basis of group differences was something that did not yet seem reasonable to students and school officials. In voting for the Color Guard, commented the school yearbook, "no boy asks himself, as he makes his choice, 'What is his race? To which religion does he belong?' No.—the selection is made on qualities anyone may possess." In short, students were exposed to and made aware of "differences" in order to teach the lesson that even the most essential differences of race, class, and national origin were, in fact, of little consequence. In a world in which God had created "all men equal," the schools, at least, were supposed to be "one world."

The use of the doctrine of toleration to achieve a larger goal, such as a unified school or a stable society, is sharply revealed in Dore Schary's film about the problems of returning veterans, *Till the End of Time.* Guy Williams, Robert Mitchum, and Bill Williams play veterans Cliff Harper, William Tabeshaw, and Perry Kincheloe, each unable to adjust to civilian life. Harper can't hold a job, bridles at his family's interference with his social life, and seems resigned to life as a beach bum. Tabeshaw lives with a metal plate in his head and a fantasy of a future on his own New Mexico ranch. An embittered paraplegic, Kincheloe at first refuses to use his artificial legs— "Twenty-one and I'm dead," he tells Harper and Tabeshaw.

The turnaround takes place in the Swan Bar, a dive where our alienated and self-pitying protagonists have taken refuge from the torments of the real world. In this vulnerable state, an unsavory representative of the proto-fascist American War Patriots tempts the vets with the prospect of a large monthly bonus and, significantly, an organization free of Catholics, blacks, and Jews. Enraged by this statement of prejudice—and having found something worth standing up for—Tabeshaw starts a fight. Kincheloe learns that even without real legs he can be effective with his fists. The next day, Harper is ready to settle down and accept the responsibilities of maturity; he now realizes that despite his problems, he is a relatively fortunate young man.

Like the Buffalo high school Color Guard, *Till the End of Time* offers toleration as a powerful, abstract idea capable of transcending the most serious social problems and dissolving even the most profound social tensions. Obviously, the film's central concern is the adjustment of white veterans; the idea of toleration has utility only as a catalyst to that adjustment. For the same reason, the film neither explores minority cultures nor treats the special problems faced by black and Jewish veterans. It is also possible that the film is not even very much interested in veterans, that it uses their special problems only to make a broader statement about the general need for unity at a time of social dislocation in the nation's transition from a war economy.

A story told by syndicated columnist Walter Winchell reinforces this interpretation. One Rudy Kovarick, thirty-six, was visiting Miami from Dearborn, Michigan, in late December 1946, when he began hemorrhaging. He needed AB–Rh positive blood, a type so rare that none was available in the area. Miami's newspapers put out a call, and the blood to save Kovarick's life was found in Georgia. As Winchell explained, Kovarick's obvious ethnicity served as a point of unity. "The local newspaper and radio," he later wrote, "aroused almost an entire nation. . . . Nobody stopped to ask, 'Is he black, brown, white, or yellow? Is he a Jew, Protestant, Catholic or atheist?'"[61] (Actually, Winchell's account tells us that people probably did ask precisely those questions, only to conclude that the answer was unimportant.)

Two years later, Harvard president James Bryant Conant made much the same argument while setting the need for "national solidarity" in a cold war context appropriate to 1948. Like Schary's film and Winchell's account of Kovarick's troubles, Conant found a potential source of unity in the nation's immigrant history and diversity of peoples. Tolerance of diversity, Conant argued, was the "bedrock" of national unity, and religious tolerance was a "unifying secular doctrine."[62] Far from being an invitation to a chaotic, decentralized, centrifugal, cultural pluralism, toleration was an ideology of universalism, a step in the direction of the culture of the whole.

The culture of the whole might best be understood as a matrix of thought through which Americans in a great variety of pursuits experienced, understood, and sought to change their world. On one level, the culture of the whole was reality itself, a composite of the increasingly frequent signs of cultural homogenization that flowed inevitably from the enormous economic and social changes required by a wartime economy. On another level, the culture of the whole was a set of ideas about organization: Jungian assertions of collective consciousness, Davis's vision of world citizenship, *Time's* prophecy of a world unified by the spectacle of television, Mead's study of the American character, and the espistemologies of system that underlay Fuller's geodesic dome, Pound's *The Pisan Cantos*, and the music of the serial composers.

Related to this penchant for higher levels of organization, the culture of the whole also meant the refusal to make or to countenance distinctions of class, race, and ethnicity. This refusal was sometimes carried out under the rubric of loyalty, by which groups or persons whose allegiances cut against the culture of the whole might be censured, and sometimes through the doctrine of toleration, which, by denying the distinctive qualities of racial and ethnic groups, generated the fiction of a unified culture. The American character studies helped create the illusion that social classes were rapidly disappearing in the solvent of abundance.

While theorists of the whole usually presented themselves, and deservedly so, as idealists in search of some obvious good, the unifying impulse that dominated the field often brought its practitioners and advocates into contact with certain ideas with fascist overtones. So it was that Pound was nearly tried for treason, that *Time* found itself drooling over the inaugural spectacle of 1949, and that Eero Saarinen designed an arch that might have been built for Mussolini.

In a sense, the effort to build a culture of the whole tracked the disintegration of world order. For example, Willkie's *One World* appeared in 1943, at the very moment when the prospects for world unity seemed bleakest. Even such intellectual games as systems theory were based on a perception of disequilibrium that was in some fundamental way inspired by the chaos of European state politics. After 6 August 1945 many considered world government essential to the survival of the human race.

Certain forms of one-world thinking should also be understood as politically motivated; that is, some stood to benefit from them more than others. The American character studies were full of assumptions of cultural superiority; they helped to win the war and justified the nation's emerging world dominance. Even Willkie's genuinely idealistic vision of one world looked to the eventual penetration of world markets by American products. Within the United States, assertions of the whole helped the dominant culture set aside the problems of returning veterans (*Till the End of Time*), technology (*Louisiana Story*), anti-Semitism (*Home of the Brave*), and social class (*Hollywood Canteen*), while the culture of the spectacular promised to open up uniform national markets composed of anyone vulnerable to the direct appeals of television.

At the deepest level, then, the culture of the whole was the result of efforts to deal—or not deal—with critical international and national problems. The potential for nuclear devastation seemed to call for a reexamination of the national systems of governance that were responsible for the bomb and its use, and that meant world government, world citizenship, the United Nations, and other manifestations of one world. The prospect of another Great Depression seemed to justify a capitalism of spectacle, as well as Willkie's interest in world markets. The wildcat strikes of 1946 were met with a mythic vision of a society of abundance and classlessness. And, as John W. Aldridge understood, the specter of the Holocaust required that every shred of difference be denied or tolerated in the cause of the new, and specious, culture of the whole.

five

Turning Inward

After long years of war, Americans turned to peace with an almost desper-ate self-consciousness, as if living itself had been suspended for the duration and might prove a custom difficult to revive. The very titles of some films—*It's a Wonderful Life*, *The Best Years of Our Lives*, *The Time of Your Life*, and *Living in a Big Way*—suggest the high level of awareness with which this project of "living" was pursued. *March of Time* programs "Life with Baby" (1946), "Life with Junior" (1948), and "Life with Grandpa" (1948) confirmed this new consciousness of life and reflected the trend in the social sciences toward studying the life cycle. Despite the recognition of man's finiteness that lay behind this emphasis on "living," the international voice of existentialism, Jean-Paul Sartre, found a new sort of Emersonian eternality in the habits of day-to-day life. "We make absolutes," he wrote. "You light your pipe and that is an absolute; you don't like oysters and that is an absolute. . . . Whether God exists or does not exist . . . nothing will ever be able to negate the fact that you passionately loved such and such a picture, such and such a cause, and such and such a woman; that you lived that love from day to day; lived it, willed it, and undertook it; and that you engaged your whole being in it."[1]

Holiday magazine, designed for those who craved more "sheer living out of life itself," greeted the readers of its first issue in March 1946 with an an-nouncement heralding another great cause of the day: happiness. "*Holiday*," wrote its editor, "is dedicated to the pursuit of happiness." In a postwar world of "stresses and strains," happiness meant recapturing, and perhaps fulfilling, the dream of adventure. "If you have heard promises in the West Wind, if you have restlessly listened to a train whistle at night, looked longingly at an

AMERICAN RIVER COLLEGE

airplane in flight, or dreamed of being cargoed to far lands on a passing ship, you will appreciate *Holiday*."[2]

When life itself is raised to cult status and happiness can be marketed like any other commodity, one may be sure that something is amiss. Perhaps, like the Keller family in Arthur Miller's *All My Sons*, millions of postwar Americans remained virtual prisoners of war and "never took up our lives again." The agenda of the panel of distinguished Americans meeting as the 1948 *Life* roundtable was to probe the "failure in America to achieve genuine happiness." But their not-so-hidden agenda was to demonstrate the fallacy of the old New Deal–Great Depression view that unhappiness was a product of flaws in the "outer world"—that is, in the nation's economic and social systems. *Life* closed its account of the Rye conference with an observation from Betsey Barton, who had lost the use of both legs in an automobile accident. "Happiness," said Barton, "is primarily an inner state, an inner achievement. . . . The Kingdom of heaven is within us."[3]

The *Life* roundtable was only one of many forums in which Americans expressed their doubts about life in an age colored by the atomic bomb and international communism, by rampant commercialism and materialism, and by a fragmentation of social and cultural life so severe that it seemed to deny people coherent personalities and stable existences. By the end of the decade, Americans were sure that theirs was a culture of anxiety; like the participants in the roundtable, many were convinced that relief from anxiety required a sharp turn inward, away from the public realm of politics and economics and toward the neurotic, troubled, fragmented, and "rootless" self. By midcentury the phrase "age of anxiety" had been used as the title of both a W. H. Auden poem and a symphonic translation of Auden's work by Leonard Bernstein, and in the title of the first chapter of Arthur M. Schlesinger, Jr.'s *The Vital Center* ("Politics in an Age of Anxiety"). Albert Camus labeled the era the "age of overt anxiety," and Rollo May offered a psychological account in *The Meaning of Anxiety* (1950), commenting on the "formless uneasiness that has dogged the footsteps of modern man." In addition, Schlesinger, the radio rabbi and self-help author Joshua Liebman, and sex-role theorists Ferdinand Lundberg and Marynia F. Farnham characterized the culture, or certain aspects of it, as essentially neurotic (characterized by an emotional state lacking an objective basis). "Neurosis," wrote Lundberg and Farnham, "is the true epidemic of our time."[4]

The culture of anxiety had so many sources that it is difficult to isolate the few worthy of special attention. One, surely, was the all too obvious failure to stabilize the world political scene—or control the forces of destruction—in ways that would allow people to live securely. In 1948 a high school sophomore penned a "Letter to God" for her school yearbook, holding the deity responsible for having broken a promise to fashion a workable peace: "You said that men of good will would live in mutual accord. But where is this concord? Where are those men of good will? Peace is freedom from fear, and yet, man fears many things." Accepting the 1950 Nobel Prize for Literature, William Faulkner called on American writers to shed their fears and to return to a literature immersed in love, compassion, and universal truth. "Our tragedy today," said Faulkner, "is a general and universal physical fear so long sustained by now that we can even bear it. There are no longer problems of the spirit. There is only the question: when will I be blown up?"[5]

Such anxieties formed the backdrop for the UFO scare of mid-1947, for the sex-crime paranoia of the late 1940s and early 1950s, for the intimidating anticommunism of the Truman administration's loyalty program and, later, of Sen. Joseph McCarthy, and for the fanatical, anticommunist opposition to the fluoridation of public water supplies. Even the humor of the age worked off fear, anxiety, and the inevitability of disaster. "All comedy," wrote "Li'l Abner" cartoonist Al Capp, "is based on man's delight in man's inhumanity to man." Full of self-doubt and desperately needing reassurance, human beings relished their relative superiority over the hapless characters that inhabited comic strips and film. "Sitting there in the theater [watching a Charlie Chaplin film]," wrote Capp in a 1949 essay that turned humor into something resembling film noir, "we are all gods on Olympus, watching an inferior being trying to escape the destiny we, in our omniscience, know must be his."[6]

Although Americans were committed to television, the automobile, the private home, and the washer and dryer, their contract with materialism, leisure, and the culture of consumption was often seen as a crucial source of anxiety. Looking back at 1947, *Time* linked the year's meager output in the arts to feelings of uncertainty that prosperity could not overcome and for which it was, conceivably, responsible. According to *Time*, "The U.S. people produced more than ever before and had more money to buy things than ever before, yet the country still did not have the happiness its boom seemed to offer." Typical of the numerous self-help books of the age were Thomas Merton's *Seeds of Contemplation* (1949), which counseled readers to avoid "the amusements and the noise and the business of men"; Joshua Liebman's *Peace of Mind* (1946), which characterized worldly acquisitions as "mere weapons of aggression and vengeance" and described the pursuit of such goods as a "pathological race" undertaken to satisfy childhood compulsions; and Dale Carnegie's *How to Stop Worrying and Start Living* (1948), whose strong producer ethic betrayed considerable uneasiness with the growing number of leisure hours available to the average American. Philosopher Erich Fromm explained how the twentieth-century "gospel of selling" had produced the "marketing orientation" of personality, with man reconstructed as an empty, role-playing commodity, bereft of individuality and fit only for the consumption of others.[7]

103

Films of the day seldom directly criticized the impulse to consume and to possess, but they often found fault with the coldly efficient systems and institutions designed to profit from the marketing and sale of goods. The department store came under scrutiny in *Good Sam* (1948), which featured Gary Cooper as Sam Clayton, a combination of department-store general manager and doe-eyed, do-good social worker ("he just loves people"). Despite his employment in the temple of consumer capitalism, Sam understands the store and the capitalist marketplace not as a modern cathedral of desire but as an old-fashioned, community-based institution where genuine needs are filled. Much to the chagrin of his boss, Sam gives his employees time off to attend a funeral in the midst of the Christmas rush, directs an old lady to another store for the purchase of eyeglasses, and, in the film's final episode, gives away his family's house fund. When the last act fortuitously leads to the return of the original investment and a tidy sum besides, Sam confronts his wife with the central irony of postwar consumer capitalism: "Lou, we made a profit on people. Now we can buy the house and live happily ever after."

Another major source of 1940s anxiety was freedom, or choice—the product of philosophical, political, and historical circumstances. One source of the anxiety of choice was the failure of history and tradition as guides to conduct. Margaret Mead had commented favorably on the restless mobility of Americans in her wartime classic, *And Keep Your Powder Dry*, describing the third-generation American as "leaving behind him all that was his past," while others, like baby doctor Benjamin Spock, sensed the need to provide "common sense" advice to the mother whose mobility and isolation from tradition had rendered her virtually helpless in the presence of a crying infant or a recalcitrant child.[8]

On the philosophical level, anxiety was an inevitable concomitant of the unanchored values of modern society (described in Chapter 2). In the absence of accepted moral and ethical principles of conduct and belief, an infinity of actions and beliefs became possible and the anxiety of choice unavoidable. For instance, consumer anxiety was experienced in a marketplace stocked with virtually indistinguishable goods, each bearing a brand name and claiming superiority over all others. The anxiety of choice can also be seen in the persona of Snoopy, the hedonistic canine of the comic strip "Peanuts," introduced in 1950. Arthur Berger describes Snoopy as "an existential hero," striving with "dogged persistance" to "overcome what seems to be his fate—that he is a dog; that he is *just* a dog. And somehow he does it!" The result was existential man (or existential dog), "the spiritually unaccommodated man," as Lionel Abel put it, for whom "nothing is impermissible. He must decide himself just what it is he forbids himself to do." Modern man, in Abel's rendering of Sartre, wishes to be "unmodern . . . for being modern is precisely not having to be anything with true 'resolute decision.' He thinks of communism and at times would like to be a Communist, but not finally. . . . If he has children, he does not know what he wants them to become. . . . What paintings please him? All sorts of paintings, but only to a limited extent." In the words of Søren Kierkegaard, whose *The Concept of Dread* (1844) was translated into English in 1944 and became a key existentialist text, "anxiety is always to be understood as oriented toward freedom."[9]

Several scholars used the idea of anxiety to help explain the great inexplicable phenomenon of the twentieth century: totalitarianism. Although the word itself did not come into general use until the late 1930s, it soon came to mean a system characterized by near total control, based on instruments of modern technology and, as in the attempt to exterminate the Jews, on large-scale organized violence. For Arthur Schlesinger, Jr., totalitarianism grew out of the anxiety of the modern existential situation. While the existentialists claimed that the idea of existence itself could function as a surrogate value system (people, they argued, could act to infuse their lives with value despite the apparent hopelessness and absurdity of such a task), Schlesinger saw this "vacuum of faith" as the spawning ground of the political religion of totalitarianism. "Free society," he wrote in *The Vital Center*, "alienates the lonely and uprooted masses; while totalitarianism, building on their frustrations and cravings, provides a structure of belief, men to worship and men to hate and rites which guarantee salvation." In *The Origins of Totalitarianism*, the most powerful postwar treatment of the subject, Hannah Arendt presented a case not unlike Schlesinger's, arguing that totalitarianism could be understood only in psychological and sociological terms as the product of modern conditions of mass alienation, loneliness, rootlessness, and superfluousness (in short, as the loss of a sense of self). Deeply influenced by existential thought, Arendt also insisted that one must face up to reality, no matter how evil or horrible that reality is—for instance, the reality that the Nazis tried to kill all the Jews and to persuade themselves that some human beings were superfluous—and that, having come to grips with the worst, one must act existentially on that knowledge in a political way, that is, without any assurance than one's actions would have any particular or even substantial effect.[10]

At the center of forties anxiety was the problem of identity. Although the word *identity* was not commonly used in the social sciences until the 1950s, the concept appeared frequently in the popular and scholarly literature of the 1940s. Under the rubric of identity, Americans identified two very different but related maladies: the fragmented self and the rootless self. Harry Emerson Fosdick explained the fragmented self in his popular book of advice, *On Being a Real Person* (1943). According to Fosdick, personality was falling apart under the pressures of modern life. "Being a real person" meant pulling oneself up by one's bootstraps and returning to the self a degree of "wholeness" and "coherence"—a project that might be understood as an internal, personal equivalent of Wendell Willkie's one world. "The central criterion of success-ful personal living," wrote Fosdick, "is somehow to pass from mere 'multiple selves' into the poise, balance, and cohesion of a unified personality." Ac-cepting—albeit somewhat reluctantly—the psychological frameworks within which modern problems were being discussed and worked out, Catholic priest and radio personality Fulton J. Sheen described the modern self in *Peace of Soul* (1949) as a "battlefield where a civil war rages between a thou-sand and one conflicting loyalties." Dissociated from history, wrenched from his own memories, and deprived of the ability to achieve wholeness in God by the shattering experience of the bomb, modern man, wrote Sheen, "is no longer a unity. . . . There is no single overall purpose in his life."[11]

Among social scientists, the fragmented self was often presented in the language of role theory, which was a way of explaining what people do by the positions (roles) they occupy in a social structure. Although the devel-opment of role theory was gradual, credit for its conceptualization is usually assigned to two books published in 1936: Ralph Linton's *The Study of Man* and Lewis Terman and Catherine Miles's *Sex and Personality*. By the 1940s both academic and popular writers had begun to use role theory to explore problems of sex-role *identity*, emphasizing the apparent distortions in men's and women's roles that cropped up as a result, especially, of the changing sex-role requirements of World War II. Thus the war produced stereotypes, such as the overbearing female parodied in the hit song "Pistol Packin' Mama" (1943) about a gun-toting woman who chases her husband's girl-friend. Behind the stereotypes, of course, was an important social reality: during the war, about six million American women left their traditional roles as homemakers to tackle industrial tasks previously done by men. While few of these women became overt feminists as a result of their new work expe-rience, there is no doubt that many men were disturbed by the challenge to their hegemony within the family.[12]

Most scholars and popular writers agreed that the new, presumably over-bearing woman of the forties had produced an identity crisis for the Ameri-can male. According to Talcott Parsons, the central problem of taking on the appropriate male sex-role identity (i.e., of becoming a man) involved over-coming a strong initial identification with the female/mother. His theory found practical expression in a variety of texts, including Philip Wylie's *Gen-eration of Vipers* (1942), which accused American women of smothering the male psyche under the skirt of "momism." During the national sex-crime panic that began in 1947, the domineering mother was identified as the pri-mary reason for the child-molesting, homosexual male who was supposedly causing all the trouble. Sex deviates were defined as those who were unwill-ing to accept gender-defined responsibilities, and long-term solutions to the problem generally involved the reapplication of traditional, balanced gender roles in child-rearing.[13]

Though Dr. Spock leaned in the other direction, toward the child's need for a "steady, loving person" (generally the mother), he, too, was concerned that the lack of precise role models might adversely affect the male child. According to *Baby and Child Care*, the boy without a father—a common enough situation during the war—ran the risk of becoming interested in his mother's world and growing up "precocious and effeminate. . . . A boy doesn't grow spiritually to be a man just because he's born with a male body. The thing that makes him feel and act like a man is being able to copy, to pattern himself after men and older boys with whom he feels friendly."[14]

After the war, sex-role experts used much the same theory to examine the related problem of hypermasculinity (extreme, possibly violent, masculine behavior), an approach that seemed to be useful in explaining such phenomena as juvenile delinquency, the attraction of males to fascism, and returning veterans who beheaded their wives with machetes. *The Authoritarian Personality*, a path-breaking study by German émigré Theodor Adorno and his associates, concluded that the hypermasculinity of the authoritarian male was really a boastful "pseudo-masculinity," designed, perhaps, to mask some underlying, and possibly feminine, passivity. Adorno's hypothesis may explain the final scene in Mickey Spillane's *I, the Jury*, in which the arguably hypermasculine Mike Hammer kills Charlotte, the object of his love and affection, in cold blood. Charlotte's transgressions are two: as a psychiatrist, she has "gone into the frailty of men and seen their weaknesses" (that is, she has seen and revealed the feminine within them—and within Hammer), and she no longer has "the social instinct of a woman—that of being dependent upon a man." For these sins against traditional models of gender, Charlotte is summarily dispatched, and appropriately so, too—with one carefully placed .45-caliber bullet in the "naked belly," that locus of sex and motherhood, the site of her confusion and failure. In short, Charlotte dies because she is at once the observer and the embodiment of the fragmented self.[15]

No less attention was devoted to the problem of female identity. Among the more remarkable documents of the period is Ferdinand Lundberg and Marynia F. Farnham's *Modern Woman: The Lost Sex*. Like Spillane's Charlotte, and embodied visually in Willem de Kooning's painting *Woman* (1949), Lundberg and Farnham's woman is a victim of role confusion, a "psychologically disordered" "bundle of anxieties" lacking the one guarantee of her happiness: secure status "as a woman, a female being." Victimized by the "deep illness" of feminism, women had repudiated the home, children, and the proper confines of gender and become "truly displaced persons" (referring to a special population of identityless peoples around the world who, in the aftermath of war, literally lacked homelands).[16]

While *Modern Woman* could be marginalized (as it was in some quarters) as the work of off-the-deep-end Freudians, Margaret Mead's *Male and Female*, which made many of the same arguments, could not be dismissed so easily. Although Mead claimed that restrictions on women's functions were ultimately dehumanizing, she also defended a very traditional model of gender "interdependence," built on the "constructive receptivity" of the female. Without stooping to characterize the sexes as equivalent to their genitals, as Lundberg and Farnham had, Mead nonetheless described the question of roles as an urgent one upon which the "survival of our civilization" depended. "Have we overdomesticated men?" she asked, and "have we cut women off from their natural closeness to their children?" To these questions she essentially answered yes, concluding that women could attain an all-important sense of "irreversible achievement" simply by being permitted to "fulfil their biological rôle[s]."[17]

By creating new roles and opportunities for women, the Second World War had encouraged women to reinvent their lives—that is, to reconsider and remake their identities. The social ferment of the war had the same impact within the black community, where it stimulated a new generation of writers, including Richard Wright and Ralph Ellison, to redefine the meaning of being black in white America. For Ellison, whose *Invisible Man* was begun in 1945, the problem was essentially one of identity—"*the* American theme," as Ellison later claimed. "The nature of our society is such that we are prevented from knowing who we are." The book chronicles the shedding of one kind of identity—an illusory and harmful identity, lodged in the expectations of others, especially whites—and the conscious taking on of another kind of identity, based in part on an appreciation of black culture. On one level, *Invisible Man* is a statement about race. Its rich description of the black experience amounts to a denunciation of the insulting picture of black culture offered by Gunnar Myrdal's *An American Dilemma*, at the same time that it prefigures the black nationalism of the 1960s. On another level, however, the book's treatment of identity seems to bypass questions of race and culture. For Ellison the problem of identity was philosophical rather than social, a matter of the existential self. His invisible man was invisible not because whites had made him so, but because of a failure of his own understanding and will. "All dreamers and sleepwalkers must pay the price," states the nameless hero, "and even the invisible victim is responsible for the fate of all. But I shirked that responsibility. . . . I was a coward." As Ellison would later explain, "The hero's invisibility is not a matter of being seen, but a refusal to run the risk of his own humanity, which involves guilt. This is not an attack upon white society. . . . [The hero] must assert and achieve his own humanity."[18]

Perceptions of the fragmented self informed two of the decade's most important efforts to understand the emergence of a modern personality. Erich Fromm's "marketing man" was little more than an empty shell, lacking any strong quality of character that might conflict with the needs of the market, with role expectations, or with the requirements of the bureaucracies within which he earned his livelihood. This emptiness allowed marketing man to function as a kind of interpersonal chameleon, ready to take on qualities—or rather, the *appearance* of qualities—as the situation demanded. As an example, Fromm compared the nineteenth-century salesman, who really *was* reliable and respectable, with his twentieth-century counterpart, "who instills confidence because he *looks* as if he had these qualities. . . . What kind of person is behind that role does not matter and is nobody's concern." Like Fromm's marketing man, David Riesman's "other-directed" man had lost the solid core of being characteristic of his "inner-directed," nineteenth-century predecessor and had become an anxious bit of social radar, attuned to the changing nuances of the external situation, "at home everywhere and nowhere, capable of a rapid if sometimes superficial intimacy with and response to everyone." Riesman's most compelling example was the American teenager, who lacked the internal gyroscope of inner-direction that might have produced genuine standards and who was therefore at the mercy of the fashion-conscious peer group, that new arbiter of musical tastes and preferences. Radio's other-directed man was Henry Aldrich, the adolescent protagonist of "The Aldrich Family" and a youth, according to one writer, whose "chief endeavor is to find out what are the mores and then to obey them."[19]

Among Hollywood's numerous treatments of identity, few dealt with the subject as successfully as *A Double Life* (1947), which starred Ronald Colman as Anthony John, a successful actor in New York's legitimate theater whose failure to separate his "real" self from his stage persona finally makes him a murderer. The consummate "Method" actor, Tony John is actually *too* good at what he does—capable, according to the play's director, of "becoming someone else . . . completely." After several hundred performances in the role of Othello, John finds himself unable to keep the character in the play out of his personal life. Othello's jealousy and rage become his own, until he commits murder in the real world. Having, like Othello, "loved not wisely but too well," and "perplexed in the extreme," he takes his own life on the stage.

More than a clever piece of cinema, *A Double Life* offers two explanations for the identity crisis that overwhelmed not only Tony John but Americans in the 1940s. The film finds fault with John's ambition and upward mobility, the driving forces behind his original desire to be an actor—to play all those ultimately harmful roles. "I had to tear myself apart and put myself together," John explains, "again and again, and the leftover pieces are all scattered somewhere between here and a thousand one-night stands." More important is the film's central argument: roles once taken on are not so easily shed; to act out a particular role is to modify one's essence, to risk an irrevocable fusion of role and self. Applied to the national situation in the late forties, this principle begs a series of questions: What was the nation's equivalent of John's Othello? What role had the nation acted out (dropping the bomb? ignoring the plight of Europe's Jews?) that threatened to determine its future conduct?

The other basic ingredient of the midcentury problem of identity, the rootless self, was a product of the modern experience of isolation and separation from every meaningful and legitimate sort of cultural bond. Man was alone and lonely—detached, according to Schlesinger, from the "grounds of [the] civilization," estranged from what Joseph Campbell described as the mythic "vitalizing connectives" that link the individual with the community and others in it, and, like the comic-book hero Superman—whose exploits thrilled a generation of American youngsters after his introduction in 1938—a schizoid persona (Superman/Clark Kent) irrevocably exiled from the past.

Many Americans experienced the rootless self through the music of Hank Williams, who translated his own unceasing loneliness into "Lovesick Blues" (1949), "Cold, Cold Heart" (1951), and other maudlin favorites of an anxious generation. Millions more felt their identities challenged by the racial, ethnic, and class homogeneity of the burgeoning postwar suburb, typified by the 17,400 standardized, single-family dwellings constructed in Levittown, Long Island, beginning in 1947. For Shelley Cousins, the protagonist of Charles Mergendahl's novel, *It's Only Temporary* (1950), life in the new suburb of Camptown required the shedding of just those qualities of distinctiveness that might have made for a stable, individual identity. "She had been unable to fit herself into the general scheme of things, into the thousands of houses all the same, into the social life that consisted of watching children and talking about popular fiction and husbands and the price of groceries. She wanted to fit. . . . But . . . she still had that feeling of temporariness, and she still felt that she was, after all, Shelley Cousins, an individual person who might someday live an individual life."[20]

For intellectuals of the Frankfurt School, themselves uprooted and transplanted like Shelley Cousins, an important source of rootlessness was the difficulty of achieving autonomy in an anonymous "mass society." Max Horkheimer, Theodor Adorno, Paul Lazarsfeld, Leo Lowenthal, and Herbert Marcuse were the most prominent members of a group of Marxist scholars who had gathered at the University of Frankfurt in Germany. Immigrating to the United States in the 1930s after Hitler's rise to power, most of the group was reassembled at Columbia University. In the American context, the traditional emphasis of Marxist analysis on the economic exploitation of the working class gave way to a new variety of Marxism, according to which the masses were victimized and dominated not by work relations but by culture. For the Frankfurt scholars, the new agencies of capitalist domination and control were the Hollywood films, comic books, popular music, and other ingredients of the modern "culture industry," which was holding the masses in a state of unthinking passivity. As Adorno and Horkheimer wrote in 1944, "Donald Duck in the cartoons and the unfortunate in real life get their thrashing so that the audience can learn to take their own punishment." By making the self into a commodity and substituting stereotypes for authentic individuals, mass culture, according to the Frankfurt School, undermined and prevented the development of a genuine self rooted in real experiences and genuine communities.[21]

Identity emerged as a special problem in the summer of 1945, when the end of the war—and the bomb that ended it—forced millions of American men into a radical rethinking of their ties to family, community, and the world. The returning veteran was torn from the easy, accepting, one-dimensional, male camaraderie of the service and set down in the alien, heterosexual landscape of domesticity and consumerism. As veteran Al Stephenson remarks in *The Best Years of Our Lives*, "Last year it was kill Japs, this year it's make money."

The postwar longing for identity is superbly captured in Carson McCullers's play *The Member of the Wedding* (written 1948, produced 1950), set in a small Southern town in August 1945, not long after the atomic bomb had been used against Japan. McCullers's protagonist is Frankie, a twelve-year-old tomboy whose brother, Jarvis, is to be married on Sunday. Much of the dialogue involves Frankie and Berenice Sadie Brown, the family's forty-five-year old black cook. Frankie's desire is for membership—that is, identity. "The trouble with me," she explains, "is that for a long time I have been just an 'I' person. All other people can say 'we.' When Berenice says 'we' she means her lodge and church and colored people. Soldiers can say 'we' and mean the army. All people belong to a 'we' except me."

The identity that Frankie envisions is a most curious and yet representative one. One part of it—the desire to find one's identity in the new, domestic, postwar America—is expressed in Frankie's wish to be a "member of the wedding"; she fully intends to go away with Jarvis and his bride in a trio of nuptial bliss. The other part of Frankie's dream combines this domestic chimera with a version of identity framed by a postnuclear politics of the universal and the spectacular. While Berenice holds tight to the real people who are all she has, Frankie fantasizes a future of fame, celebrity, and promiscuous friendship: "Mrs. Janice Addams elected Miss United Nations in beauty contest. . . . We will know decorated aviators and New York people and movie stars. We will have thousands and thousands of friends." Having failed to appreciate that one connects with others in precise if flawed and fragmentary ways, and troubled by the bomb (in one scene she anticipates taking two baths to scrub away its fallout), Frankie projects herself into a worldwide community—a community of the whole—in which national identifications have dissolved. On the road with Jarvis and Janice, Frankie will meet "Everybody . . . We will be members of the whole world." Later, perhaps dimly aware that this supraidentity is no identity at all, Frankie says, "I wish the whole world would die."[22]

The leading midcentury interpreter of the rootless self was undoubtedly the neo-Freudian psychologist Erik Erikson, whose *Childhood and Society* (1950) provided the first widely available and explicit discussion of the problem of identity. Erikson traced the current crisis in part to long-term phenomena such as industrialization, standardization, and the development of worldwide communications—aspects of the culture of the whole—which threatened identities inherited from agrarian and feudal cultures. He also recognized the special problems of identity in the United States: elaborate processes of Americanization were essentially designed to provide each and every immigrant with a "super-identity." In addition, Erikson raised the possibility that the postwar "drive for tolerance" might be the source of considerable anxiety among certain marginal people, since "the tolerant appraisal of other identities endangers one's own." Finally, Erikson suggested that the process of identity formation could be damaged by the absence of a certain kind of freedom. To "take hold of some kind of a life," as Biff put it in Miller's *Death of a Salesman*, Americans needed to believe that they were making real choices from positions of genuine autonomy.[23]

The rootless self was a favorite theme of the film noir genre. Its protagonists were invariably required to undergo their ordeals in isolation from friends, family, community, and their own history—or, at best, to be bound to the rest of humanity by the fragile electronic signal of the telephone. In films such as *D.O.A.*, a journey into the crowded anonymity of the big city (usually Los Angeles) triggers the "mass society" experience described by the Frankfurt School. Obvious identity problems abound in these films. *Out of the Past* opens in the mountain town of Bridgeport, where the character played by Robert Mitchum has been living for three years under an assumed name (that is, without his own secure identity). In *Sunset Boulevard*, the "real" self of Joseph Gillis is regularly violated by the role he must play as companion to ex–Hollywood star Norma Desmond.

From the perspective of film noir, the rootless self was a product not only of understandable phenomena such as postwar mobility but of the unfathomable mysteries of a contingent world. This is the lesson of *Detour* (1946), a low-budget wonder featuring Tom Neal as Al Roberts, who gives up his life—his identity—as a piano player in New York City to chase after his girl, who has headed for Hollywood to grab the brass ring. Roberts follows, hitching a ride in Arizona with a fellow named Haskell, who summarily and accidentally dies. Panicked that he will be held responsible, Roberts takes Haskell's driver's license, clothes, money, and car—in effect, he adopts Haskell's identity and leaves his own behind ("If they found a dead man in the gully now, it would be me"). Though Roberts intends to return to his own identity as soon as possible, his plans for doing so are thwarted by a hitchhiker, a woman (the standard forties nemesis) who sees through Roberts's scheme and insists that he carry it through to an almost absurd conclusion in order to claim Haskell's inheritance. As the film comes out of flashback, we find Roberts (or is it Haskell?) hitchhiking back East, glum, unshaven, and defeated. He is a man without an identity: as Haskell, he is afraid to return to Hollywood, where Haskell was known and he could be revealed as a fraud; as Roberts, who is "listed as dead," he does not exist at all. Al Roberts is the displaced person of American film.

So strong were midcentury anxieties about the rootless self that even historians committed to scrupulously honest retellings of the nation's past found their narratives informed by the idea of rootlessness. Such was the case with Oscar Handlin, whose study of emigration, appropriately titled *The Uprooted* (1951), won the Pulitzer Prize for history. Writing in a florid prose that at times seemed more suited to fiction than history, Handlin described the experience of emigration in the language of postnuclear catastrophe: Europe's "whole peasant order," destroyed by an "external blow," spewed victims from the community of the village to the desperate loneliness and isolation of America's teeming cities and barren plains. Where once the house and fields and trees "had had a character and identity of their own" and "had testified to the peasant's *I*, had fixed his place in the visible universe," in America the peasant was a transient in a land of "separated men." Anticipating historian Stanley Elkins's portrait of the American black slave, Handlin described a peasant without "meaningful connections in time and space . . . cut off from his surroundings." "I made the effort," explains Handlin's immigrant in a fictional soliloquy, "I . . . wished to be myself; but could not." Compounding the immigrant's crisis of identity was a helplessness born of the anxiety of contingency; every step of the journey seemed "bound up with chance," and every success or failure "altogether fortuitous." Desperately lonely and unable to affect his condition, the immigrant—and the American of the 1940s—stumbled from crisis to crisis, "past the discontinuous obstacles of a strange world."[24]

At the most basic level, the 1940s had two solutions to the burden of anxiety. One, explored in Chapter 4, and touched upon by McCullers in *The Member of the Wedding*, was to look beyond the nation to a supranational entity that could wrench "one world" from the shabby system of nation-states that to many seemed responsible for world war, the bomb, and the murder of Europe's Jews. The other solution—more satisfying in the short run and certainly more available to the average person—was to turn inward, to search the self for the wellsprings of happiness and peace of mind.

As simple as the basic idea was, the terrain of this new, interior frontier was no less complex and no more mapped than the trans-Mississippi West of 1800. Experts differed on the contours of this invisible land, on what portions of it deserved early colonization, and even on whether the self could be expected to carry the whole burden of the quest for happiness. For Dale Carnegie and William Faulkner, the self was a reservoir of strength, capable of wresting hope and victory from the jaws of desperation. If man had grown fearful in the shadow of the bomb, counseled Faulkner, "he must teach himself that the basest of all things is to be afraid; and, teaching himself that, forget it forever, leaving no room in his workshop for anything but the old verities and truths of the heart." And if, as most everyone seemed to think, the past held only fuel for anxiety, and the future only uncertainty, the self might simply resolve to live in the present, to "shut off the future," as Carnegie put it, "as tightly as the past." Alternatively, one might reconceptualize the world as a more secure place, governed less by contingency than by the "law of averages" and other comforting scientific and mathematical formulas.[25]

Others, less sure of the self's ability to carry the day yet mindful of its new isolation, helped bring on the postwar boom in expertism by seeking the advice of specialists to supplement the frail self. Because man seemed to have lost contact with traditional and customary ways of doing things, experts appeared who could soothe the anxious, comfort the insecure, and direct the confused.

Parenting was the special focus of expertism. Parents could take comfort in the "common sense" advice of Dr. Spock, who advised bewildered mothers to think of child-rearing and child development as natural processes in which children retraced "the whole past history of mankind, physically and spiritually, step by step," and yet whose own compendium of complex instructions was testimony to the unnaturalness of bringing up baby in the twentieth century. Spock joined other experts in advocating comforting "stage" theories of child development, according to which learning was a matter of the child moving through fixed and inevitable natural stages corresponding to chronological age.[26]

The ambivalent consumerism of the culture of anxiety helps explain the public's attraction to another form of expertism, embodied in several of the most popular figures of the age, including Kate Smith and Arthur Godfrey. Smith is perhaps best remembered for her 1938 recording of "God Bless America," but Americans of the early 1940s knew her as the most popular figure in commercial radio and as the nation's premier war-bond salesperson. As sociologist Robert K. Merton discovered in his 1946 study of Smith's record-setting radio war-bond marathon in 1943, the singer's charisma and public appeal were clearly multifaceted, products of her folksy image ("Hello everybody," her radio program began, "this is Kate Smith"), her facility with emotional appeals, and her manifest patriotism. Smith's most important quality, however, was one she shared with Godfrey and the fictional Sam Clayton: sincerity. Sincerity—or the image of sincerity—allowed Smith to sell the products of her commercial sponsors and to function as part of the government's propaganda apparatus, while seeming to be untouched by the undeniable instrumentalism of it all. Her principled determination to try every product before she advertised it led *Life* to conclude that "genuine interest in good food has powered Kate's commericals with a sincerity and gusto to which listeners have responded heartily." Based on extensive audience surveys, Merton argued that Smith's audience lived in a culture of anxiety: a "climate of reciprocal distrust" in which marketplace values had infiltrated human relationships and left a "craving for reassurance, an acute need to believe, a flight into faith." "Smith," argued Merton, "has become the object of this faith. She is seen as genuine by those who seek redemption from the spurious."[27]

Put another way, it was the function of Kate Smith and her male equivalent, Arthur Godfrey, to allow a generation of skeptical Americans to make the transition to a full-fledged consumer economy without feeling too guilty, too victimized, or too anxious. Godfrey's radio career began in 1929, and in 1948 he was broadcasting an astonishing seventeen and a half hours per week, including a weekday morning show and a Monday night amateur hour called "Talent Scouts." Godfrey's own version of sincerity was based on a rich, distinctive voice, a neighborly demeanor, and an engaging spontaneity with commercial copy that included occasional humanizing gibes at sponsors. Delivering his usual spiel for Chesterfield cigarettes, for instance, Godfrey once improvised, "Now what the heck do you want to buy a pack for? Buy a carton! You smoke the things all the time—why waste time and money? Go git a week's supply and forget about it."[28]

The late forties were boom years for experts in the various fields of psychology. Many were followers of Freud, who had achieved considerable popularity in the United States in the 1920s. By 1940 American Freudians were employing ideas of the subconscious, examining irrational fears, and exploring instinctual impulses in fields as diverse as advertising, industrial relations, crime prevention, and fiction writing.

Since women were deemed especially tormented in the forties, they were among the most frequent objects of expert scrutiny, a process that in Hollywood film of the decade usually takes place in the office of a male psychoanalyst or psychiatrist, whose function it is to straighten out the wayward lass and bring us all to the "truth." Predictably, the "epistemological hero" discovers that his patient has been ignoring her essential femininity and acting too much like a man; her identity crisis solved, the case is closed (a better conclusion, one might add, than being shot in the abdomen).[29]

The expertism of the psychiatrist is highlighted in the film *The Dark Past* (1948), which features Lee J. Cobb as Dr. Andrew Collins, a psychiatrist employed by a police department where everyone is a "sort of specialist, an expert." As the film reveals, however, not all experts are equal, especially in the inward-turning forties. Where the state has failed to understand and to rehabilitate cold-blooded killer Al Walker (William Holden), Collins succeeds, locating Walker's "compulsion" in a repressed primal scene in which, acting out the Oedipus complex, he had murdered his father in order to take his father's place. Having come to terms with the source of his anxiety, Walker is pronounced "cured." A final speech by Collins shifts the reason for

criminality from the outmoded depression-era explanation of economic de-
privation to the up-to-date, classless ground of psychological contingency.
"There," he says, "with very little difference in the basic human equation,
goes any one of us—or our kids."

The limits of the state and its systems are also apparent in *The Dark Mirror*
(1946), a film in which the police, unable to discern which of two identical
twins is a murderer, call on psychologist Scott Elliott to work his magic of
the mind. On one level, the film was Hollywood's most direct treatment of
the larger problem of identity; two women look and act as one. At this level,
it is Elliott's task to demonstrate that identity does exist, that "character and
personality" differ even in twins. As Elliott discovers through his Rorschach
ink blots, one of the twins is suffering from paranoid insanity.

On another level, however, the film is a narrative that reinforces the distance between the "exterior" thirties and the "interior" forties. It opens
within a legal framework, asking the state's question, "Who is guilty of a
murder?" It closes within a psychological framework, asking the therapist's
question, "Who is suffering from an illness?" The film renders irrelevant the
categories of guilt and innocence—even of murder itself—that underpin the
legal way of understanding.

While this movement toward the psychological seems sensible enough, one
wonders about its relation to the transcendent crime of the age: the murder
of six million Jews. Applied to that atrocity, did not a therapeutic framework
reduce the question of the legal guilt or innocence of the Nazis to one of
illness? Did it not trivialize the question of illness by locating it in a national
"primal scene" (e.g., the German inflation of 1922), for which no one could
in any important sense be held responsible? And, in the vein of Collins's final
plea in *The Dark Past*, did it not transmute the question of both individual
and national guilt into a universal problem of the human condition, in effect
dissolving the responsibility of Nazi Germany by spreading responsibility
around to all humanity?

One of the principal claims of the psychological film of the forties was that
the source of anxieties, traumas, and psychoses lay in one's personal past,
buried in the psyche's unconscious and beyond the reach of ordinary memory, yet reachable—and curable—through a range of psychoanalytical techniques. This was also the argument of L. Ron Hubbard's best-seller *Dianetics*
(1950), a self-proclaimed attempt to create a "science of mind" that would
match "thoughtless" advances in the physical sciences—which had put man
on the brink of annihilation—and that would enable people to pursue the
"dynamic principle of existence": survival. According to Hubbard, humans
are essentially "good" and rational creatures, whose analytical minds or "ana-
lyzers" are (in the terms of cybernetics) "perfect computers" capable of perfect logic. Hubbard's "devil" is the "reactive mind," the source of our "insane

rages," "irrational fear," and destructive behavior, and the mental villain responsible for arthritis, asthma, high blood pressure, neuroses, repressions, and other mental and physical maladies. In the reactive mind are stored "engrams": precise recordings of those moments of "unconsciousness" when the rational mind has shut down to protect itself from anxiety, pain, and trauma. Since the reactive mind held hundreds of engrams, the average person was entirely unpredictable; the "'sanest' aberree of Tuesday," wrote Hubbard, "may be a murderer on Wednesday." Fortunately, dianetic therapy makes possible the diagnosis and removal of engrams and the emergence of a completely healthy person, called a "clear." Clears are able to deal in healthy and entirely rational ways with every facet of their being, including their troubled past.[30]

The numerous solutions offered to the problem of identity might be grouped into two categories: attaining the "true" self and attaining the "integrated" self. Advocates of the former approach were optimists who shared the faith that modern psychology had made it possible to restore humans to the real and genuine state—the true self—that had reigned before they were corrupted into a series of false personae or roles, and before the rise of the "other-directed" personality type. We must, as Liebman wrote, "become *ourselves.*" While Hannah Arendt denied the idea of a fixed self, she nonetheless called for the repudiation of any idea of the self that was based on stereotyped social roles. "Since," Arendt explained, "everyone knows well enough in his own heart that he is not identical with his function [e.g., as father, husband, or president of a business] one must play at being what one '*really is*'" (emphasis added).[31] For most postwar authorities, however, the ideal true self meant precisely the stereotyped self that the existentialists loathed. To recapture this kind of secure identity, Lundberg and Farnham called for universal application of psychotherapy to restore women and men to appropriately traditional social roles.[32] Hollywood did its part to clarify and market the old-fashioned true self in such role-conscious films as *Cheaper by the Dozen* and Dore Schary's *I Remember Mama*.

Advocates of the integrated self were more likely to recognize the limitations of the self and to suggest ways in which the isolated individual might approach identity through integration with some larger, exterior entity. The secular version of the integrated self may be observed in Schlesinger's *The Vital Center*, which, for all its advocacy of the free individual, remains committed to individualism in a "social context," and specifically, to the revitalization of voluntary, associational group activities. The religious version is typified by Thomas Merton, the Trappist monk whose *Seeds of Contemplation* posed the quest for identity as a search for the true self ("For me to be a saint means to be myself"), yet found the source of that true self in a transcendent union with God and with all people. "The only true joy on earth," wrote

Merton, "is to escape from the prison of our own self-hood . . . and enter by love into union with the Life Who dwells and sings within the essence of every creature and in the core of our own souls."[33]

Joseph Campbell's *The Hero with a Thousand Faces* offered the religion of mythology, through which man might begin to understand that underlying rites and rituals of different cultures was a bond of the human spirit. Yet Campbell was not so naive as to believe that the mere publication of a compendium of the world's myths would be helpful to anyone. Because the individual had replaced the world and the group as the repository of meaning; because older mysteries associated with planting and reaping and the like had lost their ability to stimulate the modern psyche; and because the individual's ability to get at any remaining kernel of meaning had been nullified by the separation of the human psyche into conscious and unconscious, Campbell proposed a novel solution: the modern hero would be the self, whose "hero-deed" would be that of discovering, in the exile of the self, "the Self in all. . . . Wherever the hero may wander, whatever he may do, he is ever in the presence of his own essence—for he has the perfected eye to see. There is no separateness." Campbell's hero, then, was all of us, driven to search ourselves for the divinity of man. "It is not society that is to guide and save the creative hero," wrote Campbell, "but precisely the reverse. And so every one of us shares the supreme ordeal—carries the cross of the redeemer— not in the bright moments of his tribe's great victories, but in the silences of his personal despair."[34]

In the thought of Campbell and Lewis Mumford, ideas of the self come full circle: the turn inward is virtually indistinguishable from the culture of the whole, and the self becomes largely a repository of images and values that are useful in the larger project of human integration. Mumford, a New York City writer whose books on American literature, architecture, and painting had made him one of the nation's most prominent social analysts by the 1920s, had in the forties taken on the task of imagining a universal community arising out of the morally debased Western world, which was characterized by specialization, division, and sterile mechanism. In *The Conduct of Life*, Mumford presented his ideal of the "balanced man," who existed in the area between reason and emotion, individual and group, private and public, freedom and necessity. The source of this new being, Mumford argued, was not the outer world, where man functioned primarily as a tool-using animal, but the "dream-images" lodged in the individual "unconscious." It was there, in the "inner life" of symbolization and language shared by all human beings, that one could discover the creative, expressive, and imaginative commonalities that would detoxify modern existence.[35]

In the effort to relieve their anxiety, Americans of the 1940s did not entirely abandon the realm of economics and politics, which had been their major preoccupation from the Crash of 1929 to VJ-Day in 1945. Of course, the welfare state did not wither away. And the enormous sums that Americans were beginning to invest in the military-industrial complex were a sign that rising defense expenditures would be a major source of postwar security. Gone, however, was the confidence that government legislation could work a miracle, or even that one could rest secure in one's home, knowing that the Pentagon brass were busy at work. Summarizing the conclusions of its 1948 roundtable on happiness, *Life* claimed that a similar forum, held a decade earlier, would have inevitably focused on "outer reforms," and especially on the economic system. "Today," said *Life*, "it is becoming apparent to millions that economics does not in itself hold the answers to the underlying problems of democratic society. The war and its aftermath have shaken us from that position. People are searching themselves and their societies for deeper answers than the outer world alone is able to reveal." Confirming *Life*'s analysis, many leftists either abandoned Marxism altogether for new forms of social criticism based on Freudian psychology or, like the Frankfurt scholars, explored new varieties of Marxism that focused on the individual's relationship with mass culture. Americans of the 1940s were more interested in personal survival than in social progress, more concerned with exorcising demons within than with building a new world without.[36]

Abandoning the economic and political arenas that might have served as the locus of genuine social improvements, the turn inward offered no obviously workable solution to a culture in the throes of anxiety. It was not at all clear how millions of Americans were to avail themselves of necessary psychiatric services, or even what it would mean to "cure" individuals when their anxieties were bound up with the larger world. Moreover, the fact that such experts were needed to decipher the personal past or to assist an anxious mother only affirmed the inadequacy of the self in a complex world. Advocates of the integrated self at least recognized the frailty of the self and the need to forge links between one self and another. But Schlesinger's voluntary associations hardly seemed an adequate method, and Campbell's faith in the unifying power of myth, no matter how attractive and well presented, appeared incapable of moving the great mass of Americans.

There was another position, contained within the true-self and integrated-self approaches, that bypassed the most obvious sources of anxiety, finessed the problem of identity, and ignored its own role as a source of insecurity. This was the position of freedom—the autonomous self. Advocates of the autonomous self still discussed the need for a secure identity and relief from anxiety, and they often remained committed to solving those problems through turning inward and relying on the self. But the self they proclaimed was neither the tragic, victimized, warped self of some of Hollywood's psychological epics nor the frail self perpetually in need of expert assistance or links with equally frail others.

The knight of freedom was fully autonomous, a self endowed with free will and capable of free choice. For Harry Emerson Fosdick, the autonomous self was ever-present, ready to be summoned to the task of unifying the persona: "We are not marionettes, but have the power to confront life with a personal rejoinder." For Liebman and Hubbard, the autonomous self lay intact but beneath the surface, primed for release from the childhood compulsions induced by excessive competition and from the engrams that determined one's fate. As Hubbard emphasized, humans are not conditioned in a Pavlovian sense; thus, at no point are they ultimately stripped of free will. Somehow, the autonomous self was to wrest security from anxiety, and identity from role confusion. Indeed, the guru of identity, Erik Erikson, claimed that American identity depended on the individual's belief that he had "autonomous choice," that "the next step is up to him."[37]

Addressing the problem of happiness, *Life's* roundtable arrived at the same conclusion, subsuming such problems as the conflict between capital and labor and the origins of moral law under the vague banner of a Jeffersonian freedom. The roundtable's "final solution" to the nation's unhappiness took the form of the pledge of the American Heritage Foundation: "I am an American, a free American: free to speak without fear; free to worship God in my own way; free to stand for what I think right; free to oppose what I believe wrong; free to choose those who govern my country. This heritage of Freedom I pledge to uphold for myself and all mankind."[38]

six

Freedom Train

In the spring of 1948, thousands of schoolchildren found themselves on yet another field trip, this one to the railroad station to file through five sleek cars hauled by a diesel locomotive named "Spirit of 1776." The "Freedom Train," as the attraction was called, signaled the elevation of "freedom" to a position of prominence in the intellectual and cultural life of the 1940s.

To be sure, the word had been heard before in the decade, most significantly, perhaps, in *The Four Freedoms for Which We Fight*, a series of Norman Rockwell paintings printed in the *Saturday Evening Post* in early 1943. Arguably the most popular paintings in the history of American art, they presented the four freedoms—*Freedom of Speech, Freedom of Worship, Freedom from Fear*, and *Freedom from Want*—as secure possessions embedded in family and community and only marginally threatened from abroad by the existence of war; these freedoms were sure to blossom in full glory at the conflict's conclusion.

The freedom that emerged in the late 1940s was not entirely unlike Rockwell's version. Although Soviet communism had replaced German fascism and Japanese perfidy as the great enemy of the American people, the new idea of freedom was partly inspired, like the old one, by the menace of an exterior "other"; used this way, the word *freedom* evoked cold war anticommunism. What was missing, however, was the expectation of victory; the new enemy could only be held at arm's length—"contained," as George Kennan put it, through a vigil that proffered no easy ending, perhaps no ending at all. Gone, too, was Rockwell's confidence that freedom was a quality Americans possessed in abundance, if only the war could be got out of the way.

In the interval between Rockwell's *Four Freedoms* and the Freedom Train, something had happened to dispel that confidence. An example: The fear that Rockwell painted in *Freedom from Fear* was certainly real enough—two children are being tucked into one small bed under a pitched roof by their anxious father who, spectacles in hand, holds a newspaper whose headlines read "Bombings Ki . . . / Horror Hit. . . ." But it was, as that menacing roof seemed to suggest, and Stephen Vincent Benét's accompanying essay said, essentially a physical fear of exterior origin—"the fear of unprovoked attack and ghastly death for himself and for his children because of the greed and power of willful and evil men and deluded nations"—fear amenable to the military and political solutions that would produce a new set of more soothing headlines.[1]

As we have seen, postwar fear was not of the sort that could be so easily read into a comforting narrative with a reasonable ending. Nor, more importantly, was it entirely a fear of the "other." The new fear was not of "evil men" (the Nazis), who could, after all, be defeated and punished, nor of "deluded nations" (Germany and Japan), which could be stripped of the instruments of power and, through occupation, introduced to a new set of values. The new fear (or rather, anxiety, in a common distinction of the time) was that modern Americans—as well as Germans and Russians—had somehow fashioned for themselves a straitjacket of institutions and values that contained and thwarted the most basic desires for freedom of action and freedom of will. The new fear was the fear of determinism.

Determinism's foundations were gradually revealed as the argument against determinism was worked out. Science and technology, reason and the intellect, the seeming arbitrariness of history, economic, political, and social institutions and bureaucracies, systems of ideology, communication, and discourse, mass culture, an unremitting contingency—each, by one authority or another, was held responsible for man's declining sense of efficacy. A cultural rejoinder was gradually formulated and expressed. At its center, summarized by the word *freedom*, was a constellation of ideas to restore agency or, at least, to experiment with modes of acting and being that seemed to promise separation from the frameworks of determinism.

Repelled by the cold tyranny of reason, one group of Americans explored ways in which man's nonrational, intuitive, imaginative, and emotional qualities might be successfully integrated into intellectual and social life. Another group experimented with freedom as the purposeful introduction of elements of contingency and repetition; they found their efforts applauded by elitist advocates of an artistic avant-garde.

Others, including those leaders of opinion known as the "New York intellectuals," spent the decade negotiating the distance between the ideological, Marxist politics of the 1930s and a new, more conservative, and avowedly nonideological "vital center" in which freedom reigned as the value around which all right-thinking people could rally. In their search for a new framework of values anchored in the concept of freedom, the New York intellectuals gradually moved away from the frame of politics, where the most important social experimentation of the 1930s had taken place, and toward pure culture—pristine in its isolation from failed ideologies. Like most Americans, the leaders of this intellectual migration really believed that freedom and determinism were locked in mortal struggle. But their advocacy of freedom was more than a simple response to bureaucracy, technology, Soviet communism, or other "objective" sources of nonfreedom. It was also the result of a decade-long quest for a new way of understanding the world and framing its problems.

While Rockwell had posited a natural order of freedom that was ensconced in the nation's most basic institutions and ready to be released at war's end, postwar Americans in search of such freedom more often than not found themselves up against unyielding frameworks of fatalism and determinism. This was the message of novelist Nelson Algren, whose characters inevitably prove unable to shape their lives. In *The Man with the Golden Arm*, Frankie's fate is to spend his life with Sophie, whom he does not love, and apart from Molly, whom he does. This tragedy has two sources. One, a weakness of will, involves Frankie's past failure to defend Molly and escort her home after she was struck by Sophie during a quarrel. "You wanted to go home with me," Molly remembers. "It was how I wanted it too—things would have been better for me since then if you'd done like you felt instead of like other people told you you got to." The other, an automobile accident that results in Sophie's physical paralysis, and in a guilt that paralyzes Frankie just as completely, is in a bizarre way related to the atomic blasts "on the other side of the world." That is, the victim of too many drinks—Antek's A-Bomb Specials—Frankie plows his Chrysler into a streetlight. Lying on his bed trying to sort out his life, the best Frankie can do is understand his fate as the product of a series of contingencies that have conspired to deny him genuine freedom of action ("If there had been no war at all, if he hadn't volunteered, if there had been no accident, if there hadn't been this and there hadn't been that, then everything would certainly have turned out a lot better for Frankie").[2]

Determinism appeared early in the decade in the time-travel literature of science fiction, whose very function was to depict people freely choosing an environment significantly different from the natural one. While in the 1930s time-travel stories were tales of wonder featuring the exploration of past and future, by the forties such transcendent experiences were likely to result in frustration. One time traveler, advised against returning from the future at the precise moment of departure, finds himself trapped in an endlessly repeating loop of future and past (a fantasy perhaps related to the self-adjusting servo-mechanisms developed during the war and put into service in factories late in the decade). Another goes into the future only to discover his own unavoidable death at the battle of Dunkirk. Alfred Bester's "The Push of a Finger" (1942) features a computer's prediction of the end of the world. Frantic efforts to recast the future by preventing a meeting of two persons whose contact eventually produces the catastrophe only helps to usher in humanity's final moments.[3]

Others, equally convinced of the utter absence of freedom, used that conviction as the starting point for a reformism based on the "unfreedom" of behavioral modification. The utopian optimism of B. F Skinner's *Walden Two* issued, paradoxically, from the Harvard psychologist's pessimism regarding man's agency. Denying the existence of freedom and free will, Skinner argued for the use of techniques of behavioral modification that would provide the "controlled" a comfortable life with a "feeling of freedom."[4] Although few ventured as far as Skinner in denying freedom a role in human life, the mere fact of *Walden Two*'s publication, not to mention the attention it received in the popular press, reveals the potency of the determinist argument in post–World War II America.

Through the 1940s, both the high rationality of science and the high science of reason remained positive forces for most Americans. The decade's dramatic achievements—including sulfadiazine (1940), the introduction of DDT in the war against insect pests (1943), streptomycin (1944), the first automatic, general-purpose digital computer (1944), automatic pinsetting machines for bowling (1946), the Polaroid Land camera (1947), the transistor (1948), cortisone (1949), the Xerox copier (1950), and, of course, the development of the atomic bomb—encouraged the belief that smart men in white coats were astride a cornucopia of health, wealth, happiness, and security. Consumers encountered the prestige of science in advertisements that billed Gold Seal vermouth as "an achievement in wine science," claimed that "medical authorities recognize Philip Morris," and trumpeted U.S. Rubber for "serving through science to build a better world." Criminology, too, became increasingly rationalized as youngsters pored over Dick Tracy's "Crimestopper's Textbook," police departments installed laboratories for ballistics identification, serology, and toxicology, Batman (1939) prepared himself for a life of crime fighting by becoming a master scientist, and psychiatrists matched their Freudian reason against the criminal's subconscious mind.[5]

From Saarinen's gleaming St. Louis Arch to the homogenized Levittowns, from the Pentagon to the United Nations building, the most dramatic building projects of the age were spectacles of pure reason, products of investment in mathematics and organization. Similarly, representative modernist composers Milton Babbitt and Walter Piston (winner of a Pulitzer Prize in 1948) were given to rational, disciplined, systematic, "scientific" modes of composition that, like the architectural projects mentioned above, purported to divorce the product from history, politics, and society. The allure of science and technology touched even rural America: in the summer of 1945 Laura Rew Pickett, living in a house without electricity, journeyed to the grounds of the Chautauqua Institute in western New York for Grange Day, and she "enjoyed it fine. saw Goodrich Rubber exhibit, heard and saw pictures of solar homes. I saw a new recording machine demonstration on stage of Amphitheatre." Just weeks later, apparently taken with the spectacle of modernization, Pickett wrote: "The Electric Men came to wire the house. We had lights at night." Her enthusiasm was echoed at the highest level of officialdom, where in 1945 Vannevar Bush, director of the Office of Scientific Research and Development and Roosevelt's foremost science policy adviser, offered a spirited defense of science as an "endless frontier" whose development was as essential to national greatness in the twentieth century as the free land of the West had been in the nineteenth.[6]

Yet there were other voices, concerned about the consequences of unfettered and poorly focused science. Only the most astute of society's critics, such as essayist Dwight Macdonald, were able to see terror bombing, the development and use of the atomic bomb, and the Nazi concentration camps as related products of Western societies that were increasingly held hostage to bureaucratized, systematized, impersonal, irresponsible, and ultimately inhuman science. A more typical complaint was a version of the "social lag" theories popularized in the 1920s, which held that problems were often a result of the application of a process (e.g., urbanization or industrialization) that had outrun efforts at amelioration. One solution was to apply more science, not less, but only in areas where science could help redress the temporary imbalance. In the forties, this idea led to scientific study of human feelings and conduct in the hope that knowledge of human anxieties and frustrations would provide the social tools necessary to prevent war and keep science from producing weapons of destruction and instruments of genocide. Others saw the scientific mind-set as itself the problem and either advocated incorporating instruction on human values into the science curriculum or, like philosopher F. S. C. Northrop, called for more widespread application of morality and religion as a way to control "the ethically neutral instruments of scientific technology so that they are used for good rather than evil ends."[7]

The much more radical suggestion that science be controlled or somehow put on hold until human moral capacities had reached a level equal to the hazards involved, was enough to send defenders of science into spasms of concern. Acknowledging such proposals in its 1950 retrospective on the half-century, *Time* likened modern scientific and technological civilization to an "airplane in flight, supported by its forward motion. It cannot stop without falling." Thus, the solution to the problem of the earth's limited natural resources was not to curtail science but to give it free rein to "provide ample substitutes."[8]

While much of the debate over the merits of science swirled around the atomic bomb, the debate over another invention of the forties—the computer—revealed deep-seated anxieties about the survival of the human mind. Indeed, some of the darkest moments in early-1950s science fiction envisioned a self-contained, closed society in which computers had dispensed with love, imagination, creativity, and free will; humans had become machines. Press coverage of the sophisticated calculators and the earliest computers usually highlighted the machines' weaknesses and foibles. Computer stories made a special point of distinguishing between the new mechanical marvels and human thought. "Although it's easy to think of these giant pieces of machinery as 'mechanical brains' and 'electronic brains,'" reported *Popular Mechanics*, "they are purely robots and not in any sense independent thinkers. They don't formulate problems themselves."[9]

The ultimate concern of this discourse on cybernetics—the relationship between humans and machines—was whether the mind was capable of developing and producing its own superior replacement, a machine so perfect as to render its inventor superfluous. The answer—by no means offered in complete confidence—was that humans were distinguished from machines by certain, well, "human" qualities, qualities of creativity, independence, unpredictability, and moral purpose that put humans in a realm wholly separate from any machine. In a word, humans were free.

Reflected in the problem of cybernetics was a central anxiety of the age: that people had become trapped by a cold, machinelike rationality that left no room for moral sensibilities. This was the theme of "The Responsibility of Peoples" (1945), Macdonald's extraordinary effort to understand the Holocaust. In the early reports of the atrocities committed against the Jews, Macdonald found "rationality and system gone mad; the discoveries of science, the refinements of modern mass organization applied to the murder of non-combatants on a scale unknown since Genghis Khan." Based on the techniques of mass production, Nazi methods were a "sinister parody of Victorian illusions about scientific method." While other societies and peoples—including the English mill-owners of the nineteenth century—had demonstrated disregard for human life, Macdonald found the Holocaust unique. "The Nazis have not *disregarded* human life. They have, on the contrary, paid close attention to it. They have taken it for the pure, disinterested pleasure of taking it."[10]

While few Americans read Macdonald's essay, thousands were exposed to a critique of élitist rationality—albeit cleansed of its role in the Holocaust—in the film *Rope* (1948), directed by Alfred Hitchcock. The film opens in a New York City penthouse, where Brandon (John Dall) and Phillip (Farley

126

Granger), Harvard College students, are strangling their friend and peer, David Kentley (Dick Hogan). They place the dead body in a large wooden box in the living room, then use the box as a serving table for that evening's cocktail and dinner party, whose guests include the victim's father and girl-friend and Rupert Cadell (Jimmy Stewart), their prep school mentor. The murderers have adopted Cadell's rationalist, elitist, and Nietzschean ethics. Their claim is that as cultural and intellectual superiors, they are unfettered by traditional morality, by concepts of right and wrong, good and evil. They kill in part to feel "alive—truly and wonderfully alive," as Brandon explains to his more reluctant partner, but also out of a sense of rational, scientific perfectionism. They commit murder for "the experiment of committing it," as well as to demonstrate their superiority. The only crime, claims Brandon, is "making a mistake—because it's being ordinary." And the greatest mis-take—because it would suggest ordinariness and would result in detection—is to have and reveal fear, anxiety, and other emotions.

Using his rational faculties—significantly, the very ones that Brandon and Phillip have parlayed into a vicious killing—Rupert penetrates the scheme, finds the body, and denounces the perpetrators. When Brandon explains that the crime is a concrete demonstration of Rupert's own philosophy, Rupert both denies his complicity ("You've tried to twist [my words] into a cold, logical excuse for your ugly murder") and recants, dropping his rational de-meanor for a display of emotion and a tone of moral outrage; he describes the victim as a "human being" who "could live and love as you never could." Phillip, Brandon, and, until that last scene, Rupert have somehow lost those qualities of sentiment and feeling that stand between rational man and moral chaos.

The battle against the tyranny of reason affected virtually every sphere of cultural and intellectual life in the forties. Liberation from the rational was to be accomplished through the soft, nonrational, neglected side of the per-sona. As the decade wore on, writers celebrated the intuitive, emotional, "human" elements of the personality that seemed to issue from some different source than the purely rational mind. Among works of nonfiction, Catherine Drinker Bowen's *Yankee from Olympus* (1944), a biography of Supreme Court Justice Oliver Wendell Holmes, exemplifies the trend. Bowen presents Holmes as a brilliant rationalist, whose piercing and mechanical genius trou-bled even his father: "His son was quick; there was no denying it. Like light-ning his mind penetrated to the meaning of a subject, like lightning reduced it to manageable terms. But the terms themselves were cold, ruthless, intel-lectual." Holmes's avoidance of "the loose ends of sentiment, altruism," Bowen argues, put him on "a path that can lead very far from the heart, far from friendship and sympathy with one's fellow man."[11]

Although many science fiction writers continued to applaud the rational or, like Robert Heinlein, to call for the hegemony of a scientific elite, George

R. Stewart's postnuclear novel *Earth Abides* takes a different approach. As the book opens, protagonist Isherwood Williams personifies the rationalist position. Not only is he a scientist, but his first impulse in the postcatastrophic world is that of the removed observer, untouched by the trauma of genocide and even a bit thrilled by the prospect of studying a world without people. Gradually, Ish develops an emotional life, committing himself to others and coming to appreciate the benefits of living "on easy and friendly terms with people"—precisely the kinds of values that Brandon and Phillip did not possess.[12]

In the theater, actors were beginning to employ a new technique designed to allow them to feel and express emotions. "Method" acting was pioneered in turn-of-the-century Moscow by Konstantin Stanislavsky and popularized in the United States in the late 1930s by Lee Strasberg and his Group Theater and, in the late 1940s, by the Actor's Studio. Stanislavsky did not dismiss the rational mind as an acting tool—indeed, he prescribed a combination of emotion and intellect and emphasized the necessity of engaging the entire human being in the acting process. Nonetheless, the Method focused on ways of getting actors to express "real" emotions, whether by imagining emotion in some creative way or by vividly remembering some emotion experienced in the past. Actors able to express emotions "more or less 'real'" could in turn reach out to spectators who themselves had rich emotional histories. On the American stage, the Method was first applied to the plays of Clifford Odets, Arthur Miller, and Tennessee Williams. The first Method classes at the Actor's Studio were offered in 1947 and included Marlon Brando, Montgomery Clift, John Forsythe, and Mildred Dunnock.[13]

Because of the newfound interest in the emotional, authors whose work disregarded this side of the human being often became the objects of criticism. While the understated, unemotional, naturalistic tone of John Hersey's *Hiroshima* struck most reviewers as appropriate and justified, Dwight Macdonald assailed the book for its lack of "feelings of any intensity. . . . The 'little people' of Hiroshima whose suffering Hersey records in antiseptic *New Yorker* prose might just as well be white mice, for all the pity, horror, or indignation the reader—or at least this reader—is made to feel for them."[14]

A similar reaction greeted the publication of the Kinsey Report (1948 and 1953). Readers were upset that Alfred Kinsey, a biologist, had described human beings using statistical techniques deemed more appropriate to woodchucks, zebras, or insects. Kinsey came to be perceived as a real-life version of Hitchcock's Brandon: the ultrarational scientist whose facts, figures, and charts on sexual "outlets" neglected moral questions and bypassed the emotional content of the sexual experience. "Is the love of man and woman," *Reader's Digest* inquired, "merely an animal function," as the "cold, detached, scientific surveys" seemed to suggest? Or, as the *Saturday Evening Post* humorously put it, "love conquers all, excepting only the odds."[15]

The emotions were also used to highlight the postwar tension between family and career. Take, for example, the popular film treatments of the life of singer Al Jolson—*The Jolson Story* (1946) and *Jolson Sings Again* (1949)—starring Jolson himself. The Jolson films were immigrant success stories that traced the rise of Asa Yoelson to fame, glory, and a new, Americanized name. As Jolson discovers, one achieves success in the public sphere only by jeopardizing the private life of home and family. In trying to resolve this conflict, the Jolson films were arguably engaged in reconciling the publicness of life during World War II with the private tenor of postwar America. In doing so, the private Jolson—the part of him that longed for the close, personal relationships that his career made so difficult—is a figure of emotion who uses the blackface of minstrelsy to express a range of feelings often denied to urban whites or to those in the hunt for success. *Jolson Sings Again* offers a contrast between an emotional Jolson with "heart" and Bing Crosby, the easygoing, intimate, but unemotional, microphone-amplified crooner who was his real-life successor.[16]

The forties struggle between the rational and intuitive sides of the persona was also waged in the Hollywood musicals, which reached a peak of popularity in the late 1930s and 1940s. To some extent, the genre's message was encoded in its very structure, which alternated scenes of narrative realism with song-and-dance fantasies. As film critic Martin Sutton has argued, this sequencing can be interpreted in the terms of Freudian psychology: the plot sequences take the part of the "superego" (the socially derived conscience, what we are supposed to do, the voice of reason), and the dance numbers represent the stubborn and disobedient "id" (the source of instinctual energy and the emotions). Hence, the musical's central argument is that "dreams can be realised, but only within the framework of accepted values." The superego-id dichotomy can be seen in the romantic couples featured in virtually all such films: one half of the couple represents "rational cognitive thought" (in psychology, the reality principle), and the other half stands for freedom, impulse, and spontaneity (the pleasure principle).

As film scholar Jane Feuer explains, the widespread appeal of the Hollywood musical was a product of these dualisms and of the "vision of human liberation" they seemed to offer. For Feuer, however, that vision, like the musical itself, was a fraud; the freedom postulated by the musical in its musical interludes was a spurious one, the result of a series of tricks played on the naive spectator. While Hollywood musicals appeared to idealize community, they were in fact a mass-produced art that contributed to the ongoing separation of performer and audience. The aura of spontaneity and freedom that characterized Fred Astaire's dancing in *Holiday Inn* (1942), or Gene Kelly's in *Living in a Big Way* (1950), was illusory, a cloak for an underlying orchestration of mechanical and technical expertise. In some films, these efforts to deny the role of expertise, professionalism, and preparation led to scenes, often featuring Judy Garland, in which the dancing seemed amateurish. The intent, and consequence, of these obfuscations was to deprive the spectator of just the sort of knowledge necessary to genuine freedom. By preventing the audience from understanding that a Hollywood spectacle is an industrial product with bosses and its own labor force, the musical became a kind of unofficial social propaganda designed to appropriate the realm of freedom.[17]

In contrast, the extraordinarily popular films of Frank Capra were important efforts to understand the forces threatening and circumscribing freedom and to delineate the few resources remaining to the individual determined to experience it. According to film scholar Raymond Carney, Capra's films locate their protagonists in increasingly oppressive worlds in which systems of all kinds—political, technological, informational, institutional, and discursive—frustrate, negate, commodify, and destroy what remains of the free self. While early films such as *Meet John Doe* place freedom's adversaries largely in the institutional, technological, and bureaucratic settings of the public sphere, by mid-decade Capra's protagonists inhabit a world in which the systems of repression have been internalized: in *It's a Wonderful Life*, George Bailey's adversary is just another side of George Bailey. With *State of the Union* (1948), even this internal struggle has been largely dissolved; Grant Matthews (Spencer Tracy) agrees to be merchandised in return for the nomination of his political party, his dreams consigned to one scene of purely symbolic significance: he flaunts the pathetic remains of his free self, appropriately, in an airplane, far removed from the reality that oppresses him.[18]

Capra films reveal not only the ingredients of determinism but the varieties of freedom with which forties Americans fought it. For Capra, freedom involves eccentricity, desire, imagination, and a certain distance from normality, whether the social normality of George Bailey's Bedford Falls or the statistical, social-scientific normality of Kinsey's charts on sexual behavior. His freedom is not so different from the imaginative, adventurous, even manic, freedom that post–Great Depression high school youth articulated in their school yearbooks: they fancied themselves living at Sun Valley, searching for the fountain of youth, test-driving automobiles, piloting planes, mining gold in California, or parachuting from the Washington Monument. Capra's freedom is to be found and nurtured in private spaces, and it is associated with an extreme emotionality whose purpose is to confirm that qualities such as desire and imagination are real and important alternatives to being a banker (George Bailey) or to selling one's soul for political gain (Grant Matthews)—that is, to the kinds of choices that are usually presented as "real." Just as Hitchcock concluded *Rope* with a highly emotional speech (delivered, one should note, by Stewart, Capra's favorite actor) designed to disparage cold reason and validate a humanistic ethics, Capra's films frequently contained emotional episodes and concluded with wildly emotional displays. To bring off such scenes, Capra relied on a stable of actors—including Stewart, Barbara Stanwyck, and Gary Cooper—who were capable of delineating the tortured, emotional states the desperate situations of their characters required.[19]

And yet, while granting the liberating possibilities of expressing emotion in the hyper-rationalist atmosphere of the forties, one should also appreciate why many Americans were determined to keep their emotions under wraps. Take, for example, Hersey's *Hiroshima*. While critics like Dwight Macdonald found the book lacking in emotional depth, for most Americans it was a powerful reading experience—perhaps all they could absorb at that point in history, when knowing the full extent of the tragedy might well have required a certain shutting down of the emotions. Something similar can be observed in the fiction of Raymond Chandler, whose stories feature the affectless, unemotional Philip Marlowe. Marlowe is "hard-boiled" because he must be. In the contingent universe of 1940s Los Angeles, Marlowe's survival depends on remaining cool and somewhat detached so that he can negotiate the never-ending encounters with trigger-happy crooks and cops. In Chandler's story "Red Wind," the metaphor of a desert wind heightens every feeling and emotion: "It was one of those hot dry Santa Anas that come down through the mountain passes and curl your hair and make your nerves jump and your skin itch. On nights like that every booze party ends in a fight. Meek little wives feel the edge of the carving knife and study their husbands' necks. Anything can happen." While Marlowe has integrity and moral scruples, he survives because he never allows the emotions—whether fear, or love, or anger—to entirely displace his rational faculties. In the emotional maelstrom of the forties, Marlowe's relationship with detective work is the necessarily dispassionate one described in the title of one of Chandler's best-known stories: "Trouble Is My Business."[20]

The emotions were dangerous for another reason, as revealed in Arthur M. Schlesinger, Jr.'s *The Vital Center*. Writing at the peak of anticommunist hysteria in the late 1940s, Schlesinger contrasted the highly emotional substance of totalitarianism with the failure of democracy to "generate a living emotional content" that would satisfy the deep yearnings of modern people for a system of belief, a "fighting faith," capable of dispelling their anxieties. Yet Schlesinger did not explain how the anxious, neurotic victims of modernization were to be delivered from their insecurities without exposing the great and dangerous mass of them to a potentially destructive emotionalism; he could envision no safe way to integrate emotion into American political life. Rather than risk investing democracy with genuine emotional content, Schlesinger espoused a feeble system of voluntary associations that would "supply outlets for the variegated emotions of man" and in the process "siphon off emotions" that might be dangerous. This solution actually treated emotion more like a mental illness, for which Schlesinger's associations were a form of therapy.[21]

The antirational, antiscientific, antideterminist frame of mind responsible for the surge of interest in the emotions could be observed in the sphere of culture, where a self-conscious avant-garde of authors, literary critics, composers, musicians, architects, and artists explored the terrain of freedom. These explorations are usually labeled "modernism," a term that implicitly links the modernists of the 1940s with the generation of cultural critics who peopled Greenwich Village in the 1910s and the cafés of Paris in the decade after World War I. Most of those who have written about modernism in the 1940s emphasize how removed its practitioners were from the cares and concerns of ordinary people and from the products of mass culture—television, the movies, comic books—that were the stuff of everyday life. While this was obviously true in one sense—housewives were not throwing paint at huge canvases in Manhattan lofts—in another sense it misses the point: that the modernist avant-garde was articulating ideas and concerns felt by millions of people who were not, and could not be, engaged in creative and expressive activities.

Thus, the modernism of the 1940s should be seen not simply as a rejection of, or rebellion against, a dominant culture of affluence and conformity, though this was part of its sensibility. Modernism must also be understood as a more focused, more intense, and more direct investigation and articulation of the central anxieties and concerns of the age than was available in the mass media. Convinced that history was something other than a vessel for a comfortable and predictable progress, that humankind was virtually helpless before a contingent universe, and that political reformism of the New Deal variety had failed to produce a just and moral society, modernists in fields as disparate as architecture and literary criticism adopted similar strategies to describe and explain the modern world. Increasingly, they divorced their work from the historical, social, and cultural contexts that had reflected the old confidence in progress and instead produced buildings and works of art that seemed to exist beyond the familiar referents or signs that had traditionally clarified meaning and generated a feeling of security. The new frames of reference were individual, personal, introspective, idiosyncratic, and therefore ambiguous—evidence, to be sure, of the society's commitment to creative freedom, but signs, too, of a world coming apart.[22]

This exploration was well under way in December 1939, when a black saxophonist, Charlie Parker, learned to play a new kind of jazz that the next decade would know as bebop. As Parker recalled, "Now I'd been getting bored with the stereotyped changes that were being used all the time and I kept thinking there's bound to be something else. I could hear it sometimes but I couldn't play it. Well, that night I found that by using the higher intervals of a chord as a melody line and backing them with appropriately related changes I could play the thing I'd been hearing. I came alive." The big band leaders, whose authority Parker's new music threatened, were not so elated; bebop, bemoaned Tommy Dorsey, "has set music back twenty years."[23]

By the mid-1940s, Parker, trumpet player Dizzy Gillespie, drummer Max Roach, and dozens of other, mostly black musicians were playing the fast, complex, and spontaneous music by then often known simply as bop. Against the insistent 4/4 beat, predictable phrasing, and "arranged improvisation" of the big swing bands, which were then at the peak of their popularity, the smaller bop groups featured an improvised and irregular phrasing, solos that opened with mere fragments of melody, and a rhythm punctuated by irregular snare and bass drum accents or "bombs" that emphasized the music's flight from determinism and its debt to the contingent. Bop musicians also typically remained distanced from their club audiences, a posture that emphasized their refusal to conform to public expectations (to be, in David Riesman's term, "other-directed").[24]

The search for freedom in the rationalized universe of the forties was also present in the work of sculptor Alexander Calder, whose mobiles were as much a sign of the culture as Parker's rhythms. Like Parker's performances, Calder's compositions were not uncontrolled, but the control they managed depended upon the perception, at least, of disorder, disparity (in the size, weight, and color of the materials that went into them), and what Calder called "apparent accident to regularity." The playful and spontaneous qualities in Calder's work had considerable delight for Sartre, who likened a Calder mobile to "a little local merry-making" and applauded the artist for the introduction of contingency. As Sartre wrote in the catalog for Calder's 1946 Paris exhibition, "It is the time of day, the sunshine, the heat, the wind which will determine each individual dance. Thus, the object [the mobile] remains always midway between the slavishness of the statue and the independence of natural occurrences; each of its evolutions is an inspiration of the moment; one distinguishes in it the theme composed by its author, but it embroiders on that a thousand personal variations; it is a little jazz tune, unique and ephemeral, like the sky, like the morning; if you have missed it, you have lost it forever.[25]

Calder's efforts to balance agency with contingency had their dance counterpart in the work of Merce Cunningham, possibly the most innovative choreographer of the twentieth century. Cunningham studied modern dance at Mills College and Bennington School of the Dance. During the 1940s he worked for the Martha Graham company and, in 1944, began a series of collaborations with composer John Cage. He established his own dance company in 1953. Cunningham was deeply committed to freeing dance from the authority of any particular style, from the authority of narrative (that is, he

133

believed dance need not—indeed, should not—tell a story), and from narrative's handmaidens, music and meter. In the absence of music, the dancers would turn inward, creating the dance by contacting desires of the body. Cunningham also challenged the authority of the stage, allowing dancers to decide where they would move and decentering action so that no one place on the stage could be seen as primary. Like Calder, whose mobiles transcended the will of their creator by responding to the currents of air and the play of light, Cunningham sought to free himself from the agency of the choreographer—that is, from his own individual practices—by invoking a host of universal values. To do so, he employed the mechanism of chance, literally tossing pennies to determine movements and directions in compositions such as *Sixteen Dances for Soloist and Company of Three* (1951).[26]

Cage came to the techniques of chance at about the same time, joining not only Calder and Cunningham but fellow composer LaMonte Young and poet Charles Olson. Cage's *Imaginary Landscape No. 4* (1951) made music from twelve radios; another piece was performed for just as long as it took a bird, released into the room, to find an open window. For Cage as for Cunningham, the purpose of such devices was to free the composition from the agency of the composer and, beyond that, to put the individual in the proper role of object (rather than subject), adapting to the surrounding people and things.[27]

These experiments with indeterminacy were for Cage only part of a larger effort to transcend confining Western standards and traditions. Born in Los Angeles in 1912, Cage had been composing for a decade when he came to prominence in 1943 with a percussion concert at New York City's Museum of Modern Art, sensitively described by *Life* as "banging one object with another." This assessment held a kernel of truth, for Cage had turned to rhythm in an effort to free music from its traditional reliance on the manipulation of certain agreed-upon sounds into melodies (or even twelve-tone rows) that could then be understood as part of a rational, "discursive language of argument." Using chance, silence, and repetition within a structure based on durations rather than harmonics, Cage sought to disrupt and question accepted ideas of time; he hoped to divorce music from the linear structures (those with a beginning, a middle, and an end) that implied and reinforced Western notions of science, progress, rationality, and productivity. Spurning traditional harmonic structures as a form of domination consistent with Western materialism, Cage turned to the Oriental rhythmic structure as a means of bringing together even elements that "cannot and ought not to be agreed upon" (what he called "Freedom elements"). The overall goal was a noncoercive, musical equivalent of "one world"—a musical structure that was inclusive rather than exclusive, a rubric for a full-blown cultural pluralism. Freedom of expression was, as he explained in a lecture delivered at Black Mountain College in the summer of 1948, a matter of considerable importance. "In life, we would not be pleased if all of us dressed alike. Even a single individual enjoys dressing differently from one day to another. Likewise in poetry, differences of languages are not only admirable but refreshing. We feel imposed upon by G.I. clothing, Baltimore [row] housing, and we would not like poetry in standard English or Esperanto. In the area of material, we need and are enlivened by differentiation. I would say, therefore, we cannot and ought not agree on matters of material."[28]

Painting was no doubt the postwar era's most active arena of cultural opposition, for it was the locus of abstract expressionism, a movement whose participants, despite their diverse styles and approaches to the medium, were united in defiance of authority. This was not merely a defiance of the conventions of painting, although the wall-size canvases of Clyfford Still, Ad Reinhardt, Mark Rothko, Barnett Newman, Robert Motherwell, Jackson Pollock, and others helped free the work of art from the easel and frame, and from being understood as a domestic object to be hung above the couch. ("The large format," recalled Motherwell, "at one blow destroyed the century-long tendency of the French to domesticate modern painting, to make it intimate.") Even this simple innovation produced a new relationship between artist and spectator and suggested a larger field of resistance. "To be stopped by a frame's edge," explained Still, "was intolerable, a Euclidean prison, it had to be annihilated, its authoritarian implications repudiated without dissolving one's integrity and ideas in material and mannerism."[29]

The prison from which Still and others sought release was the prison of culture and history. "We are freeing ourselves," wrote Newman, "of the impediments of memory, association, nostalgia, legend, myth, or what have you, that have been the devices of Western European painting." Still's Euclidean prison, its geometry representative of a dependable, scientific, and progressive order at work in the universe, gave way to the seeming randomness of Pollock's "drip" paintings (1947–50), achieved without discernible pattern or a single straight line. Against the authority of the conscious mind—of the rational side of the psyche—Pollock, Willem de Kooning, William Baziotes, and others followed the surrealists in exploring ways of tapping the unconscious, perhaps, as Newman claimed, in search of "the absolute emotions." Pollock, in particular, piqued the public's curiosity with his efforts to bypass psychic censorship by pouring and dripping paint while in a self-imposed state of "physiological automatism."[30]

By dispensing with the familiar objects or symbols that had characterized the work of Edward Hopper and others working within the realist conventions of the 1930s, the abstract expressionists removed their work from the narrative tradition, denying art a storytelling function—denying even that there was a story out there to be told. Pollock eliminated another set of referents by dropping the names—*Night Dancer* (1944), *There Were Seven in Eight* (1945), and so on—that in mid-decade had lent his work some objective meaning, in favor of a less revealing system of numbers and dates—*Number 8, 1949* (1949), *Number 2* (1951). By the same logic, Still removed his paintings from the New York City gallery of Betty Parsons in 1948 because unauthorized titles assigned to the works gave the impression that the paintings referred to something beyond the canvas itself. Still and Pollock were among those whose paintings upset the comfortable and familiar relationship of ground and subject. Unlike works of representation, in which the artist might offer a rural landscape as the context for a farmhouse or a picnic, in paintings such as Still's *November 1950 No. 2* (1950) and Pollock's *Number 3, 1949: Tiger* (1949), ground (background, context) and subject were inseparable. The collapse of representation in painting is analogous to the decline of narrative in film and to the plotless ballets of Balanchine.[31]

The withdrawal from representation was no doubt related to the use of the atomic bomb. In the same way that Dwight Macdonald was aghast that the Pepsi-Cola company could award a prize in 1946 to Boris Deutsch for his painting *What Atomic War Will Do to You*—which depicted a subject, the horror of Hiroshima, that Macdonald believed utterly defied representation—abstract expressionism originated in the desire to create an art that would avoid representation (and its tendency to "accept the unacceptable") in favor of a style whose starting point was a figurative nuclear explosion that cleared the canvas for whatever was to follow. "The familiar identity of things," wrote Rothko, in what might have been an atomic metaphor, "has to be pulverized." Consistent with this view, one scholar has described abstract expressionism as an "art of obliteration, an art of erasure."[32]

Because abstract expressionism refused to accept the system of representation bequeathed by the culture and cultivated one that was altogether less obvious, the school was immediately vulnerable to a variety of ignorant responses and unexpected uses. It was seen as a retreat from reality, an escape from the uncertainties of the atomic age and the complexities of modern life into what one authority called "the clear and untroubled limitations of . . . craft." Led by Michigan congressman George Dondero, the nativist and anti-intellectual political right wing found in modern art just the sort of elitist disregard for artistic standards and academic traditions that could destroy the nation's cultural heritage and open the way for the triumph of an alien ideology. Nonetheless, in 1948 de Kooning's paintings could be found in the U.S. pavilion at the Venice Biennale, an international art exhibition; in 1949 *Life* transformed Pollock into a cultural hero; and by mid-1950 there was talk of including abstract expressionism in a worldwide "Marshall Plan" of ideas. In the 1950s, under the aegis of Nelson Rockefeller and the Museum of Modern Art, abstract expressionism came to stand for the best in American values—specifically, for freedom—and to represent American liberalism around the world.[33]

In retrospect, this absorption of abstract expressionism into the main-stream was inevitable. Although the freedom-centered cultural critique of the abstract expressionists was real and important, it was socially conservative in the sense that it bore no relation to the working-class struggles of the depression years or to communism, which had attracted so many prewar intellectuals. In flight from a far left that could not satisfactorily explain Soviet conduct in the burgeoning cold war, and yet repulsed by the democratized, consumer culture of modern America, the abstract expressionists sought to create a space in between—a middle ground where individuals could plumb the depths of the free self. Predictably, the subculture they created in New York was decidedly individualistic, prompting Baziotes to complain that "you can't do anything materially for someone [if] they never invite you to their place. Sometimes ten days go by and we don't see anyone." More to the point, artists threatened by the anticommunist right and criticized by elements of the mainstream middle class welcomed the definition of their work as the product of a high and creative individuality, aloof from any ideology. "Modern art," Motherwell wrote in 1944, "is related to the problem of the modern individual's freedom."[34]

Amid the frenzy of late-1940s anticommunism, it was no difficult matter for critics, scholars, and cultural authorities to appreciate these individualistic and oppositional artists as exemplars of a culture of freedom—symbols, as a contemporary put it, of the society's "infinite variety and ceaseless exploration." At the same time, to celebrate the existence of an imaginative and provocative avant-garde was to set at ease fears of a vapid and standardless "mass culture" characterized by abysmal tastes and potential authoritarianism. "A free society," as Schlesinger wrote in *The Vital Center*, "must dedicate itself to the protection of the unpopular view. It is threatening to turn us all into frightened conformists; and conformity can lead only to stagnation. We need courageous men to help us recapture a sense of the indispensability of dissent." Similarly, a potentially radical artistic vision—certainly a vision that appeared to challenge the dominant culture's most fundamental progressive myths and assumptions—was remade in the image of a Don Quixote and left to tilt against the windmills of "systems," "conformity," and other ill-defined devils that lay comfortably beyond the issues of class structure that not so long before had dominated the political scene.[35]

The movement from representation to abstract expressionism in painting had its counterpart in an intellectual migration involving a majority of the nation's writers and scholars, including Clement Greenberg, Dwight Macdonald, Lionel Trilling, Delmore Schwartz, Lionel Abel, Mary McCarthy, William Phillips, Sidney Hook, Philip Rahv, and others who wrote for New York's journals of high culture and were generally known by the 1950s as the "New York intellectuals." Although the path of this migration varied from individual to individual, it typically began from a position of Marxist radicalism in the 1930s and led, by the late 1940s, to a cold war advocacy of anticommunism and freedom. By midcentury the Old Left (as it would be known after the next generation, the New Left, produced its own version of radicalism) was virtually moribund. (By the 1980s Hook, Irving Kristol, and others among the migrants had moved beyond Schlesinger's liberalism into the neoconservative right wing of Nixon, Reagan, and the Hoover Institution.)

This devolution was a process of enormous significance; American radicalism never recovered from it. Perhaps for this reason, scholars have often been critical of its protagonists. Some have traced the sharp rightward turn to the presence in the movement of large numbers of Jews—Trilling, Daniel Bell, and Norman Podhoretz among them—estranged from their culture and perhaps, in their rootlessness, too willing to slough off radical identities to embrace mainstream values. Others have argued that intellectual radicalism was the victim of postwar affluence, which tempered critical and alternative modes of analysis and brought formerly independent writers into the security of the university, where, as John W. Aldridge recalled, the oppositional literary movement of yesteryear was reduced to "small fastidious tics experienced by graduate students in the damp undercaves of libraries. . . . Literature now was a corporate body, official, institutionalized, and closed." Still others believe that the triumph of freedom in intellectual circles was a necessary and proper response to the communist challenge in the cold war.[36]

A very different, even contrary, perspective sees the movement from social radicalism to an advocacy of freedom as absolutely necessary to the preservation of critical and independent thought in an age threatened by a media-based mass culture. The mass culture critique was framed in the decade after 1935 by Theodor Adorno, Max Horkheimer, and other scholars of the Frankfurt School. As Adorno argued in his frequent writings on music, the mass culture problem was rooted in the increasing concentration of capital, which inevitably produced a standardized, "soporific" mass entertainment (the cultural equivalent, he wrote, of Aunt Jemima's ready-mix pancakes) that undermined social consciousness and reduced its audience to infantile responses, such as listening to a complex Beethoven symphony only to hear the melody. Despite the claims that radio, for example, offered listeners numerous options, Adorno insisted that the listener, whose freedom was circumscribed by the desires of advertisers and song publishers, had "virtually . . . no choice."

The related work of Paul Lazarsfeld and Robert K. Merton probed the similarities between mass culture and propaganda, suggesting that the "narcotizing dysfunction" of mass culture phenomena such as Hollywood, New York's Radio City, and Henry Luce's *Time-Life-Fortune* empire could be "inadvertently transforming the energies of men from active participation into passive knowledge," and thus buttressing the social *status quo*. Along the same lines, a 1945 study of *Reader's Digest* (founded in 1922) depicted it as a cultural octopus, squeezing the variety out of American life and critical sensibilities out of Americans:

> Since *The Reader's Digest* has now become a way of life, it may be instructive to visualize an American home which makes us of all the facilities the *Digest* provides. Father is reading the current edition of the *Digest* while Mother is tuned to the *Digest* radio program. Brother, just home from the Army, is finishing his overseas edition. Sister is upstairs in her room studying her school edition. . . . Uncle is at the movies watching a *Digest* feature. . . . Grandfather, who has lost his sight, is enjoying the Braille edition, while Grandmother, also blind but unable to read Braille, is sitting in her room taking in the Talking-Book edition by ear.[37]

Unlike the theorists of the Frankfurt School, most critics of mass culture, including many of the New York intellectuals, located the source of the problem not in capitalist efforts to propagandize the masses (the *supply* side of culture) but in a democratized society that was incapable, according to Macdonald, of making necessary distinctions "between anything or anybody" and responsive to a marketplace dominated by working-class and middle-class consumers who had no taste (the *demand* side of culture). Eugene O'Neill found evidence of this sort of cultural decay even in the legitimate theater. "There is nothing one can do about it" he wrote in 1948. "It is simply one symptom of a world-wide passing into an existence without culture—the world of mob-destiny." Lionel Trilling agreed, taking the decline of the modern novel as a symptom of a more general cultural decadence. The novel, Trilling wrote, "has been of all literary forms the most devoted to the celebration and investigation of the human will; and the will of our society is dying of its own excess. The religious will, the political will, the sexual will, the artistic will, each is dying of its own excess."[38]

In contrast to the 1930s view of the masses as intelligent beings capable of considered judgments and rational choices, the mass culture critics of the forties wrote of ordinary people with contempt. To explain the difference between genuine culture and what he called "kitsch," Clement Greenberg described a hypothetical Russian peasant evaluating an abstract painting by Picasso and a realistic and representational one by Repin. Because the Picasso painting committed the viewer to an act of thoughtful participation, the peasant, Greenberg argued, would favor the piece by Repin, a painter who "predigests art for the spectator and spares him effort, provides him with a short cut to the pleasure of art that detours what is necessarily difficult in genuine art." "Kitsch," wrote Greenberg, "is vicarious experience and faked sensations. Kitsch changes according to style, but remains always the same. Kitsch is the epitome of all that is spurious in the life of our times. Kitsch pretends to demand nothing of its customers except their money—not even their time."[39]

Many of the issues surrounding mass culture came together in the 1940s around the figure of Arturo Toscanini, the Italian-born musician who as conductor of the NBC Symphony after 1937 achieved the status of media idol and cultural celebrity. By midcentury, his popularity cresting with television, Toscanini had taken on godlike proportions and was deemed capable, or so it seemed, of bringing the gospel of high culture to the masses of Americans. "Given a chance," commented David Sarnoff, president of RCA, NBC's parent corporation, "the average man will move slowly, perhaps falteringly, toward a selection of the best." But for Theodor Adorno and other critics of what Macdonald would later label "mid-cult," Toscanini was a disciplined, even mechanical conductor whose slick and "predetermined" performances, devoid of spontaneity, creativity, and vitality, resembled the political orchestrations depicted in Frank Capra's *Mr. Smith Goes to Washington* (1939) and *State of the Union*. "Not for nothing," wrote Adorno, "does the rule of the [Toscanini-type] conductor remind one of that of the totalitarian Führer." Adorno generalized this conclusion in *The Authoritarian Personality*, a study of the sources of fascism latent in democratic, industrialized societies.[40]

Although the anticapitalist side of mass culture theory had a certain socialist content, the mass culture critique was, on the whole, a conservative one. Its theorists advocated an elitist individualism; the free individual, critical and abstract thought, and an avant-garde were essential to a successful attack on a potentially totalitarian mass culture. For the battle against kitsch, Greenberg offered an avant-garde "in search of the absolute," engaged in the act of "creating something valid solely on its own terms." To achieve this goal, Greenberg advocated an art of pure form, thoroughly distanced from corrupt and corruptible representationalism. Greenberg's solution would find an outlet most obviously in abstract expressionism, but also in literary culture; the first issues of the *Hudson Review* (1948) featured essays by critics R. P. Blackmur (lamenting the cultural pap of the Luce publications and Hollywood while calling for a new criticism that would "compare and judge as well as analyze and elucidate") and Mark Schorer (attacking the realism of James T. Farrell and Thomas Wolfe while describing technique as "nearly everything"). The center of avant-garde free inquiry was *Partisan Review*, where Greenberg joined Harold Rosenberg, Daniel Bell, Irving Howe, William Phillips, Lionel Trilling, and Philip Rahv in a commitment to the intellectual as a social and cultural force. "The aim," as Alfred Kazin recalled, "was unlimited freedom of speculation, the union of a free radicalism with modernism."[41]

Yet freedom did not achieve its postwar prominence simply as an elitist reaction to mass culture. For most intellectuals, the growing attachment to freedom seemed a reasoned response to the cold, rigid, inflexible, overbearing, and dangerous ideologies that seemed to have got the world into so much trouble. This anti-ideological position emerged only gradually: in the late 1930s, in response to Stalin's bloody purge of political opposition and to the Nazi-Soviet Pact of 1939; during the war, when the "politics of necessity" drove American Communists and Communist sympathizers to support the nation's involvement in a conflict that only a few years previously would have been denounced as a war of capitalist, imperalist aggression, and when the doctrinal anti-Semitism of the Nazis produced the Holocaust; and after the war, when the American working class failed its final examination in elementary Marxism by refusing to act like a revolutionary proletariat, and when the emergence of the cold war fused the Nazis and the Soviets into the great, ideological enemy of totalitarianism. Max Ascoli, editor and publisher of *The Reporter*, captured the prevailing attitude toward ideology in *The Power of Freedom* (1949), describing the nations of Europe as victims of an "acid of ideas," its peoples "given in holocaust to some ideological god."[42]

Although usually associated with the decade of the 1950s, and given its ultimate expression by sociologist Daniel Bell in 1960, the idea of an "end of ideology" was widely articulated by midcentury. By that time, many Americans had chosen freedom as the centerpeice of their thought. On the popular level, the revolt against ideology could be seen in John Gunther's best-seller *Inside U.S.A.* (1947). On the surface just another American character study, Gunther's book was full of the contradictions, ironies, and paradoxes that marked the anti-ideological temper. While calling for "effective national unity," Gunther lavished praise on high individualists such as H. L. Mencken, Robert Maynard Hutchins, and Harold Stassen. Gunther reveled in what he saw as America's disdain for ideology: labor leaders were called radical, but John L. Lewis took a conservative line; despite an anti-Semitic past, Henry Ford deeply admired a Jewish colleague; call him a fascist or a Communist, but Stassen would "plug steadily down the middle."[43]

In what some scholars have seen as intellectual sleight of hand, many forties intellectuals proposed to do battle with totalitarianism not in the name of an opposing ideology such as capitalism, but by investing themselves in a series of purportedly nonideological processes: debate, inquiry, critical dialogue, discussion, the opposition of the avant-garde, dissent itself—aspects of an intellectual "freedom" that promised to hew victory out of the dense forest of competing ideas. Hence, Macdonald's post-Marxist politics called for a "negativism" that would cut against the authority of the state; Bell placed his hopes for social liberation in "the willingness of small groups of people to be themselves"; and Rahv took *Partisan Review* from deep involvement with left-wing, class politics into its new postwar role as a cultural critic, sniping away at the dominant culture from its position as outsider. Operating in the more practical arena of community organizing, an increasingly militant Saul Alinsky after 1946 asserted his independence of all "derived" (i.e., Communist) ideologies, promoting a "non-ideological" stance that emphasized technique and the "highly trained, politically sophisticated, creative organizer."[44]

The end-of-ideology theme is addressed in several works of forties fiction, among them Edmund Wilson's *Memoirs of Hecate County* (1946), Mary McCarthy's *The Oasis* (1949), and Lionel Trilling's *The Middle of the Journey* (1947). Trilling was Jewish, a New Yorker by inclination, and a frequent contributor to *The Nation*, *New Republic*, and *Partisan Review*—in many ways a typical New York intellectual. In other ways, he was not typical: at a time when most prominent intellectuals were independent of the academy, Trilling was a professor at Columbia University; and his Marxism was too tepid to hold up even in the midst of the Great Depression.[45]

Set in the mid-1930s, Trilling's novel describes the abandonment of communism by Gifford Maxim, a high-level Communist party member and a character based on Whittaker Chambers. Written in the forties, *The Middle of the Journey* also delineates the strong anti-ideological currents at work in the age of totalitarianism. Maxim's "break" with the party is accompanied by the conviction that "we are all of us, all of us, the little children of the Grand Inquisitor," and therefore, that one form of ideology—whether fascism, communism, or freedom and democracy—is as harmful as another. As Maxim explains to Arthur and Nancy Croom, who are sympathetic to communism as fellow travelers, "you think only of what the other side must do to gain its ends and you feel separated from everything that is foul in them. But I know what 'our' side must do, and not merely do; the doing would not be so terrible if we did not have to be what we do, and *I* know what we must be."

As the novel opens, John Laskell, a thirty-three-year old public housing architect, is in the final stages of recovery from a life-threatening battle with scarlet fever and about to complete his recuperation in rural Connecticut near his friends, the Crooms. Like Trilling, Laskell has never been as deeply invested in radicalism as Maxim, and he abhors doctrinal rigidities. The most significant exchange concerns the conduct of Duck Caldwell, the Crooms' sullen handyman whose function in the novel is to demonstrate that the working class is not the flawless and heroic proletariat of the left's imagination. Duck, unaware that his daughter suffers from a serious heart ailment, has brought on her death with a public slap in the face. In the debate that ensues, Nancy takes the traditional position of the idealistic left, proclaiming Caldwell's personal innocence and society's responsibility. Maxim defends his new religion of "ultimate, absolute responsibility for the individual," coupled with forgiveness. Sitting in the wings, Laskell understands the arguments as equally ideological and sees Maxim, "riding the pendulum" of the new, on the verge of laying claim to another kind of power not so different from that he exercised in the upper echelons of the party. Forced to enter the fray, Laskell occupies the pragmatic middle, refusing to absolve the people and institutions that are a part of his life, yet not being willing to deny his own will. "An absolute freedom from responsibility—that much of a child," Laskell contends, "none of us can be. An absolute responsibility—that much of a divine or metaphysical essence none of us is."[46]

Whether one agrees with Laskell's argument or, like Maxim, dismisses it as an example of mushy liberalism in flight from commitment, one can appreciate the position as a historical one, akin to Schlesinger's "vital center," Bell's "end of ideology," Gunther's world of irony and paradox, the paintings of the abstract expressionists, even Calder's mobiles. Exhausted by a decade of ideological positioning that seemed only to be responsible for death and destruction and that had failed to produce a revolutionary working class, Laskell resembled thousands of others in search of new ways of thinking about the world and their place in it. For many Americans, that new consciousness was to be experienced as a movement from left to middle, or even right, from commitment to opposition and negation, from ideology to pragmatism and ambiguity, or from communism or socialism to a home-grown freedom. Others, as we have seen, took a journey inward, from the public life of politics to the private world of the self. And the nation's schoolchildren took a day off—to meet the Freedom Train.

seven

The Age of Doubt

Long before the end of the decade—when the phrase "age of anxiety" had become de rigueur for social critics—an undertone of doubt had begun to appear beneath the optimistic surface of American culture. It was during the war that Americans began to wonder if everything would be all right. Pearl Harbor, news of the Holocaust, the slaughter on the Russian front, letters that stopped coming, a wave of juvenile delinquency, violent racial confrontations in Detroit and Harlem—these were just a few of the outward signs that something was amiss in the world that even a prosperous wartime economy could not right.

One can sense the concern—and witness the forced efforts to shore up the society's crumbling foundation of beliefs—in even the most positive and optimistic cultural moments. Elements of the age of doubt were present in 1944, when the film *Going My Way* won Academy Awards for Barry Fitzgerald as Father Fitzgibbon, the elderly and ineffectual head of the church of St. Dominic, and for Bing Crosby as Father Charles Francis Patrick O'-Malley—young, informal, an expert in human relations, and prepared to rescue the parish from a sea of red ink.

Going My Way might best be understood as an effort to dissipate a series of wartime tensions. The threat of juvenile delinquency is the first to be exiled, as O'Malley introduces an unruly gang of troublemakers to "Silent Night" in four-part harmony, thus affirming the culture's ability to socialize the young and to bring into line individuals tempted to stand apart from the group in the moment of need. The war's sexual tensions had been banished from the beginning, with O'Malley's sexual desires sublimated in the priesthood and

144

those of his ex-girlfriend tempered in an operatic career. The potential liabilities of O'Malley's most important decision—to don the uniform and deny the self—are tossed aside with a remark that affirms the survival of individualism—"At one time I had quite a decision to make: whether to write the *nation's* songs, or *go my way.*" Conflicts of class and cultures are reconciled (and the church's economic problems ostensibly solved) when the boys' choir (ex-delinquents, the working class) and the orchestra of the local opera company (culture) convince a commercial song publisher (capitalist self-interest) to buy one of O'Malley's compositions.

If *Going My Way* were just a restatement of faith in progress, or a simple affirmation of standard values, it would have ended right there. But at this moment of blissful triumph, when all seems right—when the mortgage has been paid and Father Fitzgibbon has come to terms with Father O'Malley's generation ("I feel ten years younger")—the church, an old, ornate, and in some sense irreplaceable structure, burns down. Though Father O'Malley is as optimistic as ever ("Don't worry, Father, we'll build again"), Father Fitzgibbon's faith has been shaken; while raising funds for a new church, he becomes ill. Again the boys' choir intercedes, if not quite as dramatically, and construction begins on a new church. The cold banker, whose demands for payment had brought on the first round of problems, agrees to provide a mortgage for the new structure. In every outward way, the burning of the old church has been surmounted. Yet the film ends so hastily after the catastrophe, and the destruction of the church is so unexpected and total, that the film's ultimate message is something less than completely reassuring. Despite the cheerful, buoyant confidence of Father O'Malley, the unexpected, the contingent, the catastrophic has intervened. Life will never be quite the same.

As the concerns of 1944 became the deep anxieties of midcentury, the straightforward, "objective" narrative that stood for progress and order in *Going My Way* yielded to the voice-over/flashback, the "subjective" camera, multiple storytellers, and the semidocumentary techniques of film noir. In the context of a military victory that seemed to have been won at the cost of demonstrating the inhumanity of humankind, and of a cold war that called for eternal vigilance, the ability of the cultural text to produce a conclusion consistent with, and implied in, everything that had gone before—what literary scholar Frank Kermode calls "the sense of an ending"—withered and died. Endings became beginnings, and the expectation of closure disappeared. As Richard Brooks put it in the 1945 novel *The Brick Foxhole*, "Their war was with the Japs. And after the Japs would come the Russians. And why the Russians? They couldn't tell you. It was just accepted that that would happen."[1]

The moment of the forties glimpsed in *Going My Way* and writ large in film noir was in part a moment of crisis in the national identity. Although identity was, as we have seen, normally taken up as a problem of the individual, it was also a factor in the nation's confusion. Was the United States a bastion of isolationism, as it had been in 1940, or a committed imperial power, as the Truman Doctrine and the Marshall Plan seemed to demonstrate? Was the nation committed to Franklin D. Roosevelt's New Deal welfare state—with its implied goal of economic security for all citizens—or was it, as the popularity of Ayn Rand's novels suggested, a stronghold of free-enterprise capitalism and individual responsibility, given to entrepreneurship and risk taking? Were Americans the stable, rooted beings that appeared in Norman Rockwell's paintings, or were they, as Oscar Handlin's study of immigration claimed, "the uprooted"? Were we becoming a nation of other-directed conformists, as David Riesman contended, or the collection of idiosyncratic oddities pulled together by John Gunther? While most of these were not new questions, they were asked in the forties with compelling urgency, as if events had bypassed the time for decision. Yet, despite the spate of American character studies, the nation remained confused as to its identity.

The confusion and uncertainty extended to the most basic beliefs, values, and priorities. Unsure of how to carry out the most essential and elemental social tasks, Americans welcomed the advice of experts in child-rearing, marriage, and many other fields. Yet they remained fondly attached to the folk, embracing Ted Mack's "The Original Amateur Hour" (1948) and joining Avery Brundage, head of the International Olympic Committee, in celebrating the amateur code as a kind of moral law beyond the corruptions of materialism.[2] Though convinced that science and reason were essential to progress, they could see the Nazi concentration camps as the embodiment of system and rationality (of "scientific management"), understand the bomb as a product of a science that had suddenly made all men helpless, and lament the inability of the scientific framework to encompass love and other emotions.[3] Despite the decade's heightened sense of contingency, artists as diverse as Charlie Parker, Jackson Pollock, and John Cage purposely invested their performances and compositions with elements of chance—that is, with even more contingency. Late in the decade, when cold war anxieties had produced a climate of ideological coercion—reflected in the pervasive ideal of "loyalty"—the culture perversely claimed "freedom" as its dearest possession. At the same time, the decade's contrarieties were apparent in the polar positions that characterized the culture of the whole and the culture of the self.

Such contradictions and paradoxes inevitably produced a culture committed both to the discussion of the ironic and to its presentation. In literature and film, the site of the ironic became Los Angeles, at once the repository of the American dream and—in the detective novels of Raymond Chandler and in films such as *Detour* and *D.O.A.*—the setting for a seedy reality that made a mockery of all genuine hope. There was the irony of B. F. Skinner's *Walden Two*, with its affirmation that man could achieve freedom only by yielding to a system of social engineering; of Gunther's *Inside U.S.A.*, which claimed some vision and perspective on the nation while shredding its subject into so many bits and pieces; of Lionel Trilling's *The Middle of the Journey*, whose protagonist at once affirmed and denied man's responsibility for his acts; of film noir, with its suspenseful stories whose endings we already know. The ironic was present in high school yearbooks, which were laden with man's newfound guilt and responsibilities in the atomic age, yet full of idealism and committed to the idea of progress; in the postwar pastoral musical, with its overdone and self-mocking small-town perfectionism; in the musical theories of Cage, who contested established Western dogmas yet came perilously close to the one-world position espoused by the nation's empire-builders; among literature's New Critics, who appreciated poetry as an affective, emotive alternative to scientific rationalism yet reified the poem to the point where it ordered the universe and contained contingency just as science once had. The decade's "preacher of paradox," the culture's "spokesman for the tragic sense of life," was Reinhold Niebuhr, for whom the making of the bomb, the exercise of world power, and the "vulgarization of culture" through the technology of mass communications were all incongruous and hence ironic developments, products of the "illogical and contradictory patterns of the historic drama," and of man's inherent limitations.[4]

From the welter of contradictions and ironies there was no easy escape, no easy way of feeling good about an imperfect world and a flawed humanity. One might seek to reduce life's ironic dimension by emphasizing—as did Niebuhr, Leslie Fiedler, many playwrights and novelists working in the realist vein, the foreign policy establishment, and others—the need for a new, more "realistic" perspective that would dispel the illusions that were seen as the source of humanity's disappointments.

A second stance, that of existentialism, assumed the impossibility of reconciling contradictions, clearing up ambiguities, or resolving the most perplexing issues of the day. Against this condition of continual uncertainty and doubt—in which victory of any kind, of freedom over communism, of right over wrong, of man over his doubts and anxieties, was unthinkable—one could assert only the primacy of the struggle, the value of waging the good fight for what one believed was right, if need be forever. It was this perspective that informed the "containment" strategy of George F. Kennan; the existential quest of *D.O.A.*'s Frank Bigelow; Lionel Trilling's presentation of life as an ongoing philosophical debate; Arthur M. Schlesinger, Jr.'s call for a "continuing struggle" to solve problems that were "insoluble"; and the determination of postwar parents to have children—indeed, record numbers of them—in an age so full of anxiety that poet Weldon Kees could see death in the innocence of his sleeping daughter. "There is," Schlesinger wrote in 1949, "no more exciting time in which to live—no time more crucial or more tragic. We must recognize that this is the nature of our age: that the womb has irrevocably closed behind us, that security is a foolish dream of old men, that crisis will always be with us."[5]

Chronology

1939   Inspiration for bebop strikes Charlie Parker.

1940   Germans conquer France, Belgium, Denmark, the Netherlands, Luxembourg, Norway, and Romania. First peacetime draft in U.S. history 29 October.

1941   Rachel Carson's *Under the Sea-Wind* is published. *Time* and *Life* publisher Henry Luce proclaims the "American Century." *Citizen Kane* named best film of 1941 by New York Film Critics. Japanese attack Pearl Harbor 7 December.

1942   Irving Berlin's "White Christmas" becomes best-selling song ever. Thornton Wilder's *The Skin of Our Teeth* opens on Broadway, 18 November. Margaret Mead's *And Keep Your Powder Dry* is published. Battle of Stalingrad turns tide of war on Eastern Front.

1943   John Cage directs percussion program at Museum of Modern Art. Popular Library, publisher of paperbound books, founded. Pentagon completed 15 January. Roy Stryker begins Standard Oil of New Jersey photography project. Norman Rockwell paints *Four Freedoms* for *Saturday Evening Post*. Wendell Willkie's *One World*, based on forty-nine-day tour of Allied fronts, is published. D-Day—Allied troops land at Normandy beaches 6 June. Kate Smith raises $39 million in marathon radio war-bond drive 21 September.

1944   Committee on Research in Economic History outlines entrepreneurship as field of study. Dwight Macdonald founds the journal *Politics*.

1945 "Sentimental Journey" is no. 1 popular song 13 June. Vannevar Bush confirms new role of federal government in science in report to the president, *Science: The Endless Frontier*, July. The United States drops an atomic bomb on Hiroshima 6 August. World War II ends in Europe, 8 May, and in the Pacific, 14 August. *The Lost Weekend*, a film about alcoholism, is chosen the year's best film by the New York Film Critics. *Red Pyramid*, an Alexander Calder mobile, exhibited.

1946 Dr. Benjamin Spock's *Common Sense Book of Baby and Child Care* is published. ENIAC computer developed at University of Pennsylvania. John Hersey's *Hiroshima* is published. Jean-Paul Sartre visits New York City, January. William Wyler's *The Best Years of Our Lives* is universally declared best picture of the year. French critic Nino Frank coins term *film noir.*

1947 Courses in "Western civilization" are popular on college campuses. Arthur Miller's *All My Sons* opens at Coronet Theater in New York City 29 January. Jackie Robinson, first black major-league baseball player, signs with Brooklyn Dodgers. Sex-crime "panic" begins. Ferdinand Lundberg and Marynia F. Farnham's *Modern Woman* describes woman as "the lost sex." Lionel Trilling's novel *The Middle of the Journey* is published. Mickey Spillane introduces detective Mike Hammer in *I, the Jury*. Laura Hobson's *Gentleman's Agreement*, about anti-Semitism, is a nonfiction best-seller. Truman Doctrine, to aid Greece and Turkey against communism, outlined 12 March. Christian Dior introduces the "New Look" for the "womanly woman," April. *Life with Father* sets record with 3,183 consecutive performances at the Empire Theater in New York City, 14 June. UFO scare, July. Suburban development of Levittown opens on Long Island, October. Tennessee Williams's *A Streetcar Named Desire* opens on Broadway 3 December. Bing Crosby is the nation's top money-making performer for the fourth straight year. Actor's Studio, teaching "Method" acting, opens. Bernard Baruch coins the phrase *cold war.*

1948 Television becomes a major industry. Jackson Pollock begins his "action" paintings, pioneering abstract expressionism. Alfred C. Kinsey's *Sexual Behavior in the Human Male*, the first volume of the Kinsey Report, is published. B. F. Skinner's *Walden Two* is published. Architect Eero Saarinen wins Jefferson National Expansion Memorial competition with design for parabolic arch, to be constructed in St. Louis. Ted Mack's "The Original Amateur Hour" premieres 18 January. Shirley Jackson's "The Lottery" is published in the *New Yorker.* State of Israel proclaimed 14 May. Premiere performance of Samuel Barber's cantata, *Knoxville, Summer of 1915*, with text by James Agee. *Life* roundtable, "The Pursuit of Happiness," July, Rye, New York. Berlin airlift begins 15 July. R. Buckminster Fuller builds his first geodesic dome. Robert Flaherty's documentary film *Louisiana Story* premieres 28 September. Norman Mailer's *The Naked and the Dead* and Dale Carnegie's *How to Stop Worrying and Start Living* are fiction and nonfiction best-sellers, respectively. Jack Kerouac travels the country, his adventures to be described in *On the Road* (1957). Richard Hofstader's *The American Political Tradition* is published. Arthur Godfrey's relaxed style makes him radio's biggest star. Garry Davis emerges as leader of the world citizenship movement. Norbert Wiener's *Cybernetics* is published. *Time*'s Man of the Year is Harry Truman, "Fighter in a Fighting Year."

1949   Arthur M. Schlesinger, Jr.'s *The Vital Center* and Joseph Campbell's *The Hero with a Thousand Faces* are published. Ezra Pound wins Bollingen Prize for *The Pisan Cantos*. Hank Williams becomes country star with "Lovesick Blues," released in February. First performance of Leonard Bernstein's symphony, *The Age of Anxiety*, April. North Atlantic Treaty Organization (NATO) created 4 April. Evangelist Billy Graham opens his first crusade, in Los Angeles, September. Soviets detonate atomic bomb. Pyramid friendship clubs are national rage. *Billboard* changes "race" music category to rhythm and blues. George R. Stewart's *Earth Abides* is published.

1950   Erik Erikson's *Childhood and Society* and L. Ron Hubbard's *Dianetics* are published. Muzak Corporation has 10,000 customers in 150 cities. David Riesman's *The Lonely Crowd* presents concepts of "inner-directed" and "other-directed." Theodor Adorno's *The Authoritarian Personality* is published.

1952   Reinhold Niebuhr's *The Irony of American History* is published.

Notes and References

Chapter One

1. Geoffrey Perrett, *Days of Sadness, Years of Triumph: The American People, 1939–1945* (Baltimore: Penguin Press, 1974), 123.

2. William Graebner, *The Engineering of Consent: Democracy and Authority in Twentieth-Century America* (Madison: University of Wisconsin Press, 1987), 101 (radio groups); "Town Meetings for War," in Richard Polenberg, ed., *America at War: The Home Front, 1941–1945* (Englewood Cliffs, N.J.: Prentice-Hall, 1968), 11.

3. Quoted in Graebner, *Engineering of Consent*, 104, 107–8, 105.

4. *Time*, 3 January 1944, p. 18; Pierre Couperie, et al., *A History of the Comic Strip*, trans. Eileen B. Hennessy (New York: Crown, 1968), 89; Cynthia B. Richardson, *Susie Cucumber: She Writes Letters* (New York: Samuel Gabriel Sons, 1944), (unpaginated).

5. Jeanine Basinger, *The World War II Combat Film: Anatomy of a Genre* (New York: Columbia University Press, 1986), 5.

6. Clayton R. Koppes and Gregory D. Black, *Hollywood Goes to War: How Politics, Profits, and Propaganda Shaped World War II Movies* (New York: Free Press, 1987), 37–38.

7. Allen L. Woll, *The Hollywood Musical Goes to War* (Chicago: Nelson Hall, 1983), 52; H. Wiley Hitchcock, *Music in the United States: A Historical Introduction* (Englewood Cliffs, N.J.: Prentice-Hall, 1969), 212 (marching bands); Stanford University, School of Education Faculty, *Education in Wartime and After* (New York: D. Appleton-Century, 1943), 295, 296–98.

8. John A. Kouwenhoven, *Made in America: The Arts in Modern Civilization* (1948; reprint, Garden City, N.Y.: Doubleday/Anchor, 1962), 13, 220.

9. Alfred Kazin, *New York Jew* (New York: Alfred A. Knopf, 1978), 97.

10. Ernie Pyle, *Here Is Your War: The Story of G.I. Joe* (New York: World Publishing, 1945), 99.

Notes and References

12. Robert McCloskey, *Make Way for Ducklings* (New York: Viking Press, 1946) (unpaginated).

13. John Costello, *Virtue under Fire: How World War II Changed Our Social and Sexual Attitudes* (Boston: Little, Brown, 1985), 120, and chap. 8.

14. Allan M. Winkler, *Home Front U.S.A.: America during World War II* (Arlington Heights, Ill.: Harlan Davidson, 1986), 21, 22 (Stalin quotation); Perrett, *Days of Sadness*, 255 (banners, San Quentin), 258 (*Time* quotation); Susan M. Hartmann, *The Home Front and Beyond: American Women in the 1940s* (Boston: Twayne, 1982), 21.

15. John Morton Blum, *V Was for Victory: Politics and American Culture during World War II* (New York: Harcourt Brace Jovanovich, 1976), 90, 92; Mary Ann Doane, *The Desire to Desire: The Woman's Film of the 1940s* (Bloomington: Indiana University Press, 1987), 81; advertisements for Coca-Cola and New Departure ball bearings, *Time*, 9 June 1941, 42, 46.

16. Robert B. Ray, *A Certain Tendency of the Hollywood Cinema, 1930–1980* (Princeton, N.J.: Princeton University Press, 1985), 193–94 (Capra); advertisement for Ipana, *Parents Magazine*, January 1943, 3.

17. David Cushman Coyle, "Planning a World of Plenty," *Parents Magazine*, January 1943, 19; advertisement, *Time* 21 December 1942, 3 (Revere); Brian Horrigan, "The House of Tomorrow," in *Imagining Tomorrow: History, Technology, and the American Future*, ed. Joseph J. Corn (Cambridge, Mass.: MIT Press, 1986), 158; Kenneth T. Jackson, *Crabgrass Frontier: The Suburbanization of the United States* (New York: Oxford University Press, 1985), 232.

18. Richard H. Pells, *The Liberal Mind in a Conservative Age: American Intellectuals in the 1940s and 1950s* (New York: Harper & Row, 1985), 63–71, 112 (Burnham quotation), 108–16.

19. Jerry Robinson, *The Comics: An Illustrated History of Comic Strip Art* (New York: G. P. Putnam's Sons, 1974), 141–42 ("Steve Canyon").

20. George Lipsitz, *Class and Culture in Cold War America: "A Rainbow at Midnight"* (South Hadley, Mass.: J. F. Bergin, 1982), 95–97, 112; Nelson Lichtenstein, "Life at the Rouge: A Cycle of Workers' Control," in *Life and Labor: Dimensions of American Working-Class History*, ed. Charles Stephenson and Robert Asher (Albany, N.Y.: SUNY Press, 1986), 253–54; Robert H. Wiebe, *The Segmented Society: An Introduction to the Meaning of America* (New York: Oxford University Press, 1976), 107–11, 123, 129.

21. Coca-Cola advertisement, *Time*, 10 May 1948, back cover; Chevrolet advertisement, *Newsweek*, 21 March 1949, 57.

22. Joseph C. Goulden, *The Best Years: 1945–1950* (New York: Atheneum, 1976), 173; George Lipsitz, "The Meaning of Memory: Family, Class, and Ethnicity in Early Network Television Programs," *Cultural Anthropology* 1 (November 1986): 355–87.

23. Patricia S. Warrick, *The Cybernetic Imagination in Science Fiction* (Cambridge, Mass.: MIT Press, 1980), 55–57; Reuel Denney, "The Revolt against Naturalism in the Funnies," in *The Funnies: An American Idiom*, ed. David Manning White and Robert H. Abel (New York: Free Press, 1963), 64–65; Roland Marchand, "Visions of Classlessness, Quests for Dominion: American Popular Culture, 1945–1960," in *Reshaping America: Society and Institutions, 1945–1960*, ed. Robert H. Bremner and Gary W. Reichard (Columbus: Ohio State University Press, 1982), 170–71; Brian Horri-

gan, "The Home of Tomorrow, 1927–1945," in *Imagining Tomorrow: History, Technology, and the American Future,* ed. Joseph J. Corn (Cambridge, Mass.: MIT Press, 1986), 155–57.

24. Doane, *The Desire to Desire,* 22–24.

25. "Fashion Means Business," *The March of Time* (1947). Les Daniels, *Comix: A History of Comic Books in America* (New York: Outerbridge & Dienstfrey, 1971), 54; Goulden, *The Best Years,* 156–57.

26. Goulden, *The Best Years,* 147 (pyramid friendship clubs).

27. C. W. E. Bigsby, "Drama from a Living Center," in *Arthur Miller,* ed. Harold Bloom (New York: Chelsea House, 1987), 106; Arthur Miller, *All My Sons,* in *Famous American Plays of the 1940s,* ed. Henry Hewes (New York: Dell, 1960), 236; Richard L. Neuberger, "Ah, Wilderness—New Style," *Harper's,* October 1948, 81.

28. Elaine Tyler May, *Homeward Bound: American Families in the Cold War Era* (New York: Basic Books, 1988), 10–14, 87–94.

29. Keith F. Davis, *Todd Webb: Photographs of New York and Paris, 1945–1960* (Kansas City, Mo.: Hallmark Cards, 1986), 16–19, 102 (Newhall quotation); J. P. Telotte, *Voices in the Dark: The Narrative Patterns of Film Noir* (Urbana: University of Illinois Press, 1989), 108–9.

30. Doane, *The Desire to Desire,* 118, 122, 100–101, 123–24, 134–37.

31. Edward C. McDonagh, "Television and the Family," *Sociology and Social Research* 35 (1950): 113–22; John W. Riley, Frank V. Cantwell, and Katherine F. Ruttiger, "Some Observations on the Social Effects of Television," *Public Opinion Quarterly* 13 (Summer 1949): 228, 232 (quotations), 233; Charles A. Siepmann, *Radio, Television, and Society* (New York: Oxford University Press, 1950), 270, 355, 357, 331.

32. Magnavox advertisements, ca. 1949–50 (photocopies in author's possession); General Electric advertisement, *House Beautiful,* May 1951, 20.

33. Dana Polan, *Power and Paranoia: History, Narrative, and the American Cinema, 1940–1950* (New York: Columbia University Press, 1986), 43, 78; "Mr. and Mrs. America," *The March of Time* (1942).

34. Rod Dyer and Ron Spark, *Fit to Be Tied: Vintage Ties of the Forties and Early Fifties* (New York: Abbeville Press, 1987), 35, 93.

Chapter Two

1. See the Corporal Le Van Roberts poem, "Good-By to a World," in Annette Tapert, ed., *Lines of Battle: Letters from American Servicemen, 1941–1945* (New York: Random House/Times Books, 1987), 16.

2. Ibid., 10–11, 66.

3. Paul Boyer, *By the Bomb's Early Light: American Thought and Culture at the Dawn of the Atomic Age* (New York: Pantheon, 1985), 8 (Cousins quotation). See the distinction between fear and anxiety in Paul Tillich, *The Courage to Be* (New Haven: Yale University Press, 1952), 34–35.

4. Boyer, *By the Bomb's Early Light,* 278 (Condon quotation), 281; Laura Rew Pickett diary, courtesy Jack T. Ericson, State University College, Fredonia, New York.

5. Margaret Mead, *And Keep Your Powder Dry: An Anthropologist Looks at America* (1942; reprint, New York: William Morrow, 1965), xii.

6. "Speaking of Pictures," *Life*, 21 July 1947, 14–16; "Signs, Portents, and Flying Saucers," *Newsweek*, 14 July 1947, 19–20; "Double, Double, Toil and Trouble," *Newsweek*, 14 July 1947, 30; Waldemar Kaempffert, "Remember the Flying Saucers?" *Science Digest* 22 (October 1947): 69 (condensed from *New York Times*); "The Somethings," *Time*, 14 July 1947, 18. See also Madelyn Wood, "Sudden Death from the Sky," *Coronet*, September 1948, 122–30, dealing with meteors rather than UFOs; and Susan J. Douglas, "Amateur Operators and American Broadcasting: Shaping the Future of Radio," in Corn, *Imagining Tomorrow*, 35–57, for a description of an earlier dream of sending radio waves to Mars as a function of American isolation and insecurity.

7. Estelle B. Freedman, "'Uncontrolled Desires': The Response to the Sexual Psychopath, 1920–1960," *Journal of American History* 74 (June 1987): 93 (*American Magazine* reference), 84.

8. George Chauncey, Jr., "The National Panic over 'Sex Crimes' and the Construction of Cold War Sexual Ideology, 1947–1953," paper presented at the 1986 meeting of the Organization of American Historians, 49, 5 (*Collier's* reference).

9. Freedman, "'Uncontrolled Desires,'" 84.

10. Goulden, *The Best Years*, 37–40. On readjustment problems, see the film produced by Dore Schary, *Till the End of Time*.

11. Thomas Heggen, *Mister Roberts* (Boston: Houghton Mifflin, 1946), 168, 166, 162.

12. Thomas M. Leonard, *Day by Day: The Forties* (New York: Facts on File, 1977), 895.

13. Sidney Kingsley, *Detective Story* (New York: Random House, 1949), 44, 55, 106.

14. Reinhold Niebuhr, *The Irony of American History* (New York: Charles Scribner's Sons, 1952), 79, 74, 38–39, 2, 88, 79, 42, 167, 133; Richard Wightman Fox, *Reinhold Niebuhr: A Biography* (New York: Pantheon, 1985), 166.

15. Robert G. Porfirio, "No Way out: Existential Motifs in the Film Noir," *Sight and Sound* 45 (Autumn 1976): 216–17, 215.

16. J. P. Telotte, "Film Noir and the Dangers of Discourse," *Quarterly Review of Film Studies* 9 (Spring 1984): 101–12.

17. Richard Wright, "The Man Who Killed a Shadow," *Zero* 1 (Spring 1949): 49–53; Richard Wright, *Native Son* (New York: Harper & Row, 1960); Michel Fabre, *The World of Richard Wright* (Jackson: University Press of Mississippi, 1985), 108–17.

18. Goulden, *The Best Years*, 204; Daniels, *Comix*, 13.

19. Russell W. Davenport, "The Pursuit of Happiness," *Life*, 12 July 1948, 97.

20. Ronald Lora, "Education: Schools as Crucible in Cold War America," in Bremner and Reichard, *Reshaping America*, 227–29.

21. Mortimer Smith, *And Madly Teach: A Layman Looks at Public School Education* (Chicago: Henry Regnery, 1949), 17–18, 23, 51, 24; Bernard Iddings Bell, *Crisis in Education: A Challenge to American Complacency* (New York: McGraw-Hill, 1949), 65, 145, 59.

22. Alfred C. Kinsey, Wardell B. Pomeroy, and Clyde E. Martin, *Sexual Behavior in the Human Male* (Philadelphia, W.B. Saunders, 1948); Alfred C. Kinsey, Wardell B. Pomeroy, Clyde E. Martin, and Paul H. Gebhard, *Sexual Behavior in the Human Female* (Philadelphia, W.B. Saunders, 1953); Regina Markell Morantz, "The Scientist

as Sex Crusader: Alfred C. Kinsey and American Culture," *American Quarterly* 29 (Winter 1977): 566–70, 569, 570.

23. "Plain Words from the Dean," *Time*, 1 November 1948, 67.

24. "Must We Change Our Sex Standards?" *Reader's Digest*, June 1948, quoted in Wardell B. Pomeroy, *Dr. Kinsey and the Institute for Sex Research* (New York: New American Library, 1972), 303.

25. "White House Press Release on Hiroshima, August 6, 1945," in Robert C. Williams and Philip L. Cantelon, eds., *The American Atom: A Documentary History of Nuclear Policies from the Discovery of Fission to the Present, 1939–1984* (Philadelphia: University of Pennsylvania Press, 1984), 68–70.

26. Steven L. Del Sesto, "Wasn't the Future of Nuclear Energy Wonderful?" in Corn, *Imagining Tomorrow*, 60, 61, 62; Boyer, *By the Bomb's Early Light*, 124, 112.

27. Boyer, *By the Bomb's Early Light*, 11–12, 85; Georges Bataille, *Death and Sensuality: A Study of Eroticism and the Taboo* (1962; reprint, New York: Arno Press, 1977), 171, 11–14; Photograph "1946 The Atomic Age Audit," Royal Photo Company Collection, University of Louisville Photographic Archives, Neg. No. 9033.

28. Warrick, *The Cybernetic Imagination*, 65, 66.

29. Thomas L. Haskell, ed., *The Authority of Experts: Studies in History and Theory* (Bloomington: Indiana University Press, 1984), xi–xiii.

30. "The Nation," *Time*, 3 January 1944, 16–18.

31. Boyer, *By the Bomb's Early Light*, 49–51.

32. Chauncey, "National Panic over 'Sex Crimes,'" 1, 32–33, 37.

33. *The Authoritarian Attempt to Capture Education: Papers from the Second Conference on the Scientific Spirit and Democratic Faith* (New York: King's Crown Press, 1945), 12–17, 25, 27, 78; Harold W. Stubblefield, *Towards a History of Adult Education in America: The Search for a Unifying Principle* (London: Croon Helm, 1988), 83–93, 91 (Hutchins quotation); Mark Van Doren, *Liberal Education* (New York: Henry Holt, 1945), 18–21, 24, 46.

34. Miller, *All My Sons*, in *Famous American Plays of the 1940s*, 251, 279, 280, 275, 287.

35. Tom F. Driver, "Strengths and Weaknesses in Arthur Miller," in Bloom, *Arthur Miller*, 24.

36. Ayn Rand, *The Fountainhead* (New York: Bobbs-Merrill Co., 1943); H. L. Rothman, "H. Roark, Architect," *Saturday Review*, 26 (29 May 1943): 30–31 (Roark quotation); Lorine Pruette, "Battle against Evil," *New York Times Book Review*, 16 May 1943, 7, 18.

37. Helen Sprackling, *Courtesy: A Book of Modern Manners* (New York: M. Barrows, 1944), viii, 195; Mary Beery, *Manners Made Easy* (New York: McGraw-Hill, 1949), vii–viii, 3.

38. Tennessee Williams, *A Streetcar Named Desire* (New York: New Directions, 1947), 28, 152.

39. Mickey Spillane, *I, the Jury* (1947; reprint, New York: Signet, 1975), 76, 2.

40. Richard H. Rovere, *Senator Joe McCarthy* (1960; reprint, New York: World Publishing, 1973), 49, 144 (Alsops quotation).

41. Alonzo L. Hamby, *Beyond the New Deal: Harry S. Truman and American Liberalism* (New York: Columbia University Press, 1973), 257.

42. Quoted in Bert Cochran, *Harry Truman and the Crisis Presidency* (New York: Funk and Wagnalls, 1973), 225.

43. Ralph Harper, *Existentialism: A Theory of Man* (Cambridge, Mass.: Harvard University Press, 1948), 35, 38, 36.

44. Arthur Miller, "Tragedy and the Common Man," *New York Times*, 27 February 1949, sec. 2, pp. 1, 3.

45. John McDonald, *Strategy in Poker, Business and War* (1950; New York: W.W. Norton, 1963), 121–22, 13, 14, 52, 63, 81–83, 69, 126, 97–108.

Chapter Three

1. New England Mutual advertisement, *Newsweek*, 13 October 1947, 53; Russell quoted in Goulden, *Best Years*, 5–6, 9. See also Quentin Reynolds, "The Best Years of Our Lives, II," *Reader's Digest* 50 (February 1947): 48–50; and Nicholas Lemann, *Out of the Forties* (1981; reprint, New York: Simon & Schuster, 1985).

2. Henry R. Luce, *The American Century* (New York: Farrar & Rinehart, 1941).

3. Raymond Fielding, *The American Newsreel, 1911–1967* (Norman: University of Oklahoma Press, 1972), 253, 301. *The March of Time*, "Fashion Means Business" (1947); "Americans All" (1944); "The Movies March On" (1939); "Tomorrow's Mexico" (1945).

4. Norbert Elias, *The Civilizing Process: The Development of Manners: Changes in the Code of Conduct and Feeling in Early Modern Times* (1939; reprint, New York: Urizen Books, 1978), 230; Randall Jarrell, "90 North," in *The Contemporary American Poets: American Poetry since 1940*, ed. Mark Strand (New York: New American Library, 1969), 161–62; Sidney B. Fay, "The Idea of Progress," *American Historical Review* 52 (January 1947): 231.

5. Nelson Algren, *The Man with the Golden Arm* (Greenwich, Conn.: Fawcett, 1949), 11.

6. "The House of Dior," *Life*, 24 March 1947, 65–70; "Counter-Revolution," *Time*, 15 September 1947, 87; "Manners and Morals," *Time*, 18 August 1947, 22 (*Harper's Bazaar* quotation). See also Southern Railway System advertisement, *Nation's Business* 36 (February 1948): 67.

7. *The March of Time*, "The Fight Game" (1948).

8. "Alcoholic Illness," *Time*, 3 June 1946, 95.

9. Rachel L. Carson, *Under the Sea-Wind: A Naturalist's Picture of Ocean Life* (1941; reprint, New York: Oxford University Press, 1952), 35, 50, 19, 83.

10. Rachel L. Carson, *The Sea around Us* (New York: Oxford University Press, 1951), 3, 28, 15.

11. Judy Oppenheimer, "The Haunting of Shirley Jackson," *New York Review of Books*, 3 July 1988, 16; Donald Barr, "A Talent for Irony," *New York Times Book Review*, 17 April 1949, 4; Harvey Breit, "Talk with Miss Jackson," *New York Times Book Review*, 26 June 1949, 15.

12. Spillane, *I, The Jury*, 2.

13. Leslie A. Fiedler, *An End to Innocence: Essays on Culture and Politics* (Boston: Beacon Press, 1955), 4, 21, 22, 24, 141, 142–50, 150.

14. Hannah Arendt, *The Origins of Totalitarianism* (1951; reprint, New York: Harcourt, Brace & World, 1966), xxx (preface to the first edition).

15. Arthur M. Schlesinger, Jr., *The Vital Center: The Politics of Freedom* (1949; reprint, Boston: Houghton Mifflin, 1962).

16. Quoted in Peter Novick, *That Noble Dream: The "Objectivity Question" and the*

American Historical Profession (Cambridge, England: Cambridge University Press, 1988), 333.

17. Ibid., 300 (Schlesinger quotation), 303, 325.

18. Arnold J. Toynbee, *Civilization on Trial* (New York: Oxford University Press, 1948); Arnold J. Toynbee, *A Study of History*, abridgement by D. C. Somervell of vols. 1–6 (New York: Oxford University Press, 1947); "The Challenge," *Time*, 17 March 1947, cover, 71–81. See also Paul A. Carter, *The Creation of Tomorrow: Fifty Years of Magazine Science Fiction* (New York: Columbia University Press, 1977), 222, 226.

19. Toynbee, *Civilization on Trial*, 25, 30, 37–39; Toynbee, *Study of History*, 552; "The Challenge," 71.

20. Margaret Mead, *Male and Female: A Study of the Sexes in a Changing World* (New York: William Morrow, 1949), 353, 345.

21. B. F. Skinner, *Walden Two* (1948; reprint, New York: Macmillan, 1962), 239, 174–75, 194–95.

22. George R. Stewart, *Earth Abides* (New York: Random House, 1949), 191, 133, 157, 162, 168, 319, 227.

23. Miller, *All My Sons*, 219.

24. Kingsley, *Detective Story*, 110, 140, 28.

25. On the use of the flashback in Frank Capra's *It's a Wonderful Life*, see Raymond Carney, *American Vision: The Films of Frank Capra* (Cambridge, Eng.: Cambridge University Press, 1986), 391–92.

26. Jean Kellogg, *Dark Prophets of Hope* (Chicago: Loyola University Press, 1975), 123–26, 129, 131.

27. George Bluestone, "Nelson Algren," *Western Review* 22 (Autumn 1957): 39.

28. Thomas Bender, *New York Intellect: A History of Intellectual Life in New York City from 1750 to the Beginnings of Our Own Time* (New York: Alfred A. Knopf, 1987), 338.

29. William Harmon, *Time in Ezra Pound's Work* (Chapel Hill: University of North Carolina Press, 1977), 106 (quotation); Marianne Korn, *Ezra Pound: Purpose/Form/Meaning* (London: Pembridge Press, 1983), 123–30.

30. Bender, *New York Intellect*, 338; John Hersey, *Hiroshima* (1946; reprint, New York: Bantam, 1985).

31. Boyer, *By the Bomb's Early Light*, 204; Hersey, *Hiroshima*, 36, 1.

32. Boyer, *By the Bomb's Early Light*, 206 (Macdonald and McCarthy quotations).

33. Carl E. Schorske, "A Life of Learning," Charles Homer Haskins Lecture, American Council of Learned Societies, Washington, D.C., 23 April 1987 (ACLS occasional paper no. 1) (n.p., n.d.), 12.

34. Christopher Brookeman, *American Culture and Society since the 1930s* (New York: Schocken Books, 1984), 37; James E. Magner, Jr., *John Crowe Ransom: Critical Principles and Preoccupations* (Paris: Mouton, 1971), 12.

35. Benjamin Spock, *The Common Sense Book of Baby and Child Care* (New York: Duell, Sloan & Pearce, 1946), 259, 26, 39.

36. Erik H. Erikson, *Childhood and Society* (1950; 2d ed., rev., New York: W. W. Norton, 1963), 155.

37. Thornton Wilder, *The Skin of Our Teeth*, in Hewes, *Famous American Plays of the 1940s*, 28, 32.

38. Philip Rahv, quoted in Brookeman, *American Culture and Society since the 1930s*, 5–6.

39. Hitchcock, *Music in the United States*, 200–201, 205.

40. Jane Feuer, *The Hollywood Musical* (Bloomington: Indiana University Press, 1982), 18–22.

41. "A Young Girl's Fancy," *Ladies' Home Journal*, March 1943, 43; "The Best Modern Architecture Has Its Roots in Our Own Soil," *House Beautiful*, December 1946, 160–61.

42. Virginia Lee Burton, *The Little House* (Boston: Houghton Mifflin, 1942). The mythology of country life was explored more cynically in Betty MacDonald's *The Egg and I* (New York: J. B. Lippincott, 1945), a top-ten nonfiction best-seller in 1945, 1946 (when it was number 1), and 1947.

43. Jackson, *Crabgrass Frontier*, 240.

44. W. J. Stuckey, *The Pulitzer Prize Novels: A Critical Backward Look* (Norman: University of Oklahoma Press, 1966), 152, 155; Henry Nash Smith, *Virgin Land: The American West as Symbol and Myth* (Cambridge, Mass.: Harvard University Press, 1950).

45. "Jefferson Memorial Competition Winners," *Architectural Record* 103 (April 1948): 92–103; "Competition: Jefferson National Expansion Memorial," *Progressive Architecture* 29 (May 1948): 51–73; "Jefferson National Expansion Memorial Competition Winners Announced," *Progressive Architecture* 29 (March 1948): 18; "Arch Argument," *Life*, 8 March 1948, 113.

46. George Nelson and Henry Wright, *Tomorrow's House: A Complete Guide for the Home-Builder* (New York: Simon & Schuster, 1946), 2, 4.

47. Nathan Broder, *Samuel Barber* (New York: G. Schirmer, 1954), 63–64; *New Records* 19 (May 1951): 13.

48. Bruce Babington and Peter William Evans, *Blue Skies and Silver Linings: Aspects of the Hollywood Musical* (Manchester, Eng.: Manchester University Press, 1985), 141–63.

49. Joshua Loth Liebman, *Peace of Mind* (New York: Simon & Schuster, 1946); Norman Vincent Peale, *A Guide to Confident Living* (New York: Prentice-Hall, 1948); Sydney E. Ahlstrom, *A Religious History of the American People* (New Haven, Conn.: Yale University Press, 1972), 950–63; William L. O'Neill, *American High: The Years of Confidence, 1945–1960* (New York: Free Press, 1986), 212; Winthrop S. Hudson, *Religion in America: An Historical Account of the Development of American Religious Life*, 2d ed. (New York: Charles Scribner's Sons, 1973), 389.

50. Fox, *Reinhold Niebuhr*, p. ix; John Patrick Diggins, *The Proud Decades: America in War and Peace, 1941–1960* (New York: W. W. Norton, 1988), 172–73; Paul Tillich, *The Power of Being* (New Haven, Conn.: Yale University Press, 1952), 144–47, 139, 140, 153, 176 ("meaningless"); Paul Tillich, "The New Being" (1950), reprinted in H. Shelton Smith, Robert T. Handy, and Lefferts A. Loetscher, *American Christianity: An Historical Interpretation with Representative Documents*, vol. 2 (New York: Charles Scribner's Sons, 1963), 465–71.

51. "Heaven, Hell and Judgment Day," *Time*, 20 March 1950, 73 (Graham quotation); "Sickle for the Harvest," *Time*, 14 November 1949, 63–64.

52. Willmar L. Thorkelson, "'Billy' Graham Draws Throngs," *Christian Century*, 25 October 1950, 1270; "Billy in Dixie," *Life*, 27 March 1950, 55; Nathaniel M. Guptill, "Graham Tornado Brushes Maine," *Christian Century*, 26 April 1950, 534.

53. "President and Evangelist Pray in the White House," *New York Times*, 15 July 1950, 11; William E. Leuchtenburg, "Give 'em Harry," *New Republic*, 21 May 1984, 19.

54. Rovere, *Senator Joe McCarthy*, 122.

55. Joseph McCarthy speech at Wheeling, West Virginia, excerpted in William H. Chafe and Harvard Sitkoff, *A History of Our Time: Readings on Postwar America*, 2d ed. (New York: Oxford University Press, 1987), 64–67. This desire for renewal is not necessarily inconsistent with social conservatism. According to Jane De Hart Mathews, the anticommunist crusade could be interpreted as "a revitalization movement designed to eliminate foreign influences and revive traditional values and beliefs in a period of societal stress" ("Art and Politics in Cold War America," *American Historical Review* 81 [October 1976]: 787).

56. Steven A. Sass, *Entrepreneurial Historians and History: Leadership and Rationality in American Economic Historiography, 1940–1960* (New York: Garland Publishing, 1986), 54–58, 71, 83, 89.

57. Hugh G. J. Aitken, "The Entrepreneurial Approach to Economic History," in *Approaches to Economic History*, ed. G. R. Taylor and L. F. Ellsworth (Charlottesville: University Press of Virginia/Eleutherian Mills-Hagley Foundation, 1971), 5; Joseph A. Schumpeter, "The Creative Response in Economic History," *Journal of Economic History* 7 (November 1947): 150, 152–53.

58. Sass, *Entrepreneurial Historians and History*, p. 153; Thomas Cochran, *Railroad Leaders, 1845–1890: The Business Mind in Action* (Cambridge, Mass.: Harvard University Press, 1953); Thomas Cochran, "Role and Sanction in American Entrepreneurial History," in Harvard University Research Center in Entrepreneurial History, *Change and the Entrepreneur* (Cambridge, Mass.: Harvard University Press, 1949), 93–95.

59. "Fighter in a Fighting Year," *Time*, 3 January 1949, 10. The music speedup had been going on at least since 1944, when Benny Goodman's trio recorded "After You've Gone" at 165 beats per minute, as opposed to the 120 tempo of the group's 1935 version (Hitchcock, *Music in the United States*, 217).

60. Selection from Cabell Phillips, *The Truman Presidency: The History of a Triumphant Succession* (New York: Macmillan, 1966), reprinted in J. Joseph Huthmacher, ed., *The Truman Years: The Reconstruction of Postwar America* (Hinsdale, Ill.: Dryden Press, 1972), 125–27.

61. Jack Kerouac, *On the Road* (New York: New American Library, 1957), 111.

62. On the postwar cult of the automobile, see O'Neill, *American High*, 29–32, and Elliot Willensky, *When Brooklyn Was the World, 1920–1957* (New York: Harmony, 1986), 113 (photograph).

63. Catherine Drinker Bowen, *Yankee from Olympus: Justice Holmes and His Family* (Boston: Little, Brown, 1945), xii. On action painting, see Annette Cox, *Art-as-Politics: The Abstract Expressionist Avant-Garde and Society* (Ann Arbor: University of Michigan Research Press, 1982), 4, 11, 66 (Rosenberg quotation), 79, 83–84, 134; Lionel Abel, *The Intellectual Follies: A Memoir of the Literary Venture in New York and Paris* (New York: W. W. Norton, 1984), 210. Abel argues that the abstract expressionist movement involved "a certain Dionysian feeling of renewal" (217).

64. Williams, *Streetcar Named Desire*, 71.

65. Eugene Lewis, *Public Entrepreneurship: Toward a Theory of Bureaucratic Power: The Organizational Lives of Hyman Rickover, J. Edgar Hoover, and Robert Moses* (Bloom-

ington: Indiana University Press, 1980), 7–10, 193, 201 ("'can do' industrialization"), 202, 231–33, 241–44; Robert Moses, *Working for the People: Promise and Performance in Public Service* (New York: Harper & Brothers, 1956), 1.

66. "Preventive Medicine," *Time*, 7 January 1946, 22–24; 6 January 1947, 25–26.

67. "The Year of Decision," *Time*, 5 January 1948, 18–21.

68. Dale Carnegie, *How to Stop Worrying and Start Living* (New York: Simon & Schuster, 1948), xv.

69. Jack Schaefer, *Shane* (New York: Bantam, 1950), 17, 30, 105, 118.

70. Quoted in *New York Times Book Review*, 15 January 1989, 39.

Chapter Four

1. Wendell L. Willkie, *One World* (New York: Simon & Schuster, 1943), 1, 2, 26–27, 140, 159–60, 204–5; Alice Payne Hackett and James Henry Burke, *Eighty Years of Best Sellers, 1895–1975* (New York: R. R. Bowker, 1977), 135–36.

2. Golden MacDonald, *The Little Island* (New York: Doubleday, 1946) (unpaginated).

3. My account of Zanuck's project is adapted from John B. Wiseman, "Darryl F. Zanuck and the Failure of 'One World,' 1943–1945," *Historical Journal of Film, Radio, and Television* 7 (1987): 279–87, 283 (Willkie quotation).

4. Serge Guilbaut, *How New York Stole the Idea of Modern Art: Abstract Expressionism, Freedom, and the Cold War* (Chicago: University of Chicago Press, 1983), 102–5, 105 (Macdonald quotation).

5. *New York Times*, 27 May 1948, 11 (Davis quotations), 28 May 1948, 25, 16 June 1948, 28 (UWF quotation), 8 September 1948, 14, 24 February 1950, 11, 2 October 1950, 6; "Citizen of the World," *Time*, 7 June 1948, 28; *New Yorker*, 5 June 1948, 21; "The Little Man," *Time*, 10 January 1949, 21–22 (Einstein quotation); "Gary Davis Cult Spreads in Europe," *Life*, 24 January 1949, 28–29; "World Citizen Davis Returns," *Life*, 10 April 1950, 47–50.

6. Lewis Mumford, "The Sky Line," *New Yorker*, 25 October 1947, 54–57; "'An Act of Faith,'" *UN Bulletin* 7 (1 November 1949); 495 (Romulo quotation); Ed. Allen, "Capital for the United Nations," *Architectural Record* 99 (March 1946): 85 ("strict functionalism"); "Workshop for the World," *Time*, 2 June 1947, 53 (Wright quotation); "UN Headquarters Report Receives Wide Acclaim," *American City* 62 (September 1947): 117. For a link between the United Nations and Marshall McLuhan's concept of the "global village," see Brookeman, *American Culture and Society*, 133.

7. Buffalo Technical High School, *The Techtonian*, 1947, 9. Riverside High School, *The Skipper*, 1947, 4–5. Warren I. Susman, *Culture as History: The Transformation of American Society in the Twentieth Century* (New York: Pantheon, 1984), 207, 203, and especially chap. 10.

8. Joseph Campbell, *The Hero with a Thousand Faces* (1949; 2d ed., Princeton, N.J.: Princeton University Press, 1968), viii, 385–88.

9. Guilbaut, *How New York Stole the Idea of Modern Art*, 49, 69 (catalog quotation).

10. Cox, *Art-as-Politics*, 43, 74.

11. Motherwell quotation from Robert Motherwell, "What Abstract Art Means to Me," *Arts Digest*, February 1951, 27, quoted in Ann Gibson, "The Rhetoric of Abstract Expressionism," in *Abstract Expressionism: The Critical Developments*, ed. Michael Auping (New York: Harry N. Abrams, 1987), 66–67.

12. Auping, *Abstract Expressionism*, 261.

13. Susman, *Culture as History*, 203–7.

14. Mead, *And Keep Your Powder Dry*, 14, 25, 31, 39, 58, 66, 177, 188–89.

15. Carl Van Doren, "A Vision of the Whole," *Good Housekeeping*, April 1946, 23, 242–43; André Maurois, "What I Learned About America," *Reader's Digest*, March 1947, 25.

16. Geoffrey Gorer, *The American People: A Study in National Character* (1948; rev. ed., New York: W. W. Norton, 1964), 32–33, 36, 40–42, 145–46, 103, 107, 188, 221, 223.

17. David Riesman, with Nathan Glazer and Reuel Denney, *The Lonely Crowd: A Study of the Changing American Character* (1950; abr. ed., New York: Doubleday/ Anchor, 1953), 151. Based on lectures delivered in 1950, David Potter's *People of Plenty: Economic Abundance and the American Character* (1954; Chicago: University of Chicago Press, 1965) was an essentially conservative search for a "unifying factor" or "unifying theme" that would smother incipient cultural fragmentation and allow historians to reassemble the past around a particular vision of the culture of the whole— in this case, the comfortably traditional framework of the nation *People of Plenty* (67, 102, 137, 29–31); Robert M. Collins, "David Potter's *People of Plenty* and the Recycling of Consensus History," *Reviews in American History* 1 (June 1988): 321–36.

18. Carleton S. Coon, "What Type American Are You?" *American Magazine* 141 (June 1946): 52–53, 128–30.

19. Susman, *Culture as History*, 154–59, 205; "First Lady of Radio Takes New Sunday Night Spot," *Life*, 18 September 1944, 58.

20. Roland Marchand, "Visions of Classlessness, Quests for Dominion: American Popular Culture, 1945–1960," in Bremner and Reichard, *Reshaping America*, 165.

21. Nelson George, *The Death of Rhythm & Blues* (New York: Pantheon, 1988), 24–28, 39–49; Marchand, "Visions of Classlessness," 178; Charlie Gillett, *The Sound of the City: The Rise of Rock and Roll* (1970; rev. ed., New York: Pantheon, 1983), 133–34.

22. Marchand, "Visions of Classlessness," 178; Bill C. Malone, *Country Music, U.S.A.* (1968; rev. ed., Austin: University of Texas Press, 1985), 178, 181–83, 205, 211, 236–37; Roger M. Williams, *Sing a Sad Song: The Life of Hank Williams* (1971; 2d ed., Urbana: University of Illinois Press, 1981), 118.

23. Lawrence Lader, "Music That Nobody Hears," *Nation's Business* 38 (September 1950): 58–61; "Music Piped to Apartment Houses," *Business Week*, 14 September 1940, 44–45.

24. Judy Fireman, ed., *TV Book* (New York: Workman Publishing, 1977), 6–11.

25. Phil Glanzer, "Postwar Television," *Radio News*, March 1944, 46, 61; Will Baltin, "Television—for Industry and Home," *Radio News*, January 1945, 53; Hazel Cooley, *Vision in Television* (New York: Channel, 1952), 25–35.

26. "Television," *Life*, 4 September 1944, 85; RCA Victor advertisement, *New York Times*, 13 June 1948, 58; "Hail to the Chief," *Time*, 31 January 1949, 55.

27. Guy DeBord, *Society of the Spectacle* (1967; rev. ed., Detroit: Red and Black,

1983). On the destruction of group life under fascism, see Mario Einaudi, "Fascism," *International Encyclopedia of the Social Sciences*, vol. 5 (N.p.: Macmillan Co. and The Free Press, 1968), 335–41.

28. Lewis H. Titterton, "Radio and Its Progeny," *American Scholar* 10 (October 1942): 499.

29. Charles Norman, *The Case of Ezra Pound* (New York: Bodley Press, 1948), 17–21, 32–42; E. Fuller Torrey, *The Roots of Treason: Ezra Pound and the Secret of St. Elizabeths* (New York: McGraw-Hill, 1984), 134–35 (Pound quotation on presidents); Robert A. Corrigan, "Ezra Pound and the Bollingen Prize Controversy," in *The Forties: Fiction, Poetry, Drama*, ed. Warren French (Deland, Fla.: Everett/Edwards, 1969), 288.

30. The *Saturday Review* and Viereck quotations are in Corrigan, "Ezra Pound and the Bollingen Prize Controversy," 288–90; Korn, *Ezra Pound*, 129–30.

31. Forrest Read, *'76: One World and The Cantos of Ezra Pound* (Chapel Hill: University of North Carolina Press, 1981), 3, 431–39; Korn, *Ezra Pound*, 129, 131; R. Buckminster Fuller, Third Annual Pound Lecture, 7 April 1977, University of Idaho, 3, 7; Norman, *The Case of Ezra Pound*, 60 (man in the abstract).

32. Norman Mailer, *The Naked and the Dead* (New York: New American Library, 1948); Robert Merrill, *Norman Mailer* (Boston: Twayne, 1978), 32–40; Stanley T. Gutman, *Mankind in Barbary: The Individual and Society in the Novels of Norman Mailer* (Hanover, N.H.: University Press of New England, 1975), 13–25; Chester E. Eisinger, *Fiction of the Forties* (Chicago: University of Chicago Press, 1963), 33–38.

33. "Competition: Jefferson National Expansion Memorial," *Progressive Architecture* 29 (May 1948): 52; "Jefferson Memorial Competition Winners," *Architectural Record* 103 (April 1948): 93; "Arch of St. Louis," *Newsweek*, 1 March 1948, 73.

34. Rothko quoted in Michael Auping, "Beyond the Sublime," in Auping, *Abstract Expressionism*, 148; Lewis S. Baer, Chief, Screening Unit, Motion Picture Section, Department of the Army, letter to Robert Flaherty, n.d. [1948], and Al Lewin, MGM, letter to Robert Flaherty, 23 July 1948, both in Standard Oil of New Jersey Papers, University of Louisville, Photographic Archives, Louisville, Kentucky.

35. "Arch Argument," *Life*, 8 March 1948, 113; Stuart Ewen, *All Consuming Images: The Politics of Style in Contemporary Culture* (New York: Basic Books, 1988), 222; Carney, *American Vision*, 372–74; Skinner, *Walden Two*, 42.

36. Warrick, *The Cybernetic Imagination*, 15–16; Ludwig von Bertalanffy, *Robots, Men, and Minds: Psychology in the Modern World* (New York: George Braziller, 1967), 12–13, 17–18, 22, 58–60; Ervin Laszlo, *The Systems View of the World: The Natural Philosophy of the New Developments in the Sciences* (New York: George Braziller, 1972), 79.

37. Definition of cybernetics quoted in Warrick, *The Cybernetic Imagination*, 8; Norbert Wiener, *Cybernetics: Or Control and Communication in the Animal and the Machine* (New York: John Wiley, 1948), 19, 15, 27, 38, 39.

38. J. P. Chaplin and T. S. Krawiec, *Systems and Theories of Psychology* (2d ed., New York: Holt, Rinehart & Winston, 1968), 55–57; Rudolf Arnheim, "The Gestalt Theory of Expression," reprinted in *Documents of Gestalt Psychology*, ed. Mary Henle (Berkeley and Los Angeles: University of California Press, 1961), 316–17; Wolfgang Köhler, "Gestalt Psychology Today," in Henle, *Documents of Gestalt Psychology*, 4.

39. J. Feibleman and J. W. Friend, "The Structure and Function of Organiza-

tion," *Philosophical Review* (1945), reprinted in *Systems Thinking: Selected Readings*, ed., F. E. Emery (Harmondsworth, Eng.: Penguin, 1969), 40, 43, 53.

40. Phillip Selznick, "Foundations of the Theory of Organizations," *American Sociological Review* (1948), reprinted in Emery, *Systems Thinking*, 261–63, 265–69.

41. Walter B. Cannon, *The Wisdom of the Body* (New York: W. W. Norton, 1932); Warrick, *The Cybernetic Imagination*, 9–10; Wiener, *Cybernetics*, 188–89; Stephen J. Cross and William R. Albury, "Walter B. Cannon, L. J. Henderson, and the Organic Analogy," *Osiris* 3, 2d series (1987): 165–92; Selznick, "Foundations of the Theory of Organizations," 267–68.

42. Terry Eagleton, *Literary Theory: An Introduction* (Minneapolis: University of Minnesota Press, 1983), 49, 47.

43. John Kenneth Galbraith, *American Capitalism: The Concept of Countervailing Power* (1952; reprint, Boston: Houghton Mifflin, 1956), 151.

44. Alden Hatch, *Buckminster Fuller: At Home in the Universe* (New York: Crown, 1974), 189 (Cage quotation), 191–92, 204.

45. Hatch, *Buckminster Fuller*, 187; "R. Buckminster Fuller," in Adolf C. Placzek, ed., *Macmillan Encyclopedia of Architects*, vol. 2 (New York: The Free Press, 1982), 125–27; John McHale, *R. Buckminster Fuller* (New York: George Braziller, 1962), 29–31, 42.

46. Gilbert Chase, *America's Music: From the Pilgrims to the Present* (New York: McGraw-Hill, 1955), 599, 603, 608, 612; Nicholas E. Tawa, *A Most Wondrous Babble: American Art Composers, Their Music, and the American Scene, 1950–1985* (Westport, Conn.: Greenwood Press, 1987), 4–5.

47. Hitchcock, *Music in the United States*, 222–23, 230–31, 236.

48. Walter A. Jackson, "The Carnegie Corporation and Gunnar Myrdal's *An American Dilemma*," paper presented at the History of Science Society annual meeting, Raleigh, North Carolina, October 1987, 5; Walter A. Jackson, "The Making of a Social Science Classic: Gunnar Myrdal's *An American Dilemma*," *Perspectives in American History* 2, new series, (1985): 257–58, 264; Gunnar Myrdal, *An American Dilemma: The Negro Problem and Modern Democracy* (New York: Harper & Row, 1944), 56; Walter A. Jackson, "The American Creed from a Swedish Perspective: Gunnar Myrdal's *An American Dilemma*," paper presented at the Southern Historical Association meeting, New Orleans, Louisiana, November 1987, 21. Sociologist William H. Whyte brought some of Myrdal's assimilationist logic to bear on the questions of ethnicity and class in *Street Corner Society: The Social Structure of an Italian Slum* (1943; Chicago: University of Chicago Press, 1964), his influential study of an Italian "slum" called "Cornerville."

49. John W. Aldridge, *In Search of Heresy: American Literature in an Age of Conformity* (1956; reprint, Port Washington, N.Y.: Kennikat Press, 1967), 71–72; Kazin, *New York Jew*, p. 27.

50. Lester D. Friedman, *Hollywood's Image of the Jew* (New York: Frederick Ungar, 1982), 100, 91, 118, 114, 127, 129.

51. For the story of the nation's failure to act on behalf of the Jews, see David S. Wyman, *The Abandonment of the Jews: America and the Holocaust, 1941–1945* (New York: Pantheon, 1984).

52. Arthur Laurents, *Home of the Brave*, in Hewes, *Famous American Plays of the 1940s*, 117, 122, 140, 147, 173, 175, 182.

53. Cox, *Art-as-Politics*, 147–48; David A. Hollinger, "Ethnic Diversity, Cos-

mopolitanism, and the Emergence of the American Liberal Intelligentsia," *American Quarterly* 27 (May 1975): 133–51, 143 (Trilling quotation).

54. Basinger, *The World War II Combat Film*, 53; Woll, *The Hollywood Musical Goes to War*, 136.

55. Frederic Wakeman, *The Hucksters* (New York: Rinehart & Company, 1946); Stephen L. Del Sesto, "Wasn't the Future of Nuclear Energy Wonderful?" in Corn, *Imagining Tomorrow*, 61, 69; Gorer, *The American People*, 212.

56. Roland Marchand, "Visions of Classlessness," in Bremner and Reichard, *Reshaping America*, 169; C. Wright Mills, *White Collar: The American Middle Classes* (1951; reprint, New York: Oxford University Press, 1967), ix.

57. Clifton Daniel, ed., *Chronicle of the Twentieth Century* (Mount Kisco, N.Y.: Chronicle Publications, 1987), 642.

58. The discussion of secret societies is adapted from William Graebner, "Outlawing Teenage Populism: The Campaign against Secret Societies in the American High School, 1900–1960," *Journal of American History* 74 (September 1987): 411–35.

59. A similar constellation of fears and anxieties can be seen in the concept of "mafia," which was revived in the late 1940s and early 1950s after decades of disuse to describe certain forms of criminal activity. Like "secret society," the term "mafia" suggested an ethnic-based group to which members granted an excessive and misplaced loyalty (Dwight C. Smith, Jr., *The Mafia Mystique* [New York: Basic Books, 1975], 7–8, 22, 79, 83–85, 121, 126, 129).

60. This discussion of toleration is adapted from William Graebner, *Coming of Age in Buffalo: Youth and Authority in the Postwar Era* (Philadelphia: Temple University Press, 1990), 112–13.

61. Walter Winchell, *Winchell Exclusive* (Englewood Cliffs, N.J.: Prentice-Hall, 1975), 194–96.

62. James Bryant Conant, "Challenge of the Times," *Vital Speeches* 14 (15 August 1948): 644.

Chapter Five

1. Jean-Paul Sartre, "We Write for Our Own Time," *Virginia Quarterly Review* (Spring 1947): 237–38.

2. *Holiday*, March 1946, 3.

3. Davenport, "The Pursuit of Happiness," 98, 113.

4. Rollo May, *The Meaning of Anxiety* (1950; rev. ed., New York: W. W. Norton, 1977), ix, x, 4, 6–7; Schlesinger, *The Vital Center*, 1, 246; Joshua Loth Liebman, *Peace of Mind* (New York: Simon & Schuster, 1946), 87, 90; Ferdinand Lundberg and Marynia F. Farnham, *Modern Woman: The Lost Sex* (New York: Harper & Brothers, 1947), 47–48. For another perspective, see O'Neill, *American High*, especially p. 7.

5. "A Letter to God," 1948 *Bennett Beacon*, Bennett High School, Buffalo, New York, 8; William Faulkner Nobel Prize acceptance speech, reprinted in "Trade Winds," *Saturday Review of Literature* 34 (3 February 1951): 5.

6. Al Capp, "The Comedy of Charlie Chaplin," *Atlantic Monthly* (February 1950): 25–29, reprinted in White and Abel, *The Funnies*, 265, 268–69. On the fluoridation controversy, see "The Battle for Sound Teeth," *American Journal of Public Health* 42 (October 1952): 1304–6.

7. "The Year of Decision," *Time*, 5 January 1948, 21, 20; Thomas Merton, *Seeds*

of Contemplation (1949; reprint, New York: Dell, 1960), 54; Liebman, *Peace of Mind*, 101–2; Carnegie, *How to Stop Worrying*, 49–50; Erich Fromm, *Man for Himself: An Inquiry into the Psychology of Ethics* (New York: Rinehart, 1947), 76–78, 81–82.

8. Mead, *And Keep Your Powder Dry*, 37.

9. Arthur Asa Berger, *The Comic-Stripped American* (New York: Walker, 1973), 192; Abel, *The Intellectual Follies*, 128–29; Søren Kierkegaard, *The Concept of Dread*, quoted in May, *The Meaning of Anxiety*, 37.

10. Hannah Arendt, "French Existentialism," *The Nation* 162 (23 February 1946): 227; May, *The Meaning of Anxiety*, x, 12 ("vacuum of faith"); Schlesinger, *The Vital Center*, 246, 244; John P. Diggins, *Mussolini and Fascism: The View from America* (Princeton, N.J.: Princeton University Press, 1972), 489–90. See also "Hannah Arendt" and "Totalitarianism" in *International Encyclopedia of the Social Sciences*.

11. Philip Gleason, "Identifying Identity: A Semantic History," *Journal of American History* 69 (March 1983): 910–31; Harry Emerson Fosdick, *On Being a Real Person* (New York: Harper & Row, 1943), 28, 30; Fulton J. Sheen, *Peace of Soul* (New York: McGraw-Hill, 1949), 7–8.

12. Ralph Linton, *The Study of Man: An Introduction* (New York: D. Appleton-Century, 1936), 113–31; Lewis M. Terman and Catherine Cox Miles, *Sex and Personality: Studies in Masculinity and Femininity* (New York: McGraw-Hill, 1936); Joseph H. Pleck, "The Theory of Male Sex Role Identity: Its Rise and Fall, 1936 to the Present," in *In the Shadow of the Past: Psychology Portrays the Sexes*, ed. Miriam Lewin (New York: Columbia University Press, 1983), 207; Malone, *Country Music, U.S.A.*, 196.

13. Pleck, "Theory of Male Sex Role Identity," 213–14; Philip Wylie, *Generation of Vipers* (New York: Rinehart, 1942), 184–204; Chauncey, "The National Panic over 'Sex Crimes,'" 1, 27, 41–43.

14. Spock, *The Common Sense Book of Baby and Child Care*, 484, 492, 254.

15. Pleck, "Theory of Male Sex Role Identity," 215–16; Chauncey, "The National Panic over 'Sex Crimes,'" 38; T. W. Adorno, Else Frenkel-Brunswik, Daniel J. Levinson, R. Nevitt Sanford, *The Authoritarian Personality* (New York: Harper & Row, 1950), 428; Spillane, *I, the Jury*, 236, 246, 116. On hypermasculinity, see also Freedman, "'Uncontrolled Desires,'" 96.

16. Lundberg and Farnham, *Modern Woman*, v, 10, 117, 118.

17. Margaret Mead, *Male and Female: A Study of the Sexes in a Changing World* (New York: William Morrow, 1949), 382, 368, 371, 160.

18. Ralph Ellison, "The Art of Fiction: An Interview," in *The Merrill Studies in Invisible Man*, ed. Ronald Gottesman (Columbus, Ohio: Charles E. Merrill Publishing, 1971), 45; Ralph Ellison, *Invisible Man* (New York: New American Library, 1952), 17; John S. Wright, "To the Battle Royal: Ralph Ellison and the Quest for Black Leadership in Postwar America," in *Recasting America: Culture and Politics in the Age of Cold War*, ed. Lary May (Chicago: University of Chicago, 1989), 246–66; Ellison, "Art of Fiction," 47.

19. Fromm, *Man for Himself*, 76–82; Riesman, Glazer, and Denney, *The Lonely Crowd*, 41–42, 86–100; Bell, *Crisis in Education*, 13.

20. Schlesinger, *The Vital Center*, 1; Campbell, *The Hero with a Thousand Faces*, 383; Berger, *The Comic-Stripped American*, 153, 157–58; Williams, *Sing a Sad Song*, 82, 118; Charles Mergendahl, *It's Only Temporary* (Garden City, N.Y.: Doubleday, 1950); Jackson, *Crabgrass Frontier*, 235, 241–42.

21. Gleason, "Identifying Identity," 927–28; Theodor Adorno and Max Hork-heimer, *Dialectic of Enlightenment* (1944; London: Verso 1979), 138; Brookeman, *American Culture and Society*, 83–84.

22. Carson McCullers, *The Member of the Wedding*, in Hewes, *Famous American Plays of the 1940s*, 404, 427–28, 437.

23. Erikson, *Childhood and Society*, 262, 282, 419, 307 (Biff quotation); Arthur Miller, *Death of a Salesman* (1949; New York: Viking Press, 1967); Liebman, *Peace of Mind*, 60; Schlesinger, *The Vital Center*, 247.

24. Oscar Handlin, *The Uprooted* (1951; 2d ed., Boston: Little, Brown, 1973), 22, 94–95, 271, 95, 269, 96–97, 271–72.

25. Faulkner quoted in "Trade Winds," *Saturday Review of Literature* 34 (3 February 1951): 4; Carnegie, *How to Stop Worrying*, 2, 66 ("law of averages").

26. Spock, *The Common Sense Book of Baby and Child Care*, 145, 3, 20.

27. Kate Smith, *Upon My Lips a Song* (New York: Funk & Wagnall's, 1960), 90, 155; "First Lady of Radio Takes New Sunday Night Spot," *Life*, 18 September 1944, 58; Robert K. Merton, *Mass Persuasion: The Social Psychology of a War Bond Drive* (New York: Harper & Brothers, 1946), 80, 83–84, 142, 143.

28. Ernest Havemann, "How Did That Guy Get on the Radio," *Reader's Digest*, September 1948, 64; Carol Hughes, "What's the Secret of King Arthur Godfrey," *Coronet*, December 1949, 160–61 (Godfrey quotation).

29. Doane, *The Desire to Desire*, 41–47.

30. L. Ron Hubbard, *Dianetics: The Modern Science of Mental Health* (1950; reprint, Los Angeles: Bridge Publications, 1985), 7, 9, 29, 62, 71, 76, 98, 101, 232, 20–21; see also Liebman, *Peace of Mind*, 28.

31. Liebman, *Peace of Mind*, 12; Hannah Arendt, "French Existentialism," *The Nation* 162 (23 February 1946): 226, 227.

32. Lundberg and Farnham, *Modern Woman*, 356–57.

33. Schlesinger, *The Vital Center*, 248, 253; Merton, *Seeds of Contemplation*, 20, 28, 16.

34. Campbell, *The Hero with a Thousand Faces*, 388, 386, 391.

35. Lewis Mumford, *The Conduct of Life* (New York: Harcourt, Brace, 1951), 190–91, 129–30, 23, 92–94, 7–8, 40–45.

36. Davenport, "Pursuit of Happiness," 113; Tom Bottomore, *The Frankfurt School* (Chichester, Eng.: Ellis Horwood, 1984), 19–20.

37. Liebman, *Peace of Mind*, 18, 101–2; Fosdick, *Being a Real Person*, 8; Hubbard, *Dianetics*, 192–93; Erikson, *Childhood and Society*, 286, 38. Davenport, "Pursuit of Happiness," 110.

Chapter Six

1. *Saturday Evening Post*, 20 February 1943, 12–13; 27 February 1943, 12–13; 6 March 1943, 12–13; 13 March 1943, 12–13; "U.S. Artist," *New Yorker*, 17 March 1945, 34, 38, 41. Stephen Vincent Benét, essay accompanying Rockwell photo "Freedom from Fear," *Saturday Evening Post*, 13 March 1943, 12. Having once failed to appreciate the potential in Rockwell's early sketches for the series, government officials reversed their course and found a use for the paintings in the marketing of war bonds; the Office of War Information distributed some four million sets.

2. Nelson Algren, *The Man with the Golden Arm*, 154, 75–76, 123. See also

Stewart H. Benedict, "The Pattern of Determinism in J. P. Marquand's Novels," *Ball State Teachers College Forum* 2 (Winter 1961–62): 60–64.

3. Paul A. Carter, *The Creation of Tomorrow: Fifty Years of Magazine Science Fiction* (New York: Columbia University Press, 1977), 96, 100, 101–2; David F. Noble, *Forces of Production: A Social History of Industrial Automation* (New York: Oxford University Press, 1986), 36, 47.

4. Skinner, *Walden Two*, 115, 257, 263.

5. Gold Seal vermouth advertisement, *Time*, 9 June 1941, 64; Philip Morris and U.S. Rubber advertisements, *Saturday Evening Post*, 28 October 1944, 39, 40; Eugene J. Watts, "Cop and Crooks: The War at Home," in Bremner and Reichard, *Reshaping America*, 292; Jules Feiffer, *The Great Comic Book Heroes* (New York: Bonanza Press, 1965), 69–70.

6. Charles Hamm, "Music and American Society, 1945–1960," seminar paper (n.d.), Music Library, State University of New York at Buffalo, 23–26, 37; entries for 18 August and 4 October 1945, Laura Rew Pickett diary, in possession of Jack T. Ericson, State University College, Fredonia, New York; Vannevar Bush, *Science: The Endless Frontier. A Report to the President* (Washington, D.C.: GPO, July 1945), 1, 5–6.

7. Robert Westbrook, "Horrors—Theirs and Ours: The *Politics* Circle and the Good War," *Radical History Review* 36 (September 1986): 16–21; Lyman Bryson, Louis Finkelstein, and R. M. MacIver, eds., *Conflicts of Power in Modern Culture*, Seventh Symposium of the Conference on Science, Technology and Religion (1947; reprint, New York: Cooper Square Publishers, 1964), 71, 356 (Northrop quotation).

8. "Steep Curve to Level Four," *Time*, 2 January 1950, 39.

9. Warrick, *The Cybernetic Imagination*, 131–34; Andrew Hamilton, "Brains That Click," *Popular Mechanics*, March 1949, 165; "Machines Can Play Chess, but Human Should Win," *Science News Letter* 58 (30 December 1950): 418.

10. Dwight Macdonald, "The Responsibility of Peoples," reprinted in Dwight Macdonald, *The Responsibility of Peoples: And Other Essays in Political Criticism* (1957; reprint, Westport, Conn.: Greenwood Press, 1974), 12, 14, 19.

11. Bowen, *Yankee from Olympus*, 220, 248.

12. H. Bruce Franklin, *Robert A. Heinlein: America as Science Fiction* (New York: Oxford University Press, 1980), 94–95; Stewart, *Earth Abides*, 4, 5, 18, 162, 191.

13. Charles Marowitz, *The Method as Means: An Acting Survey* (London: Herbert Jenkins, 1961), 34–39; Konstantin Stanislavsky, *Building a Character*, trans. Elizabeth Reynolds Hapgood (New York: Theatre Arts Books, 1949), x, 47, 76, 280; H. D. Albright, *Working up a Part: A Manual for the Beginning Actor* (Boston: Houghton Mifflin, 1947), 86–90; Stanley Kahan, *Introduction to Acting* (New York: Harcourt, Brace & World, 1962), 40.

14. Boyer, *By the Bomb's Early Light*, 205–6.

15. Wardell B. Pomeroy, *Dr. Kinsey and the Institute for Sex Research* (New York: New American Library, 1972), 303; "Our 'Unsavory Character' Resents Speed Ratings Applied to Women," *Saturday Evening Post*, 3 October 1953, 12.

16. Babington and Evans, *Blue Skies and Silver Linings*, 114, 119, 123, 130, 137, 125.

17. Martin Sutton, "Patterns of Meaning in the Musical," in *Genre: The Musical*, ed. Rick Altman (London: Routledge & Kegan Paul, 1981), 191, 196; Feuer, *The Hollywood Musical*, 71, 84, 2–5, 9, 13–15.

18. Carney, *American Vision*, 301, 351, 380, 449, 452, 459, 343, 325–30.

19. William Graebner, "The Apple Boy: Individual and Community in the Era of the Second World War," *New York Folklore* 10 (Summer–Fall 1984): 84.

20. Raymond Chandler, *Trouble Is My Business* (1950; reprint, New York: Vintage Books, 1988), 590.

21. Schlesinger, *The Vital Center*, 243–56.

22. See especially Brookeman, *American Culture and Society*, 188–202, and Lary May's Introduction and the essays by Erika Doss and Lewis A. Erenberg in May, *Recasting America*.

23. Parker quoted in Max Harrison, *Charlie Parker* (New York: A. S. Barnes, 1961), 8–9; Dorsey quoted in Ross Russell, *Bird Lives! The High Life and Hard Times of Charlie (Yardbird) Parker* (New York: Charterhouse, 1973), 173.

24. Russell, *Bird Lives!*, 198, 190; Harrison, *Charlie Parker*, 33, 45; Hitchcock, *Music in the United States*, 218; H. Wiley Hitchcock and Stanley Sadie, eds., *The New Grove Dictionary of American Music*, vol. 1 (London: Macmillan, 1986), 260–61; Lewis A. Erenberg, "Things to Come: Swing Bands, Bebop, and the Rise of a Postwar Jazz Scene," in May, *Recasting America*, 221–45.

25. James Johnson Sweeney, *Alexander Calder* (New York: Museum of Modern Art, 1951), 70, 64–66 (Sartre quotation).

26. James Klotsky, ed., *Merce Cunningham* (New York: E. P. Dutton, 1975), 12, 23, 13.

27. Ilene Strelitz, "'Repetition' as Cultural Rebellion: 'Boredom,' the Avant-Garde, and Rock and Roll," *OneTwoThreeFour: A Rock 'n' Roll Quarterly* 4 (Winter 1987): 45; "Cage," Hitchcock and Sadie, *New Grove Dictionary of American Music*.

28. "Percussion Concert," *Life*, 15 March 1943, reprinted in *John Cage*, ed. Richard E. Kostelanetz (New York: Praeger, 1970) (unpaginated); Michael Nyman, *Experimental Music: Cage and Beyond* (New York: Schirmer Books, 1974), 28 ("discursive language"); Strelitz, "'Repetition' as Cultural Rebellion," 43; William Brooks, "Choice and Change in Cage's Recent Music," in *A John Cage Reader*, ed. Peter Gena and Jonathan Brent (New York: C. F. Peters, 1982), 85–86, 96; "Interview with Roger Reynolds" (1961), in *John Cage* (New York: Henmar Press, 1962), 47–48; John Cage, "Defense of Satie," in Kostelanetz, *John Cage*, 84 ("freedom elements"), 79 ("differentiation").

29. Brookeman, *American Culture and Society*, 199 (Motherwell quotation); Guilbaut, *How New York Stole the Idea of Modern Art*, 142 (Still quotation).

30. Ann Gibson, "The Rhetoric of Abstract Expressionism," in Auping, *Abstract Expressionism*, 78 (Newman quotation); Cox, *Art-as-Politics*, 69; Elizabeth Frank, *Jackson Pollock* (New York: Abbeville Press, 1983), 66; Rudolf E. Kuenzli, "Pollock's Mural," in *Human Rights/Human Wrongs: Art and Social Change*, ed. Robert Hobbs and Frederick Woodard (Ames: University of Iowa Museum of Art, 1986), 122–23; Marcelin Pleynet, "For an Approach to Abstract Expressionism," in Auping, *Abstract Expressionism*, 42.

31. Gibson, "Rhetoric of Abstract Expressionism," 83.

32. Bender, *New York Intellect*, 338; Guilbaut, *How New York Stole the Idea of Modern Art*, 158 (Rothko quotation), 197–98 ("art of erasure"). See also Clement Greenberg, "Towards a Newer Laocoon," reprinted in *Pollock and After: The Critical Debate*, ed. Francis Frascina (New York: Harper & Row, 1985), 39.

33. Milton W. Brown, "After Three Years," *Magazine of Art* 39 (April 1946): 138

("limitations of craft"); Mathews, "Art and Politics in Cold War America," 772–73, 780; Eva Cockcroft, "Abstract Expressionism, Weapon of the Cold War," in Frascina, *Pollock and After*, 129–31; Guilbaut, *How New York Stole the Idea of Modern Art*, 193.

34. Michael Leja, "The Formation of an Avant-Garde in New York," in Auping, *Abstract Expressionism*, 20–21 (Baziotes quotation); Guilbaut, *How New York Stole the Idea of Modern Art*, 181; Max Kozloff, "American Painting during the Cold War," in Frascina, *Pollock and After*, 111 (Motherwell quotation).

35. Guilbaut, *How New York Stole the Idea of Modern Art*, 189 ("ceaseless exploration"); 202 (Schlesinger quotation); Cox, *Art-as-Politics*, 134.

36. Russell Jacoby, *The Last Intellectuals: American Culture in the Age of Academe* (New York: Basic Books, 1987), 90, 32; Aldridge, *In Search of Heresy*, 17; Alan M. Wald, *The New York Intellectuals: The Rise and Decline of the Anti-Stalinist Left from the 1930s to the 1980s* (Chapel Hill: University of North Carolina Press, 1987), 218; Pells, *The Liberal Mind in a Conservative Age*, 117–82.

37. T. W. Adorno, "A Social Critique of Radio Music," *Kenyon Review* 7 (1944): 210–16; Paul F. Lazarsfeld and Robert K. Merton, "Mass Communication, Popular Taste, and Organized Social Action" (1948), reprinted in Bernard Rosenberg and David Manning White, *Mass Culture: The Popular Arts in America* (Glencoe, Ill.: Free Press, 1957), 457, 459, 464, 472–73; John Bainbridge, *Little Wonder, or, The Reader's Digest and How It Grew* (New York: Reynal & Hitchcock, 1945), 131–32.

38. Brookeman, *American Culture and Society*, 52 (Macdonald quotation), 50; James J. Martine, ed., *Critical Essays on Eugene O'Neill* (Boston: G. K. Hall, 1984), p. 52 (O'Neill quotation); Jackson Lears, "A Matter of Taste: Corporate Cultural Hegemony in a Mass-Consumption Society," in May, *Recasting America*, 46 (Trilling quotation).

39. Clement Greenberg, "Avant-Garde and Kitsch," reprinted in Frascina, *Pollock and After*, 30, 25.

40. Joseph Horowitz, *Understanding Toscanini: How He Became an American Culture-God and Helped Create a New Audience for Old Music* (Minneapolis: University of Minnesota Press, 1988), 268–69, 227 (Sarnoff quotation), 237 (Adorno quotation); Theodor Adorno, et al., *The Authoritarian Personality*.

41. Greenberg, "Avant-Garde and Kitsch," 23; R. P. Blackmur, "A Burden for Critics," *Hudson Review* 1 (Summer 1948): 173, 180; Mark Schorer, "Technique as Discovery," *Hudson Review* 1 (Spring 1948): 81, 67; Kazin, *New York Jew*, 44.

42. Max Ascoli, *The Power of Freedom* (New York: Farrar, Straus, 1949), 34.

43. Daniel Bell, *The End of Ideology: On the Exhaustion of Political Ideas in the Fifties* (1960; rev. ed., New York: Free Press, 1965); John Gunther, *Inside U.S.A.* (New York: Harper & Brothers, 1947), 638, 375, 303, 916, 404–5, 305.

44. Gene Wise, *American Historical Explanations: A Strategy for Grounded Inquiry* (2d ed. rev., Minneapolis: University of Minnesota Press, 1980), 226; Howard Brick, *Daniel Bell and the Decline of Intellectual Radicalism: Social Theory and Political Reconciliation in the 1940s* (Madison: University of Wisconsin Press, 1986), 121–22 ("negativism," Bell quotation); Wald, *New York Intellectuals*, 220–21; Robert Fisher and Joseph M. Kling, "Leading the People: Two Approaches to the Role of Ideology in Community Organizing," *Radical America* 21 (January–February 1987): 41 (Alinsky quotation).

45. Edmund Wilson, *Memoirs of Hecate County* (Garden City, N.Y.: Doubleday

& Co., 1946); Mary McCarthy, *The Oasis* (New York: Random House, 1949); Wald, *New York Intellectuals*, 239; Stephen L. Tanner, *Lionel Trilling* (Boston: Twayne, 1988), 23, 19.

46. Lionel Trilling, *The Middle of the Journey* (1947; reprint, New York: Avon Library, 1966), 228, 229, 307, 309, 310.

Chapter Seven

1. Frank Kermode, *The Sense of an Ending: Studies in the Theory of Fiction* (New York: Oxford University Press, 1967); Polan, *Power and Paranoia*, 222, 223.

2. Allen Guttmann, *The Games Must Go On: Avery Brundage and the Olympic Movement* (New York: Columbia University Press, 1984), 116.

3. Westbrook, "Horrors—Theirs and Ours," 16, 19.

4. Bernard DeVoto, *The Year of Decision: 1846* (Boston: Little, Brown, 1943), 5; Eagleton, *Literary Theory*, 46–50; William E. Leuchtenburg, "Preacher of Paradox," review of Fox, *Reinhold Niebuhr*, *Atlantic Monthly*, January 1986, 93–95; Fox, *Reinhold Niebuhr*, 234 ("tragic sense"); Niebuhr, *The Irony of American History*, 59, 88, 133.

5. Wise, *American Historical Explanations*, 224, 226; Weldon Kees, "For My Daughter" (1943), in *The Contemporary American Poets*, 178; Schlesinger, *The Vital Center*, 254, 10.

Bibliographic Essay

Three chronological reviews of the 1940s are especially useful. James Trager, ed., *The People's Chronology: A Year-by-Year Record of Human Events from Prehistory to the Present* (New York: Holt, Rinehart & Winston, 1979), is strong on cultural developments; Thomas M. Leonard, *Day by Day: The Forties* (New York: Facts on File, 1977) can help in establishing an event's precise relation to contemporaneous developments in other fields; Clifton Daniel, ed., *Chronicle of the Twentieth Century* (Mount Kisco, N. Y.: Chronicle Publications, 1987), will irritate some readers with its glosses of events in a newspaper article format, but an hour spent with its 167 pages on the forties provides an overview of the decade not available elsewhere.

There is no existing history of American thought and culture in the 1940s. Because 1945 has traditionally been used as the end of one age and the beginning of another, only a handful of books treat the decade as a unit. Warren French, ed., *The Forties: Fiction, Poetry, Drama* (Deland, Fla.: Everett/Edwards, 1969), is a collection of scholarly essays on major figures and events. Chester E. Eisinger, *Fiction of the Forties* (Chicago: University of Chicago Press, 1963), treats the forties as an age marked by "incoherence and uncertainty"; it remains the starting point for an examination of the novel. *Out of the Forties* (1981; reprint, New York: Simon & Schuster, 1985) by journalist Nicholas Lemann is a more positive assessment based on the Standard Oil photographic collection at the University of Louisville Photographic Archives. For Lemann the extraordinary series of photographs taken for Standard Oil of New Jersey under the direction of Roy Stryker capture the watershed of the immediate postwar years, "the end of a long bad time and the beginning of a time of great confidence, prosperity, and change." Film studies, the area of the most creative and challenging recent scholarship, has given us Mary Ann Doane, *The Desire to Desire: The Woman's Film of the 1940s* (Bloomington: Indiana University Press, 1987), which employs the theory of the gaze (who looks at whom) to explain how the cinema has elaborated and contained female subjectivity, and Dana Polan's *Power and Paranoia: History, Narra-*

tive, and the American Cinema, 1940–1950 (New York: Columbia University Press, 1986), which suggests that the forties, far from being divided at its midpoint between wartime consensus and postwar conflict, was a decade unified by its troubled relationship with narrative systems and structures.

Some of the best introductions to the thought and culture of the forties are to be found in books with a larger focus. John Patrick Diggins, *The Proud Decades: America in War and in Peace, 1941–1960* (New York: W. W. Norton, 1988), distinguishes between an optimistic popular culture and a pessimistic high culture; it is particularly strong on the latter, especially on the role of the refugee intellectuals. Lary May has assembled a superb collection of essays in *Recasting America: Culture and Politics in the Age of Cold War* (Chicago: University of Chicago Press, 1989); almost all touch on the 1940s. Christopher Brookeman, *American Culture and Society since the 1930s* (New York: Schocken Books, 1984), is very strong on the Frankfurt School, the mass culture debate, the New Criticism, and modernism. Geoffrey Perrett, *Days of Sadness, Years of Triumph: The American People, 1939–1945* (Baltimore: Penguin Books, 1974), has revealing chapters on education, democracy, leisure, and racial discrimination. John Morton Blum, *V Was for Victory: Politics and American Culture during World War II* (New York: Harcourt Brace Jovanovich, 1976), is especially vivid on wartime psychology, literature, heroism, and consumerism. Focusing on the 1950s, William L. O'Neill's *American High: The Years of Confidence, 1945–1960* (New York: Free Press, 1986) presents a case counter to my own; it also slights cultural and intellectual history. *Reshaping America: Society and Institutions, 1945–1960*, edited by Robert H. Bremner and Gary W. Reichard (Columbus: Ohio State University Press, 1982), contains several relevant essays, especially Roland Marchand's on popular culture. Warren I. Susman describes the forties as an age of participation and adjustment in "Culture and Commitment," a chapter in his *Culture as History: The Transformation of American Society in the Twentieth Century* (New York: Pantheon Books, 1984). Though not written for scholars, Joseph C. Goulden, *The Best Years, 1945–1950* (New York: Atheneum, 1976), is engaging and informative; the chapters on afternoon soap operas and early television are especially good. George Lipsitz, *Class and Culture in Cold War America: "A Rainbow at Midnight"* (South Hadley, Mass.: J. F. Bergin, 1982), successfully links such cultural phenomena as rhythm and blues and film noir to the mass demonstrations and wildcat strikes of the postwar era.

Though they do not treat intellectual and cultural history to any significant extent, Richard Polenberg's books are useful in understanding the period. See his *One Nation Divisible: Class, Race, and Ethnicity in the United States since 1938* (New York: Penguin, 1980); *War and Society: The United States, 1941–1945* (New York: J. B. Lippincott, 1972), especially the chapter "Civil Liberties and Concentration Camps"; and *America at War: The Home Front, 1941–1945* (Englewood Cliffs, N.J.: Prentice-Hall, 1968), a valuable collection of primary and secondary materials. Ross Gregory, *America 1941: A Nation at the Crossroads* (New York: Free Press, 1989), is full of relatively undigested information on sports, leisure, religion, and sexual attitudes. Dyed-in-the-wool Manhattanites may find a nugget or two in Jan Morris, *Manhattan '45* (New York: Oxford University Press, 1987). *Time's* man-of-the-year essays, which appear in the first issue of each year, offer still another avenue into the culture of the forties.

On the war, see David S. Wyman, *The Abandonment of the Jews: America and the Holocaust, 1941–1945* (New York: Pantheon, 1984), which reveals the nation's sordid failure to help the Jews. Paul Boyer's *By the Bomb's Early Light: American Thought and Culture at the Dawn of the Atomic Age* (New York: Pantheon, 1985) is by far the best book on the cultural impact of the bomb in the late 1940s, though John Hersey's novel *Hiroshima* (1946; reprint, New York: Bantam, 1985) remains a revealing account of how Americans were able to absorb the knowledge of what they had done. The decade's reconstruction of sexual and gender relations has been thoroughly studied. See John Costello, *Virtue under Fire: How World War II Changed Our Social and Sexual Attitudes* (Boston: Little, Brown, 1985), and Susan M. Hartmann, *The Home Front and Beyond: American Women in the 1940s* (Boston: Twayne, 1982), especially the chapter, "Models of Womanhood in the Popular Culture," which argues the centrality of domesticity even during the war.

In addition to the May collection, the relationship between culture and the cold war has been explored in James Gilbert, *A Cycle of Outrage: America's Reaction to the Juvenile Delinquent in the 1950s* (New York: Oxford University Press, 1986). Jane De Hart Mathews locates the hostility to abstract expressionism in the desire for certitude and control in "Art and Politics in Cold War America," *American Historical Review* 81 (October 1976): 762–87. Estelle B. Freedman explains how the sex-crime panics redefined sexual normality and elevated the status of psychiatrists in "'Uncontrolled Desires': The Response to the Sexual Psychopath, 1920–1960," *Journal of American History* 74 (June 1987): 83–106. Stanley I. Kutler deals provocatively with the story of Ezra Pound in *The American Inquisition: Justice and Injustice in the Cold War* (New York: Hill and Wang, 1982). Richard H. Rovere, *Senator Joe McCarthy* (1960; reprint, New York: World Publishing, 1973), presents McCarthy as having been in opposition to the dominant conformist impulses of the age.

Film has produced a rich literature, most of it within film criticism rather than history. Besides the Doane and Polan books, students of the period must read Raymond Carney, *American Vision: The Films of Frank Capra* (Cambridge, Eng.: Cambridge University Press, 1986), which presents Capra as a spokesperson for the individual imagination in a world threatened by the forces of control, and J. P. Telotte, *Voices in the Dark: The Narrative Patterns of Film Noir* (Urbana: University of Illinois Press, 1989). Robert B. Ray, *A Certain Tendency of the Hollywood Cinema, 1930–1980* (Princeton, N.J.: Princeton University Press, 1985), explores ways in which even Hollywood productions could subvert the society's dominant ideology. Hollywood's relationship with the wartime propaganda apparatus is treated in Clayton R. Koppes and Gregory D. Black, *Hollywood Goes to War: How Politics, Profits, and Propaganda Shaped World War II Movies* (New York: Free Press, 1987), and Jeanine Basinger defines and interprets a particular genre in *The World War II Combat Film: Anatomy of a Genre* (New York: Columbia University Press, 1986). Bruce Babington and Peter William Evans offer readings of two Jolson films and the musical *Summer Holiday* in *Blue Skies and Silver Linings: Aspects of the Hollywood Musical* (Manchester, Eng.: Manchester University Press, 1985), and Jane Feuer analyzes the mystifying purpose of film in *The Hollywood Musical* (Bloomington: Indiana University Press, 1982). Also useful are Lester D. Friedman, *Hollywood's Image of the Jew* (New York: Frederick Ungar, 1982); Robert G. Porfirio, "No Way out: Existential Motifs in the Film Noir," *Sight and Sound* 45 (Autumn 1976): 212–17; and June Sochen, "*Mildred Pierce* and Women in Film," *American Quarterly* 30 (Spring 1978): 3–20, as well as the Winter 1979 issue of *American Quarterly*, which includes essays on three forties films.

Abstract expressionism has received as much if not more scholarly attention than film. One can begin with two collections of essays: Michael Auping, ed., *Abstract Expressionism: The Critical Developments* (New York: Harry N. Abrams, 1987), and Francis Frascina, ed., *Pollock and After: The Critical Debate* (New York: Harper & Row, 1985), which emphasizes the alienation and engagement of this group of artists. Annette Cox, *Art-as-Politics: The Abstract Expressionist Avant-Garde and Society* (Ann Arbor: University of Michigan Research Press, 1982), emphasizes abstract expressionism's debt to surrealism, while Rudolf E. Kuenzli, "Pollock's *Mural*," in *Human Rights/Human Wrongs: Art and Social Change*, ed. Robert Hobbs and Frederick Woodard (Ames: University of Iowa Museum of Art, 1986), makes the connection to jazz. The richest analysis of the relationship between the cold war and abstract expressionism is Serge Guilbaut, *How New York Stole the Idea of Modern Art: Abstract Expressionism, Freedom, and the Cold War* (Chicago: University of Chicago Press, 1983). For a good introduction to Jackson Pollock, see Elizabeth Frank, *Jackson Pollock* (New York: Abbeville Press, 1983).

Forties architecture remains an unstudied field. Suburbia has been treated in Gwendolyn Wright, *Building the Dream: A Social History of Housing in America* (New York: Pantheon, 1981), and Kenneth T. Jackson, *Crabgrass Frontier: The Suburbanization of the United States* (New York: Oxford University Press, 1985). The competition that produced the St. Louis Arch must be approached through primary sources, including the pages of *Architectural Record*, *Life*, and *Progressive Architecture*. John McHale, *R. Buckminster Fuller* (New York: George Braziller, 1962), provides an adequate introduction to its subject's life and work. Stuart Ewen's sweeping study of style, *All Consuming Images: The Politics of Style in Contemporary Culture* (New York: Basic Books, 1988), sees the forties as a decade of reaction against the excesses of modernism in architecture and other fields, a theme echoed in Brian Horrigan, "The Home of Tomorrow, 1927–1945," in *Imagining Tomorrow: History, Technology, and the American Future*, ed. Joseph J. Corn (Cambridge, Mass.: MIT Press, 1986), 137–63. Essays by Esther McCoy and Rosemarie Haag Bletter in David Hanks, et al., *High Styles: Twentieth-Century American Design* (New York: Whitney Museum of American Art, 1985), provide a solid introduction to American ideas on the design of furniture, automobiles, homes, and other commodities.

Major developments in music can be traced in H. Wiley Hitchcock, *Music in the United States: A Historical Introduction* (Englewood Cliffs, N.J.: Prentice-Hall, 1969); Gilbert Chase, *America's Music: From the Pilgrims to the Present* (New York McGraw-Hill, 1955); Wilfrid Mellers, *Music in a New Found Land: Themes and Developments in the History of American Music* (New York: Alfred A. Knopf, 1965); and Nicholas E. Tawa, *A Most Wondrous Babble: American Art Composers, Their Music, and the American Scene, 1950–1985* (Westport, Conn.: Greenwood Press, 1987). Michael Nyman, *Experimental Music: Cage and Beyond* (New York: Schirmer Books, 1974), sets Cage in an interdisciplinary group that includes Pollock and Alexander Calder. Cage's career and thought can best be approached through Peter Gena and Jonathan Brent, eds., *A John Cage Reader* (New York: C. F. Peters, 1982), and Richard E. Kostelanetz, ed., *John Cage* (New York: Praeger, 1970), which contains a selection of primary sources from the 1940s.

Joseph Horowitz's revealing book, *Understanding Toscanini: How He Became an American Culture-God and Helped Create a New Audience for Old Music* (Minneapolis: University of Minnesota Press, 1988), traverses the fault line between long-hair and popular music, examining the cult surrounding the world's most famous classical musician as a function of mass spectacle and cultural iconography. The chapter "Stone, Steel, and Jazz" in John A. Kouwenhoven's *Made in America: The Arts in Modern Civilization* (1948; reprint, Garden City, N. Y.: Doubleday/Anchor, 1962) remains one of the most provocative efforts to set jazz within a cultural context. Charlie Parker deserves more scholarly attention than he has received, but one can begin to gain an understanding of his music from Max Harrison, *Charlie Parker* (New York: A. S. Barnes, 1961); Ross Russell, *Bird Lives! The High Life and Hard Times of Charlie (Yardbird) Parker* (New York: Charterhouse, 1973); Ross Russell, "Bebop," in *The Art of Jazz*, ed. Martin T. Williams (New York: Oxford University Press, 1959), 187–214; and Lewis A. Erenberg's essay in the Lary May collection, *Recasting America*. The source of Kate Smith's appeal can be gleaned from her *Upon My Lips a Song* (New York: Funk & Wagnall's, 1960) and from Robert K. Merton's account of the World War II war bond drives, *Mass Persuasion: The Social Psychology of a War Bond Drive* (New York: Harper & Brothers, 1946). On Hank Williams, see Roger M. Williams, *Sing a Sad Song: The Life of Hank Williams* (1971; 2d ed., Urbana: University of Illinois Press, 1981).

Except for film, the emergence of a visual culture is poorly documented. Raymond Fielding, *The March of Time, 1935–1951* (New York: Oxford University Press, 1978), does little more than tell the basic story; the newsreel series can best be approached by viewing the original episodes, many of which are available on video. James L. Baughman's *Henry R. Luce and the Rise of the American News Media* (Boston: Twayne, 1987) also favors the narrative approach over interpretation. Keith F. Davis, *Todd Webb: Photographs of New York and Paris, 1945–1960* (Kansas City, Mo.: Hallmark Cards, 1986), is an evocative and interpretive collection, and Steven W. Plattner, *Roy Stryker: U.S.A., 1943–1950* (Austin: University of Texas Press, 1983), introduces the photography project of Standard Oil of New Jersey. On forties television, there is George Lipsitz's penetrating essay, "The Meaning of Memory: Family, Class, and Ethnicity in Early Network Television Programs," *Cultural Anthropology* 1 (November 1986): 355–87. Though Roland Marchand's important history, *Advertising the American Dream: Making Way for Modernity, 1920–1940* (Berkeley and Los Angeles: University of California Press, 1985), ends with the previous decade, its concluding pages suggest advertising's future role as therapy for anxious moderns. The early development of the Polaroid Land camera is traced in Mark Olshaker, *The Instant Image: Edwin Land and the Polaroid Experience* (New York: Stein and Day, 1978).

While the thirties is considered the golden age of the comic strip, the significant interest shown in this field has yielded works that illuminate popular culture in the forties as well. Jerry Robinson, *The Comics: An Illustrated History of Comic Strip Art* (New York: G. P. Putnam's Sons, 1974), provides a solid if unspectacular grounding. David Manning White and Robert H. Abel, eds., *The Funnies: An American Idiom* (New York: Free Press, 1963), is a fine collection of interpretive essays; Heinz Politzer's on "Li'l Abner" and Reuel Denney's on "Pogo" are especially provocative. Less even but useful is Arthur Asa Berger, *The Comic-Stripped American* (New York: Walker, 1973), and Les Daniels, *Comix: A History of Comic Books in America* (New York: Outerbridge & Dienstfrey, 1971). Mickey Spillane's detective hero Mike Hammer is seen as a moralistic vigilante in Charles J. Rolo, "Simenon and Spillane: The Metaphysics of Murder for the Millions," in *Mass Culture: The Popular Arts in America*, ed.

Bernard Rosenberg and David Manning White (Glencoe, Ill.: Free Press, 1957), 165–75, and the Los Angeles environment of Raymond Chandler's Philip Marlowe is interpreted as the corruption of the American dream in Joseph C. Porter, "The End of the Trail: The American West of Dashiell Hammett and Raymond Chandler," *Western Historical Quarterly* 6 (October 1975): 411–24.

Though often mentioned in the literature of the forties, fashion's New Look of 1947 has not received scholarly treatment. See "The House of Dior," *Life*, 24 March 1947, 65–70, and "Revolution," *Time*, 18 August 1947, 22. The rise and fall of the wide and colorful cravat is covered in Rod Dyer and Ron Spark, *Fit to Be Tied: Vintage Ties of the Forties and Early Fifties* (New York: Abbeville Press, 1987). Alison Lurie, *The Language of Clothes* (New York: Random House, 1981), is good on the links between fashion and subculture.

Index

nuclear fission, 30, 95
nuclear utopianism. *See* atomic bomb: reimagined
Number 2 (Pollock), 136
Number 3, 1949: Tiger (Pollock), 136
Number 8, 1949 (Pollock), 136

Oasis, The (McCarthy), 142
O'Brien, Edmund, 38
Odets, Clifford, 128
Office of Civilian Defense, 2
Office of Scientific Research and Development, 125
Office of War Information, 6
Oklahoma!, 75
Olson, Charles, 134
O'Neill, Eugene, 56, 139
"one world," 18, 50, 80–81, 106, 113, 147; and Cage, 134
One World (Willkie), 70–71, 74, 100
On the Road (Kerouac), 65
"open door," the, 70–71
organizations: theory of, 87–88
organized labor, 10
"Original Amateur Hour, The," 146
Origins of Totalitarianism, The (Arendt), 48, 105
Outlaw, The, 8
Out of the Past, 55, 112
"Over There," 6

pacifism, 4
Page, Patti, 79
painting, 10, 75, 85–86, 89, 121. *See also* particular artists; abstract expressionism
paradox, 62
paralysis, 123
paranoia, 24
Parker, Charlie, 132–33, 146
Parsons, Betty, 136
Parsons, Talcott, 42, 90; on sex roles, 106; and systems theory, 86
Partisan Review, 140–42
Pasadena, California, 27
past: threatening, 53, 55
patriarchy, 12
peace, culture of, 1
Peace of Mind (Liebman), 61, 103
Peace of Soul (Sheen), 106
Peale, Norman Vincent, 61

"Peanuts," 104
Pearl Harbor, 20, 144
Peck, Gregory, 93
pensions: growth of, 19
Pentagon, 69, 78, 89, 124
People of Plenty (Potter), 162n17
Perec, Georges, 68
perfectibility, 47
personality: disintegration of, 105–106; other-directed, 117, 133, 146; types of, 77
Phillips, William, 137, 140
philosophy, 103; and morality, 125. *See also* existentialism
photography, 14
physiology, 88, 135
Pickett, Laura Rew, 125
"Pilgrim Psalms" (Finney), 59
pinsetting (bowling), 124
Pisan Cantos, The (Pound), 56, 83–84
"Pistol Packin' Mama," 106
Piston, Walter, 124
pluralism, 91, 95, 97
Plymouth Theater, 58
Podhoretz, Norman, 138
poetry, 42, 56, 75, 82–84, 134, 147, 148; and systems theory, 88
"Pogo": and affluence, 11
Polaroid Land camera, 17, 124
Politics, 56
politics: declining interest in, 123
Pollock, Jackson, 65–66, 75, 135–36, 146
polls. *See* public opinion polls
Popper, Karl, 50
Popular Front, 71
Popular Mechanics, 30
population: migration of, 69
Portable Faulkner, The (Cowley), 55
Potter, David, 162n17
Pound, Ezra, 56, 82–84
Power, Tyrone, 47
Power of Being, The (Tillich), 62
Power of Freedom, The (Ascoli), 141
price-fixing, 2
production, 1, 8; and consumption, 7. *See also* consumerism
progress, 18, 40–68, 125–26
progressive education, 27–28
Progressive party, 9
Protestantism: consolidation of, 62
psychiatrists, 22, 32; as experts, 32

The Author

William Graebner is professor of history at the State University of New York, College at Fredonia. He has written on a variety of aspects of twentieth-century American history. His books include *Coal-Mining Safety in the Progressive Period* (1976), a history of political reform in a federalism framework for which he received the Frederick Jackson Turner Award of the Organization of American Historians; *A History of Retirement* (1980), a study of the idea and ideology of retirement over the last century, written under a grant from the American Council of Learned Societies; *The Engineering of Consent: Democracy and Authority in Twentieth-Century America* (1987), a history of America's distinctive brand of "democratic" social engineering; and *Coming of Age in Buffalo* (1990), a photo-essay on youth culture and adult authority in the 1940s and 1950s. With Leonard Richards, he was the editor of *The American Record: Images of the Nation's Past* (1987), a compilation of primary and secondary sources for the college classroom. He currently serves on the editorial board of *American Studies*. He lives in Buffalo, New York, with his wife, Dianne Bennett, and his children, Bennett and Riley.